Oliver P. William

Phila, 1974

Presidential Power and Accountability

Charles M. Hardin

PRESIDENTIAL POWER & ACCOUNTABILITY

Toward a New Constitution

The University of Chicago Press
Chicago and London

CHARLES M. HARDIN is professor of political science at the University of California at Davis. His books include *Politics of Agriculture, Food and Fiber in the Nation's Politics,* and *Freedom in Agricultural Education.* [1974]

The University of Chicago Press, Chicago 60637
The University of Chicago Press, Ltd., London
© 1974 by The University of Chicago
All rights reserved. Published 1974
Printed in the United States of America
International Standard Book Number: 0–226–31623–8
Library of Congress Catalog Card Number: 73–92022

For our grandchildren,
Sara and Charles Hansen

Contents

Acknowledgments

In a long term endeavor one's debts accumulate. I have had valuable support from the University of Chicago, the University of California at Davis, the Ford and Rockefeller Foundations and the Center for the Study of Democratic Institutions. My professional obligations, inadequately acknowledged in the notes, cannot be fully listed here. Nevertheless, and without implicating them in the result, I appreciate the encouragement of James MacGregor Burns, of Williams College, of colleagues at the University of California at Davis, especially Alexander J. Groth and John R. Owens, and of colleagues at the Center for the Study of Democratic Institutions, especially Robert M. Hutchins and Rexford G. Tugwell. Above all I am grateful to my wife.

Introduction
The Crisis and Its Cure

When a nation has cause for political philosophy, nothing can
stop it from producing it, and the cue to its absence from America
lies in the absence of a cause.—*Louis Hartz*

In 1973 America was gripped by its gravest political crisis since the
Civil War. The president all too often was out of control. Unbridled
bureaucracies acted with the arrogance befitting their autonomy. Many
pressure groups exercised appalling political leverage. Increasingly
disorganized, the public felt deceived and disillusioned. The threat of
an inquisitorial government's espionage—and even of armed attacks
by its minions, regardless of constitutional guarantees—was in the
air. A former high official of the Nixon White House, asked by a
Senate Watergate Committee member what advice he would give
young people inquiring about careers in government, replied—"Stay
away!" The audience rocked with cynical laughter. The heritage of
Washington, Jefferson, and Lincoln—so long miraculously intact—
was crumbling to dust.

A sense of the need for fundamental changes was abroad. Recent
presidents—Eisenhower, Kennedy, and Lyndon B. Johnson—had
considered and some had urged basic constitutional reforms. In 1973
Richard M. Nixon endorsed a single six-year term for presidents
coupled with a four-year term for congressmen. Ironically, his suggestion coincided with the most serious discussion of presidential impeachment since Andrew Johnson. The thought of impeachment made
many persons shudder. And yet there was the haunting nightmare of a
discredited president continuing in office for forty months. Senator
Edward M. Kennedy and ABC commentator Howard K. Smith
pointed out that the parliamentary system would enable the displace-
ment of a politically disabled president by political means and for
political reasons—a great improvement over impeachment. Clark
Clifford, formerly special counsel to President Truman and Secretary
of Defense under President Johnson, called for the president and vice-

president to resign pursuant to the Twenty-fifth Amendment. Among those who denounced Clifford was Arthur H. Dean, formerly negotiator at Panmunjom for the United States and sixteen other nations, American ambassador to South Korea, and holder of many other distinguished assignments. But all that was in the summer; by November 1973 Vice-President Spiro T. Agnew had resigned, the House of Representatives was inquiring through its Committee on the Judiciary into the evidence for impeaching the president, and the chorus of voices calling for the president to resign had swelled while those opposing resignation had fallen virtually silent.

In this period a number of people, including CBS commentator Eric Sevareid, urged Congress to reassert itself, forgetting that Congress had repeatedly proven unable to provide the concerted leadership required by the times. Former Senator Eugene McCarthy advocated "depersonalizing" the presidency in order to free the energies, "intellectual, spiritual, and moral," of the people. In reality what emerged from the people was a collective sense of the inevitable and virtually ubiquitous crookedness of politicians.

In this situation, two facts were of first importance. First, the crisis of 1973 had been foreshadowed. Presidential abuse of power, though seriously worsened, had been visible for decades; the inadequacy of Congress to provide an alternative to presidential government had been shown from the close of the Civil War to the end of the nineteenth century and fitfully demonstrated again thereafter; and the malaise of public opinion had appeared in the late 1960s. In other words, the problems were long-standing and were rooted in structural faults; they were not associated with one administration and one series of events. Second, there was—there is—a way out, painful, difficult, and dangerous as it may be. It will require constitutional surgery at least as severe as that of 1787. The end result can be briefly stated as "Presidential Power and Accountability" or, to put it another way, as presidential leadership and party government.

It will be useful to set forth the diagnosis and the prescription in an outline:

1. A foremost requirement of a great power is strong executive leadership. The political demand for it, manifest world-wide, arises from the present condition of international relationships, given the state of the military arts; from the inexorable need to develop and use

science to maintain national security; and from the nature of modern economic and social organization especially when coupled with emergent ecological considerations.

2. America met the first requirement by its presidency; but in recent decades the presidency has escaped the political controls essential to constitutional, i.e., *limited,* government. New controls must be found.

3. The search for controls is complicated by the danger that curbs may diminish the effectiveness of the presidency. The executive needs energy today at least as much as in the critical years immediately following 1787 when the Framers concluded that it should be wielded by a single pair of hands to achieve the "Decision, activity, secrecy [yes, secrecy!], and despatch" essential in safeguarding the Republic. How to maintain the full force and effect of the presidency and yet to restrain those presidential excesses so generously demonstrated in this century?

4. The beginning of the answer lies in the relationship between the president and the people. The controlling principle has been *vox populi, vox dei.* The voice of the people is the voice of God. This has been the major premise of our theory of representation; for the people cannot govern, and the president has become their surrogate. Accordingly, he personifies their political authority. When he speaks *ex cathedra* from atop his pyramid of forty million votes, with the bulk of the populace reportedly behind him, he is awe-inspiring. His infallibility especially impresses those closest to him whose approval if not their adulation convinces him that he is larger than life. And yet all this authority may dissolve if the public turns against him. The people's choice becomes the people's curse. We have seen it happen four times in this century. The results of an abrupt decline in presidential power are often unfortunate and may be disastrous.

5. It follows (although the logic may be clear only after further reading and reflection) that a measure of control over the president can be provided by subjecting him to the criticism of an organized, focused opposition with leadership centered in one person who will be continuously visible and vocal as the alternative to the president. As the presidency is unified, so should the opposition be unified. As the president speaks with a single voice, so should he be answered by a single voice instead of a clamor of discordant and little-known voices

in a legislative body whose present genius is the dispersion of power. If a focused opposition can be achieved, the crucial relationship between the public and its government will begin to change.

6. To establish an opposition we must turn to Congress, and the first step is to contradict the myth that the end of providing greater controls over the president without unduly undermining his power may be accomplished merely by increasing the weight of Congress. When powers are separated they are ordinarily less shared than displaced. Either power resides in the presidency with some congressional criticism and subject to some bargaining or it shifts to the bureaucracy, defined as comprising a conglomerate of power among agencies, strategic congressmen, and interest groups. It must be understood that the genius of Congress is opposite to that of the presidency. Where the presidency comes to life in the unification of power, Congress disperses power among a hundred leaders each with his own base in seniority and in sectional jurisdiction (over taxation, finance, transportation, military, labor, and judiciary or whatever). It appears to be impossible to organize in Congress a concentration of power sufficient to provide an orchestrated and programmatic opposition—let alone a centralized executive government.

7. The nature of Congress is strongly influenced by the manner of its selection—staggered terms for senators, two-year terms for representatives. As with the president, this situation induces a particular relationship between Congress and the public. Where the president is elected as the nonpareil, the father, the leader, the magic helper, the incarnation of the infallible goodness and wisdom of the people, congressmen and senators tend to be chosen as a means of assuring their constituents' shares of the national largesse. Henry Adams cynically wrote, "A Congressman is like a hog. You have to kick him in the snout." The grain of truth in his statement exists by virtue of the congressman's expression of the sacred demands of the public. The voter's political obligation in electing congressmen is held to be exhausted when he communicates his wants to government. The voter has no share in the responsibility of government. Indeed, the "responsible electorate" has been authoritatively defined as one that knows on which side its bread is buttered.[1] The logical outcome for public opinion is that Congress "as a whole" is despised because congressmen are generally seen as serving the interests of others—but individual con-

gressmen are typically admired and appreciated by the active and knowledgeable among their constituents.

8. The first reform then must strike at the relationships not only between president and Congress but also between both and the public. The president and Congress should be elected for simultaneous four-year terms. In addition, the defeated candidate for the presidency should have a seat in the House of Representatives, priority in committees and on the floor, and a staff, offices, and other prerequisites suitable to his position as the leader of the opposition.

9. Candidates for Congress of both parties, including a generous slate of candidates running at large on a national ticket, should constitute the nominating conventions for presidential candidates so that when people vote or otherwise share in nominations of congressmen they know that they are also naming those who will nominate for the presidency. The office of vice-president should be abolished. Other reforms will be explained in the last chapter—especially the steps to reduce the political leverage of the Senate; the introduction of national at-large candidates in a manner that will ensure the winning presidential candidate a working majority in the House of Representatives; and the provision that the minority party in Congress may remove the defeated presidential candidate as leader of the opposition but that it must replace him with another leader.

10. These changes should give the voters a new sense of their function and of their relationship to government. They will be able to realize a political responsibility that the present constitution denies them, namely, that they share in the selection of a government—or, equally important, of an opposition. This action is rich in significance. *First,* it will cause a salutary change in a basic premise of American political thought. Implicit in the new electoral system is the realization that government—far from being "the greatest of all reflections on human nature"—is a necessity if people are to dwell, as they must as human beings, in communities. *Second,* these changes will give voters the experience that will vindicate an improved theory of representation. Instead of perpetuating the myth that people in general are in position and sufficiently informed to make all political decisions—the idea of the General Will and of the initiative and referendum dear to the Progressives—the new assumption will be in accordance with a sensible division of political labor: the people will elect a government

—and an opposition—and hold them accountable, the one for governing, the other for systematically criticizing government during its term
in office. A workable theory of representative democracy should
emerge. *Third,* an extremely significant step will be taken to restore
political controls over the president without diminishing his essential
power. He would be seen as the necessary and legitimate leader for a
given period rather than as the personification of the deity domiciled
in the collective breast of the populace. Instead of governmental decisions resting on the ultimate sanction of the popular will, they would
rest on a majority, a sufficiently legitimizing concept, but one that takes
into account the fact that nearly half the people will consider the president to be politically fallible—and one that will prevail merely for the
good and democratic reason that in a civilized community there must
be some way other than violence to settle disputes. Control over the
president derived from these propositions will be enhanced by the
presence of the leader of the opposition and the alternative government that he heads. The tendency for the instincts, the whims, the
idiosyncrasies, or the mind-sets of presidents to become manifest in
dangerous initiatives should be greatly reduced. *Fourth,* the sovereign
right of the majority to choose a government that, on balance, it
considers more favorable to its interests would not be denied; but the
emphasis would be placed, where it should be if the public is to have a
practicable and active share in the awful responsibility of modern
government, on the choice of who shall rule. *Fifth,* the divisions in
the campaign should persist during the period of governance, subject,
of course, to accretion and erosion of political parties "like a ball of
sticky popcorn;"[2] and this quality of persistence, along with previous
characteristics of the new public, will further rationalize the relationship of the people to their government.

11. The new framework of government will increase the ability of
politicians to bring bureaucracy as it has crystallized in America under
control. And the balance of power between public government and
private groups, which is unfortunately tipped toward private groups
in the traditional polity of America, will be redressed.

12. Beyond these considerations looms the inability of the American system to replace a president who has become politically discredited. Impeachment is inadequate. The fault of impeachment for
removing presidents lies essentially in its juridical character, its legal
procedures, its indictments and its trial according to the rules of evi-

dence, to ascertain the *individual's* criminal guilt or innocence. But emphasis on the *legal* criminality of *individuals* hides and even denies the *political* responsibility that must be *collective*. In the modern age the intricate and complex problems of government require a collegial approach (as the current political argot recognizes—the White House team, the task forces, the national security council, the domestic council, the presidential game plan). Political adequacy is judged not by weighing individual guilt or innocence according to the rules of evidence but rather by political procedures for testing confidence in the prudence and judgment of government. Legal guilt by association is anathema; political liability by association is essential. The political process should be capable of registering the collective judgment of responsible politicians—who, in turn, are informed by their sense of public opinion—on the prudence and wisdom of governments. The legality of a president's acts may figure in such judgments, but more important are decisions on presidential prudence, grasp of events, will, wisdom, and self-control.

The reforms proposed will not in themselves provide a vote of confidence, but they will create the setting in which such votes should naturally evolve. For an essential assumption would be that a president needs a majority in the House of Representatives to govern. If he loses the majority he will be incapacitated and it would be logical for him to resign. It will be argued that the experience of parliamentary regimes shows governments to be extremely durable: prime ministers no longer get ousted because they lose majorities. And yet prime ministers do resign because they have to retain the leadership at least of their own party; and there are ways short of defection in which party members can convey to the prime minister their loss of confidence.

13. Replacement of the president by an adverse vote of confidence —or by so obvious a disintegration in the loyalty of his supporters that he feels compelled to resign—should make way for another evolutionary step, namely, dissolving government and holding new elections. Once this step is taken, it is hoped, it will become the normal way that one government ends and another is chosen. When this happens, the endless nominating and electoral campaigns will be compressed into a few weeks. One benefit will be the reduction of the cost of campaigns and of the leverage of money in politics. Stringent laws on campaign financing will become enforceable.

14. Finally, there is the promise of more honest politics and less

corruptible politicians. This result will come from the collegial responsibility of party government toward which all the reforms suggested
above will work. The inherited American system puts all stress on the
individual. He can keep himself clean, untainted by the sordid acts of
the grafters who surround him, each of whom may profit individually
from his crimes—but also may be apprehended, convicted, and sen-
tenced. In the new system members of a government will understand
that, just as they govern collectively, so they will be judged collectively
for the shortcomings of their colleagues. Party government will provide strong incentives for obedience to a code of political ethics.

1 The Constitutional Potential of Party Government

. . . we must never forget . . . that it is a constitution we are expounding.—John Marshall

A dangerous initiative has been vested in the president of the United States. Sweeping powers given him by the Constitution and by Supreme Court decisions and enlarged by his predecessors enable him to take the first crucial steps in foreign affairs. He can recognize foreign governments or withdraw recognition. He can make agreements with the force of treaties that pledge the honor, blood, and treasure of this country to protect any or all nations from foreign aggression or domestic subversion, however conveniently defined. The country's military might is his to dispose, without limits, in fulfilling his initiative.[1] His power to act domestically against the law and even to disregard the guarantees of the Bill of Rights was asserted in 1973 to be plenary, so long as he claims to act against a foreign threat, however remote, to the security of the United States.[2] "Initiative" is the right word because, once a course of action is undertaken and an organization created to carry it out, presidential control may disappear in bureaucratic independence or be lost in the labyrinth of government.

The national blindness to the dangers of presidential initiative stems from the narcissism that colors the appraisals of our own political genius. Then, too, the fault looms starkly only with vast and recent changes in the nature and distribution of world political power. Recognition has to contend with the eloquent teaching that, with all his fierce aspect, the president in domestic politics has often only the power to persuade.[3] Even more fundamentally, we have learned repeatedly that the safety of the Republic depends on a presidency capable of "Decision, activity, secrecy, and despatch."[4] Mainly this lesson has been manifest in the deeds of incumbents—"men . . . of the sort of action that makes for enlightenment";[5] but its wisdom has often been underlined by commentators.[6]

Nevertheless, the broad international commitments begun under President Truman, greatly expanded by President Eisenhower, and further increased by subsequent presidents have awakened the nation to the astounding reach of presidential initiative in foreign and military affairs.[7] It was widely believed in the early 1970s that foreign reverses, national budgetary and economic problems, the decline of morale in the armed forces, and much domestic divisiveness were rooted in an excess of armed intervention abroad.

Cry now that "The president is out of control!" and the response— from many, at least—is "Yes!" But it is not enough to cry out. To prescribe correctives requires an understanding of what is meant by loss of control as well as a wariness of overreaction in light of the demonstrated value to the nation of a unified and vigorous presidency. The answer to both problems—maintenance of presidential leadership *and* its control—lies in party government. Moreover, continuation of a strong presidency in an evolving government organized by centralized, disciplined, and competing parties will help to cope with a series of other problems. These are bureaucracy-out-of-control, insufficient coherence in public policy, excessive vulnerability to group pressures, and the travail of public opinion.

The Nature of Party Government

Party government? *Party government!* To some these are fighting words, to some a rallying slogan, to some an invitation to exhume a horse only too happily deceased; but to most people the words must be simply perplexing. What do you mean? Isn't that what we have now? A two-party system?

The answer is that party government would build on the two major parties, but they would become more than (as they are now) aggregations of voters and interests to win elections. They would be the agencies of majority government—and of minority opposition. They would concert policies for enactment; and they would unite the government to ensure that the policies would be accepted and carried out by the bureaucracy.

In order to do these things, parties will have to change fundamentally. The first question to ask if one wants to understand where power lies in parties is: Who makes nominations? If they are going to shape policies, national parties must have final control over the votes of legislative members; therefore, they must have a veto over the nominations of congressmen and senators in order to exclude those who refuse to conform to the parties' stands on policies. This would not mean the end of bargaining and compromise but rather their transfer, at least in the conclusive stages of policy formation, to the party caucuses. The present degree of influence of congressional committees, and of the interests associated with them, would be sharply cut.

But party government means more than this. The aim of the proposal is to create political conditions to enable the national community that exists in the hearts of the people to emerge. We have been somberly told of a "massive erosion of the trust the American people have in their Government."[8] Since ours is a government of, by, and for the people, this may amount to a loss of confidence in ourselves as a nation. America begins to unravel into its constituent groups. The "mystic cords of memory" that have enabled the tribes, clans, and interests to live together are replaced by envy, contempt, and hatred. All this is encouraged by the nature of certain of our political institutions as well as by the theories that explain and justify their operation. Against these trends we must be prepared to assert that we live not just in groups but in communities and above all in the national community, "the one club to which we all belong,"[9] which must be the primary theater for achieving the noble purposes set forth in the preamble of the Constitution of the United States.

But if there is the Scylla of group solipsism,* there is also the Charybdis of consensus. Consensus holds that sweet reason will so illuminate all issues that the wise and honest will invariably recognize the true anwers. Anyone who refuses agreement is either a fool or a knave. Consensus has a powerful hold on our thoughts: it is, for example, the rationale of a bipartisanship that, despite its acclaim, has often had mischievous effects. And the rationale carries over to create an establishmentarian mentality, with the result that disastrous poli-

---

*Solipsism is the theory that the self can know nothing but its own modifications and that the self is the only existent thing. We have only to substitute *group* for *self* to understand one of the grevious ills of American politics.

cies may go unchallenged for a generation simply because the "wise and the good" agree that they are right.[10]

Just as it collects the forces that degenerate into group solipsism in order to rebuild the community, so also party government breaks the stranglehold of consensus. It does so by insisting that—except for the nucleus of self-evident truths enshrined in the Declaration of Independence and the guarantees set forth in the Bill of Rights—political conclusions are provisional, contingent on conditions, and affected by group and partisan interests. To bring this fact to life the Constitution engraved on the hearts of men must recognize the function of the opposition that contending parties will incorporate as an indispensable part of government.

And finally party government will give the citizen his due share in both political power *and* responsibility. It will do so by giving him a recognizable, understandable role in the awesome task of creating a government—or an opposition. It will end the present malaise of public opinion that results from the fiction that each citizen is the sovereign arbiter of all issues—and the fact that each is caught in a political labyrinth that frustrates his efforts and stultifies his thought.

Thus the words "presidential leadership and party government" raise the most important secular questions of our time. Discussion must be thorough, detailed, and, at times, complex. Analysis must produce enough evidence to engage the reader's most serious consideration.

And now to return to the bill of particulars, which will be elaborated in following chapters.

The Lack of Presidential Debate

The president stands on an incomparable political pinnacle. Only he is elected nationally. We, the people, choose him to run our more perfect union. In our government of, by, and for the people, he alone is elevated by the support of forty million. No one else can rival him. His opponent, the only other person in the country who can speak from atop a comparable monument of votes, is in political discard. Nor is there a forum, unless it is an academic "forum of history," in which the president can be challenged effectively. There is no hall, no house, no court, no consecrated room in which the president can be confronted by a rival mounted on his own separate political base and with his own men rallied around to cheer *his* attack. No one can call the president to account and force him to explain his actions.

In consequence—and to a degree that is both disquieting and astounding—the president's whim controls, or his impulses and idiosyncrasies may be decisive. Surrounded as he is by able men, they are still *his* men. Blocked though he may be in domestic matters and controlled in foreign affairs by outside forces, including those he and his predecessors have helped to set in motion, still he is served by men who are conditioned and even constrained to agree, to acclaim, and to applaud—but not to argue. They are creatures of his appointment and dismissal. They compete for his favor and are subject to the relentless appeal of loyalty. They are awed by the man and the institution.[11]

The country needs to change some things about its government. It needs a forum where the president must come to explain his actions under the critical examination of political rivals intent on replacing him. It needs an opposition capable of countering the major themes of the administration—and not simply a number of congressional obstacles each manned by an insider who can be bought off. It needs an institutionalized opportunity for an alternate leader to exclaim, "I beseeech you, in the bowels of Christ, think it possible that you may be mistaken."[12] No staff system, nor all the essence of ivied wisdom multiplied by the craft of Wall Street, can satisfy the need for *political* confrontation.

What-might-be is party government. It is a government of national political parties whose leaders choose *their* leader—choose him and can, in an extreme situation, depose him. A ruling party, legitimized by a majority of votes, is needed; but the degree of excellence would be insufficient unless a second party, capable of commanding a majority itself someday, is incorporated in the same governmental institution and empowered to counterpose its own leader in the ultimate debate.

The vaunted advisory system built around the president has been congenitally unable to check government by whim and idiosyncrasy. Lyndon B. Johnson is a tempting target for analysis.[13] Adlai Stevenson's memoir is especially illuminating. On 28 April 1965, President Johnson announced that troops would land in Santo Domingo to save American lives threatened by civil violence. A White House meeting attended by Vice-President Hubert H. Humphrey, Secretary of State Dean Rusk, Special Presidential Assistant McGeorge Bundy, Ambassador Stevenson, and others considered how to amplify the statement. Johnson's draft went beyond rescuing Americans to include a sentence suggesting the need for preventing a Communist coup. Stevenson asked for clarification. Johnson frowned. Stevenson looked around for support and urged Humphrey to "say something!" Humphrey "put his finger to his lips and shook his head." Stevenson turned to Bundy: "What do you think?" True to his motto, to keep the options open, Bundy said "I am of twin minds." Johnson temporarily deleted the sentence—but put it back in a much stronger form when he addressed the nation on Sunday: the Communists had taken control of the Dominican rebellion, he proclaimed, and the United States would not tolerate another Cuba.

But if the initiative was the president's the action was soon in the hands of the military, which apparently preempted control[14]—and this leads us to a second problem.

Bureaucracy-out-of-control

Despite his dangerously untrammeled initiative, the president's power often disappears in bureaucratic independence. Since World War II, great public agencies have broken out of effective political control. Bureaucracy refers to a combination of agency leaders with strategically located congressmen and often with the heads of organized groups directly affected by the policies in question.[15] When bureaucracy gets out of control, the definition and execution of public policy shifts from the hands of elected politicians, either Congress (in the sense of a collective body) or the president, and into the hands of assistant secretaries and bureau chiefs, congressional committee chairmen, and sometimes the heads of interest groups. Escape from control comes out of the defeat that president and Congress inflict on each other when each tries to control the bureaucracy by characteristically different methods.

The president's nature is unity; that of Congress, diversity. The president endeavors to control by trying to make sure that the budgetary demands of each agency are weighed against the demands of other agencies and are appraised in terms of governmental fiscal and monetary policy; by trying to ascertain that minor policy departures are not in conflict with major policies under which they are subsumed; and by striving for a degree of coordination among policies. The president's chief instruments are his personal staff and the Office of Management and Budget (a perennial villain in congressional eyes).

In its turn, Congress strives for control by dividing up problems and parceling them out among committees and subcommittees. With the recent upthrust of bureaucracy, however, Congress finds insufficient its usual control through chartering agencies, defining their statutory powers, annually financing them, and investigating them.

Indeed, the great bureaucracies not only (in effect) defy the president, but play the president off against Congress, pit the two houses of Congress against each other,[16] and fatten on the rivalries of congressional committees. In their frustration, Congress and the president struggle against each other for the control of the bureaucracy—and therefore of policy; but bureaucracy escapes.

Illustrations abound. Spending programs take on a life of their own, often hindering a shift in priorities to cope with new problems. Bureaucracy shapes substantive policies. For example, it has helped the arms race get out of hand, has concentrated on building dams to the derogation of other means of conserving and managing water resources, and has maintained farm price supports at a level that requires disproportionate budgetary outlays and brought on an unfortunate inflation of farm real-estate values.

To cope with bureaucracy, politicians in the White House and Congress have been urged to unite. The obvious road to union is through political parties. But it will not be enough for both ends of Pennsylvania Avenue to join hands. Bureaucracy permeates the land. The counter-organization must not only emerge in Washington. It has to flourish at the grass roots as well—a fact that reinforces the need for union through political parties that are effectively organized not only at the center of government but in communities spread over the country.

Undue Influence of Private Groups

Bureaucracy could be discussed under the heading of group politics, a term that tends to swallow up all political phenomena. Nevertheless, there is enough difference in the response of government to organized group interests to call for separate analysis. In bureaucracy-out-of-control the locus of power moves significantly from a central direction but remains lodged in its own bastions in government. Meanwhile there is another face of power that shows itself in the ability of private interests to twist governmental policies to their own ends, or to stunt their effects, or to fence them out of certain private preserves, or even to kill them off entirely.

The role of pressure groups has long been subject to lively debate. A probe of pressure politics in the United States produces illustrations of the apparent effects of pressure on policy. Among many possible examples are these: the ability of the oil interests to maintain scandalously favorable tax treatment; the influence of the National Rifle Association in combating gun-control legislation; and the share of the Farm Bureau in inhibiting historical governmental efforts to reach the rural poor with the kind of public assistance that has become virtually the heritage of the well-to-do.

All this provokes comparison with Great Britain to see whether their version of party government provides a superior defense against pressure politics. The apparent answer is that it does; but the analysis presses out to embrace the role of producing and consuming groups in the collectivist age of modern government. The inference is that the great industrial communities require systematic policies in welfare and the management of the economy. Collectivist economic and social problems require a collectivist politics. Policies must be coherent, a fact that calls for an integrated government; but they must also be held to be conditional and contingent, a fact that calls for a concerted opposition. Once more the interpretation favors government by parties; but the parties themselves must have broad and fairly dependable bases in the electorate—and this leads us to examine the state of the public.

The Travail of Public Opinion

In the United States, public opinion is nothing and everything. It is nothing because government in the sense of the power to make binding decisions is handed over to individuals, especially the president but also a number of others—congressmen, bureaucrats, and politicians in strategic positions—to say what government shall and shall not do. But the myth is that public opinion rules. The people are the one and only authoritative voice.

One result is to increase the tensions of citizens. Despite years of lament for the overburdened voters, elections and referendums continue to proliferate. Public indifference is often manifest. Public ignorance of issues is legendary and has been repeatedly demonstrated. And yet government summons individual voters to answer the most abstruse kinds of questions about policy.[17] And when elections end, pollsters enter with their unremitting questions.

The tension of citizens is the product of ambivalence. On the one hand they are told that their highest duty is to pursue their selfish interests—politically as well as economically, in groups as well as individuals. They are urged to organize and to look after their own. No group is enjoined to look to the common good just as no congressman is compelled to have a national point of view.[18] The single-minded pursuit of group selfishness has been justified by theories that a "hidden hand" is at work to ensure that the best of all possible worlds emerges from the interplay of selfish interests.

But this brave new world gets lost in the smog or the traffic snarl or the deterioration of communities, and people become conscious of a contradictory injunction: to look to the general welfare or the public interest. The people share this duty with the president. If the joint product of group pressures fails to cure public ills, America has been said to have a providential corrective. When the "scuffle of local interests" dissolves in economic depression or verges into warfare, we turn to the president.[19] *Along with the people—and alone with them— the president is responsible for the general welfare or the public interest. People and president share an obligation from which the interests are excused: a responsibility to the political community as a whole.*

Whereas the people cannot act the president can, if he has the power. Whether he has depends on his public prestige.[20] Overwhelmed by their own helplessness, in the face of their impossible responsibilities to achieve the general welfare, people may transfer their guilt and their expectations to him. If he brings peace, prosperity, safety, and tranquillity, he may enjoy their rapturous support. And yet the link between president and people is more complicated than this implies. Frustrated and anxious though they may be, the people are also indifferent and inattentive to the specifics of government until public actions press on private lives. In times of trouble over rising prices, precarious jobs, and unemployment, fear of violence, or sons at war, the president can get the public's ear. His temptation is to manipulate the gut issues or to smother them in patriotism. But his policies may fail. Pressures on citizens rise. Presidential prestige falters. The vibrant national leader whose strength was almost palpable in the living rooms over the nation and whose voice could clutch the spine is now a ghost. We have experienced it three times since 1950.

The travail of public opinion will yield to party government. In democracies the people are entitled to a decisive voice in deciding who shall rule. This birthright can best be had through an election that will provide them with a sense of sharing the powers—and the responsibilities—of governance. Centralized and disciplined parties to which not only governors but citizens belong can provide the link. They can also reduce the public tensions arising from the ambivalence between the group's drives for privilege and the citizen's obligation to seek the common good. For political parties can enable and require the citizens to subordinate their legitimate push to satisfy their interests to an overriding sense of responsibility to the public welfare. At the same time, party government can conserve the values of a vigorous and unified presidency while providing a safe and appropriate connection between president and people to replace the dangerous and improper one that now exists.

This list of problems is not exhaustive—the concluding chapter will briefly raise two others, the inability to replace presidents who are politically disabled and the disadvantages that have recently become apparent in calendar elections. These difficulties also appear amenable to party government. But now the overriding question of feasibility can no longer be postponed.

Will Party Government Work?

One of the most rewarding things about the research for this study has been to find that many political scientists, from the most magisterial to those precisely oriented toward salient aspects of the polity, lend support to the plea for party government. When one turns to the question of feasibility, however, the weight of professional opinion seems to hold that the American public is too divided—too distributed among shifting, conflicting, and overlapping groups—to provide the social bases for durable political parties capable of reasonably stable majority government.

To deal with that question one must first ask what the prospects are that both major parties will be able to build majority support in Congress. The answer turns on Republican chances in the South. A confident affirmative cannot be given. And yet the outlook of the GOP is not entirely hopeless. Some secular trends may work to its advantage. The Democratic party appears to command an impressive southern congressional majority, present and prospective; but the tides may shift. Meanwhile, a provision can be made that will ensure that a newly elected president will enjoy a congressional majority.

On the second and more fundamental question, whether social divisions are deep enough to condemn party government as impracticable, an examination of the studies of American political attitudes and partisan behavior leads to an optimistic conclusion. Given institutional changes that would enable the test to be made, there is much evidence to suggest that the American electorate would provide a stable majority and, equally essential, an organized opposition effectively monopolized by a single alternative party.

Conclusion: The Need for Reform

John Marshall wrote: ". . . we must never forget . . . that it is a *constitution* we are expounding."[21] The essence of constitutional democracy is limited government. Both words are critical. Without government there is anarchy. Order disappears except for Spinoza's law of nature in which the big fish swallow the little fish. No common defense prevails against foreign enemies; there is nothing common to defend. Government without limits, on the other hand, is tyranny and torture, fawning and favoritism, repression and humiliation. No commonwealth exists to establish justice and to define and try to achieve the general welfare.

The linchpin of limited government is the lively understanding shared by citizens of its needs and nature.[22] A government must govern, but a limited government will act subject to open and organized criticism. "To find out whether a people is free it is necessary only to ask if there is an Opposition and, if there is, to ask where it is."[23] Government and opposition both flourish in the establishment of due procedures that become known, accepted, and matters of habit.

Fundamental changes are recommended to provide America with appropriate procedures. To maintain and control a vigorous president; to reestablish the writ of the general government over the bureaucracy;

to invest public policy with greater internal coherence and more pre-eminence over the importunities of pressures groups—all these justify major constitutional adjustments. So does the need to resolve the social and psychological tensions that arise when a limited and divided—indeed, a splintered—government confronts the problems of a collectivist age. None of these statements will dissipate the danger inherent in sweeping reforms; but they should obviate any attempt to kill them off with the pejorative tag that they are merely "tinkering with the machinery."

So far as the specifics go, the proposals are highly debatable. The intention of this book is to contribute to public acceptance of the need for serious consideration of fundamental constitutional change. Indeed, one dares to hope to inform the spirit in which change is approached in the belief that the self-fulfilling prophecy contained in the search will be in proportion to the inspiration, integrity, and soundness of the analysis on which it is based. Above all, any proposals for reforms must be constrained by the first premises of constitutional democracy as a marriage of the popular will to limited government.

2 On the Difficulty of Arguing With Presidents

King John: Hadst thou but shook thy head or made a pause
When I spake darkly what I purposed,
Or turn'd an eye of doubt upon my face,
As bid me tell my tale in express words,
Deep shame had struck me dumb, made me break off,
And those thy fears might have wrought fear in me:
But thou didst understand me by my signs
And didst in signs again parley with sin;
Yea, without stop, didst let thy heart consent,
And consequently thy rude hand to act
The deed, which both our tongues held vile to name.
Out of my sight, and never see me more!
—Shakespeare, *King John*

To a ludicrous degree, Americans are governed by presidential instincts, whims, idiosyncrasies, or mind-sets. It is ludicrous because America is the cradle of democracy, a political theory that celebrates appeals to reason exemplified in the "decent respect for the opinions of mankind" of the Declaration of Independence. Our judicial processes require adversary procedures. If the life of the law is experience rather than logic, logic must compare the virtues of different experiences and select those to repeat and improve. Legislatures employ rational examination of proposals, committee study and reports, debates, and conferences. Electoral campaigns produce platforms, examination of records, and the attacks and counterattacks of rival candidates. However filled with distortion and deception or laced with appeals to emotion, prejudice, or hatred, the legal, legislative, and electoral processes all bring adversaries to face each other with argument a significant factor in reaching decisions. If the principle of opposition falters (as in one-party states) the results are commonly deplored.

Similar ideas pervade the professions and academia where students are educated by challenge, debate, and examination—and practitioners rise by making contributions to their professions under the critical scrutiny of their peers. In businesses, in universities, and in philanthropic foundations, officers have to justify their policies to governing boards that, if not captive or corrupt, act in an examining and questioning capacity. Outside of most labor unions, the hierarchy of the Catholic church, and the military, the classical virtues of the dialogue have been widely adopted in America—except for the institution that under modern conditions looms as the most important of all in the secular life of the nation: the presidency.

More than ludicrous, it is dangerous. The president becomes virtually insulated from debate. Erected on an incomparable pyramid of votes that convey the ultimate democratic sanction, he becomes the living embodiment of popular sovereignty. He attracts persons who, however invidious their mutual regard, accord him great loyalty. He selects persons who share his views. Associates shield him from serious dissent, anticipate and spring to meet his desires, and bathe him in a corrupting admiration. "Flatter the prince," the oldest and sagest advice to courtiers everywhere (and useful in all organizations wherein aspirations are structured hierarchically), is proportionally amplified in significance for the entourage of presidents by the unparalleled power and influence of the office. The danger lies in presidential initiatives essentially uncontrolled.

Some will deny the argument on the ground that it is nonsense.[1] The answer to them will lie in the evidence of this and the next chapter. Others will say that the interpretation errs because it hides the most significant problem of the presidency, that, paradoxically, the president all too often has only the power to persuade and insufficient power to do that. His legal "powers" may fail when his commands must be fulfilled by persons who, theoretically subordinate, have actually acquired vested power positions in their own right.[2] With regard to this criticism, I agree that in addition to uncontrolled presidential initiative there is a second flaw in the contemporary American Constitution. Our great bureaucracies, understood as combinations of agencies, congressional leaders, and heads of interest groups, often become autonomous enough to harm the polity. Later chapters will deal with the problem of bureaucracy.

Another demurral may come from those who say that the fault lies less in the constitutional rigidities than in the character of the presidents themselves. One such interpretation identifies four character traits: active and passive, positive and negative.[3] The nation is best served by active-positive presidents, men who move happily and confidently to meet issues and to take charge of events. The worst of luck is for the oval office to be occupied by an active-negative president. His genius will be to act, but his fundamental failure to be confident in himself—his lack of ego strength—may force him to cling to bankrupt policies far too long or, worse, tempt him to pyramid one outrageous adventure on top of another until he leads the nation to disaster—all in the hopeless search to "prove himself."

Powerful as this interpretation is, it has two faults. First, it is a counsel of despair. Regardless of the state of health of our institutions, our fate depends on the luck of the draw; for it is inconceivable that presidential candidates would ever submit to the proper psychological tests even if they could be devised. In the sixty-five years since the ascendancy of William Howard Taft, according to this analysis, we have been favored by active-positive presidents only 35 percent of the time; and we have had the worst combination, active-negative, in Wilson (with his dogged rigidity on his own formulation of the Versailles Treaty and the League of Nations), in Herbert Hoover (blindly devoted to his failing strategy for the Great Depression), in Lyndon B. Johnson (fatally committed to the folly of Vietnam), and in Richard M. Nixon. Second, even the presidents accorded the highest character ratings in this analysis have succumbed to the autocratic aura of the office I have earlier described; the best of them have led us down the garden path.

Evidence

The evidence for the proposition that American institutions lend themselves to government by presidential instinct is strengthened by George Reedy, formerly press secretary to President Johnson, in *The Twilight of the Presidency*,[4] but his point has been noted by other students of the presidency as well.[5] Although Reedy generalized the concept, his own vivid experience had come from President Johnson. For many readers, experience under President Richard M. Nixon will be persuasive. The invasion of Cambodia in 1970 and the paroxysm on university campuses; the bombing of North Vietnam in December 1972; its continuation in Cambodia in 1973 after the cease-fire, the return of prisoners of war, and the withdrawal of American troops; the assertion that the president's power to make war is virtually unlimited—all these events are fresh in our minds. Domestically, Nixon has asserted, and acted upon, an unprecedented breadth of authority in the impoundment of appropriated funds, an authority sufficient to centralize the nation's entire fiscal policy, on the expenditure side, in his hands. At one point, his administration expanded the concept of executive privilege—that presidents and some close associates can refuse on grounds of national security to answer congressional inquiries—to the entire executive branch on any matter that the president might designate. The extent of the protective umbrella was indicated by the speech on Watergate given on 23 May 1973, in which Mr. Nixon invoked "national security," or a synonym, thirty-one times in defense or explanation of his questionable actions. All these examples fall short of the spectacle of the office of the president using any means, legal or illegal, to incapacitate its opponents and to maintain itself in power. If the indictments are harsh they have been made eloquently by ranking Republicans. President Malcolm Moos of the University of Minnesota, formerly administrative assistant to President Eisenhower, declared:

It must be faced that the sum of all the allegations is that we were the victims of a coup d'état or an attempted coup. I weigh my words carefully. I am aware that the strict definition of a coup d'état is a "sudden exercise of force whereby the existing government is subverted." But, surely, an attempt to capture or retain control of a government by illegal means is action of the same genre.[6]

Richard M. Nixon's contributions to our understanding of the problems of the president as the embodiment of democratic divinity should not mislead us into thinking that everything hinges on his retention or removal or on that of any incumbent. The flaw lies deep in the institution itself, in the manner of election of the president, in the failure of an organized opposition that will provide an alternative leader who is his peer and can call him to account, and in the relationship of the president to public opinion. This chapter will draw on experience from Franklin D. Roosevelt through John F. Kennedy to show how prone our institutions are now to elevate modern presidents into positions of unseemly power—at least of initiative. The following chapter will offer examples of policies in which presidential instincts or whims seem to dominate and will suggest the structure of a corrective. A later chapter will discuss the relationship of the president to public opinion.

I shall draw on the experience of members of the presidents' staff as well as on cabinet members and on the cabinet itself. Presidential staff members—those closest to him who see him most often and are in position to disagree with him most effectively—rarely if ever argue vehemently with him and probably never attack him with scorn and derision, hammering the table and telling him that if he persists in a course of action he is a fool. On the contrary, disagreements are subtle and muted. After all, staff members are chosen to help the president do what he wants rather than to express differences of opinion. If they disagree, they may gently protest, but when the president makes up his mind, they accept the result or—extremely rarely—they resign or are replaced. The same generalizations apply, although not so forcefully, to cabinet members who do not see the president so often and who, if successful, build their own bases in their own departments whose breadth and scope become a measure of their own influence.

If advisers appear to influence presidents, an examination will usually—one is tempted to say always—show that the advice concurs with what the president wants in his own mind. This seems to be true, for example, of Rexford Guy Tugwell or Harry Hopkins and Roosevelt, of Clark Clifford and Truman, of Sherman Adams and Eisenhower, of Theodore Sorensen and Kennedy—or of the relationships of such redoubtable cabinet secretaries as Harold Ickes or Henry A. Wallace or Henry L. Stimson and Roosevelt; as Dean Acheson and Truman; and as John Foster Dulles or George Humphrey and Eisenhower.

Franklin D. Roosevelt

Of Roosevelt, Rexford Guy Tugwell,[7] one of the original "Brains Trust," conjectured that those who stayed with him longest were allowed to remain "because they did not try to understand or probe [his mind] but rather because they gave him an unquestioning service." As governor of New York, Roosevelt had come to

regard criticism as unfriendly at best and malicious at worst.
He decidedly did not like any probing of his intentions or any inquiry about his motives . . . the implication was that he felt himself entitled to privilege, the privilege of one who was exempt from criticism. Those who did not recognize this and grant the immunity he needed were ticketed in his memory. He had an elephant's recall for injury.

Tugwell made his decision in 1932 to give Roosevelt unswerving loyalty in order to further Roosevelt's bid for the presidency as the best means of achieving the ends Tugwell sought. He was guided by the examples of such veteran Roosevelt staff members as Samuel I. Rosenman and D. (Doc) Basil O'Connor who had "long ago made up their minds that what they wanted to see done was most likely to be done by helping Roosevelt reach a position of power."[8]

Raymond Moley, also a Brains Truster, conceived his role in the same way. His job, beginning in the campaign of 1932 and continuing for four years, "was to sift proposals for [Roosevelt], discuss facts and ideas with him, and help him crystallize his own policy. At the end of this process we were generally in agreement. But when we were not, and after I had stated my case as well as I could, it was my business to see that his ideas were presented as attractively as possible. . . ."[9] When Moley decided to resign in 1936, Tom Corcoran, a young recruit to the Roosevelt staff, urged him to remain and exploit his intimacy to influence Roosevelt. " 'You write the music,' Tom said, 'He merely sings it.' " Moley exploded. He told Corcoran that he had obtained his entree to the White House "to serve Roosevelt's ideas, not yours. . . . Remember, when you get to work on the speeches, that you're a clerk, not a statesman." Nevertheless, Moley summed up his judgment of the effect of the presidency on the incumbent's character:

> Power itself has ways of closing the windows of a President's mind to fresh, invigorating currents of opinion from the outside. The most important of these ways is the subtle flattery with which the succession of those who see the President day after day treat him. Nine out of ten of those who see a President want something of him, and, because they do, they are likely to tell him something pleasant, something to cozen his good will. They are likely to agree with him, rather than disagree with him. If a man is told he is right by people day after day, he will, unless he has extraordinary defenses, ultimately believe he can never be wrong.[10]

The most durable adviser and speech-writer, who served from 1928 when FDR was elected governor of New York until FDR died in 1945, was Samuel I. Rosenman. Nearly all presidential speeches are policy-making, and those who help carry them through their many drafts "are in a peculiarly strategic position to shape . . . policy."

I do not mean to imply that any of the people who helped in the preparation of speeches would try to impose their own views on the

President or to slip them in. Even if they tried, they would have failed. We always informed him of any contrary view expressed to us by one of his associates and it would be fully and frankly discussed.[11]

Harry Hopkins, Roosevelt's most celebrated assistant, "would not utter one decisive word based on guesswork as to his Chief's policies and purposes. Hopkins ventured on no ground that Roosevelt had not charted." And again:

Harry Hopkins did not originate policy, then convince Roosevelt it was right. He had too much intelligence as well as respect for his chief to attempt the role of mastermind. He made it his job to provide a sounding board for discussions of the best means of obtaining the goals that the President set for himself. Roosevelt liked to think out loud, but his greatest difficulty was finding a listener who was both understanding and entirely trustworthy. That was Hopkins.[12]

Sometimes Hopkins may have done a little charting himself—but only in the direction FDR intended to go. When the German battleship *Bismarck* sailed into the Atlantic in May 1941, in order to intercept and sink American convoys and thereby intimidate the United States, Harry Hopkins told Rosenman and Robert E. Sherwood (the playwright was serving as a speech-writer) that he thought FDR had now decided to proclaim an Unlimited National Emergency (in 1939, a Limited National Emergency had been declared). When the speech-writers prepared a draft for the President, Hopkins urged inclusion of the proclamation. On seeing the draft, Sumner Welles, Under Secretary of State, and Adolph A. Berle, Assistant Secretary of State and one of the original Brains Trust, were astounded. Reading it, Roosevelt came to the last sentence, "I hereby proclaim that an Unlimited National Emergency exists . . ." and asked, "What's *this*?" And then: "Hasn't somebody been taking some liberties?"

I managed to explain, in a strangled tone, that Harry had told us that the President wanted something along these general lines. I am sure that Welles and Berle expected that Rosenman's and my heads were about to come off but there was not another word about the proclamation; it remained in the speech.[13]

Cabinet secretaries differ from White House staff members. Often the secretaries have their own political bases. Except for the Secretary of State, their perspectives are usually narrower than those of the White House. In defense of their departmental interests they will commonly fight anyone, including the president himself (but if they fight him it is typically by indirection, inaction, diversion, or some other devious means, rather than head-on argument). If they are the president's men, they have also been called "his natural enemies."

In Roosevelt's cabinet, Secretary of Labor Frances Perkins and National Industrial Recovery Act Administrator Hugh Johnson vied with each other to influence Roosevelt's policy on minimum wages.[14] Secretary of the Interior Harold L. Ickes and Secretary of Agriculture Henry A. Wallace maintained a running battle over the control of the Forest Service, involving whether Roosevelt would transfer it from Agriculture to Interior.[15] Secretary of the Treasury Henry Morgenthau threatened to resign when Roosevelt resumed deficit spending in 1938. Roosevelt told Morgenthau that he would be quitting under fire. Morgenthau stayed.[16] Jesse H. Jones, president of the Reconstruction Finance Corporation and Secretary of Commerce, was greatly influential in Congress (where he was once estimated to control ten Senate and forty House votes). He used his political leverage to protect Commerce agencies from budgetary cuts and the RFC from the Board of Economic Warfare.[17]

I shall disregard Secretary of State Cordell Hull and the debatable question of the degree of his influence on foreign policy in order to discuss the unrivaled experience of Henry L. Stimson who had been Taft's Secretary of War, Coolidge's Governor General of the Philippines, and Hoover's Secretary of State. Stimson had long known how hard it is to argue with presidents. Believing that few loyalties were more binding than those of cabinet officers to their chiefs "and that no obligations were more compelling than that of respect for the President of the United States," Stimson found it difficult to report the deep divisions in principle and attitude that arose between President Hoover and himself. Stimson had been convinced that America should prevent the victory of aggressors; Hoover (until Pearl Harbor), that America could and should stay aloof—this was the root of their disagreement over war debts, the Far East, disarmament, and international commitments generally.

In every case of direct conflict, Stimson followed Mr. Hoover's wishes, and time and again he acted as public advocate for courses which his own fundamental principles could hardly have justified. Occasionally he was even persuaded by forces which every lawyer loyal to his clients will understand, into a genuine belief in policies which later seemed to him insufficient and even wrong.[18]

Stimson seemed to be a likely candidate for initiating a debate with Roosevelt. Senior, experienced, prestigious, opinionated, and purposeful, Stimson was also a Republican with significant political support independent of the president. By necessity he focused on the same issues Roosevelt did, but often with different ideas about timing, strategy, and procedures. All the more striking then is Stimson's diffidence toward Roosevelt. In promoting the Selective Service Act of 1940, in pressing for the "over-age" destroyer deal with Britain, in nudging the president to take more decisive steps against Germany on the high seas, and in many other matters throughout the war Stimson was the soul of caution.[19]

After Pearl Harbor, conflicts arose over grand strategy both within the administration and, more especially, between the United States and Britain.[20] Prime Minister Winston Churchill wanted to attack through the Mediterranean and thence into the Balkans. Stimson and Chief of Staff General George C. Marshall were determined to move across the Channel toward France. After listening to Roosevelt discourse on the alternatives on 25 March 1942, Stimson and Marshall "edged the discussion over into the Atlantic and held him there." Nevertheless, the move into North Africa was made and finally approved over Stimson's opposition.

As late as July 1943, Stimson on a trip to England was faced once more with Churchill's argument against a direct assault across the Channel and in favor of operations against the "soft under-belly" of the Continent.

This stirred me up and for a few minutes we had at it hammer and tongs. I directly charged him that he was not in favor of the [cross-Channel] operation and that such statements as he made were "like hitting us in the eye" in respect to a project which we had all deliberately adopted and in which we were comrades . . .

Later, Stimson wrote that he had been able to oppose Churchill so vigorously because between such strong friends there could be "no falling out." And then this: "Stimson argued with Mr. Churchill more bluntly than he ever did with Mr. Roosevelt; he could cut loose at the Englishman as he never felt free to do with his Chief."[21]

Turning from Roosevelt's individual cabinet members to the cabinet as a whole, let me quickly dismiss the idea that the cabinet has an innate capacity for collective responsibility. The idea dies hard. Harry S. Truman declared that he regarded his cabinet as a board of directors in which the "best minds" would collectively discuss policies and advise the president on them "whether he likes it or not."[22] Dwight D. Eisenhower asserted that his cabinet was a council "met to consider together questions of public concern and to give me recommendations on new government-wide policies and institutions."[23] Richard M. Nixon began his first term with the assumption that he would run foreign affairs and let the cabinet deal with domestic matters. "I've always thought this country could run itself domestically without a President. . . . All you need is a competent Cabinet. . . ."[24] None of these dreams of collegial policy-making proved viable.[25] More in keeping with reality was John F. Kennedy's rejection of the cabinet's and the National Security Council's "making group decisions like corporate Boards of Directors."[26]

The cabinet is not a collegial body.

In matters of prestige, partisan politics, and legislative relations alike, the Cabinet as a collectivity has only a symbolic value, a value which readily disappears when the need for action supersedes the need for a show window. In the day to day work of the Cabinet, each man fends for himself without much consideration for Cabinet unity.[27]

Harry S. Truman

The most democratic and approachable of presidents, Harry S. Truman, still inspired the customary awe in associates. It took a bold or reckless man to collide with him. Admiral Sydney W. Souers, secretary of the National Security Council (NSC) under Truman, testified before the Jackson subcommittee on the issue of reductions in the military budget of the late 1940s that had become a subject of recrimination in the near-hysteria of the missile-gap illusion of the late 1950s. Some blamed the budget cuts on Truman's Budget Director James E. Webb. Senator Edmund S. Muskie (D., Maine) inquired whether Webb had made his decision before or after the NSC had recommended force levels to the president. Admiral Souers said:

That is a very delicate subject. Mr. Forrestal's memoirs show his concern with the 15 billion budget in 1948–1949 . . . The assumption was that the Budget Bureau fixed the amount and we had to plan our defense to suit it. Actually, the President made that figure. He named the figure and he stuck to the figure. I do not believe the

Director of the Budget could have changed his mind no matter how hard he tried. The matter was studied in the [National Security] Council.

Senator Muskie then asked whether President Truman listened to the council's recommendations before making up his mind. "Which one did he listen to last?" Admiral Souers replied, "It is pretty hard to delve into the mind of a President."[28]

Another example occurred in a staff meeting of 28 November 1950, when a request by big steel for authorization to raise prices in anticipation of future wage increases was discussed. The steel companies argued that general wage increases would cause their costs to rise because their business was largely on future orders at present prices; hence they wanted price rises now. Dr. John R. Steelman brought up the issue.

The President broke in quickly. "Stu [W. Stuart Symington, Chairman of the National Security Resources Board] started to talk with me about that, and I expressed such a violent opinion"—Truman smiled—"that I don't think he dared go any further with the thing." Steelman, seeing that the President's mind was made up, dropped the matter. . . .[29]

Occasionally Charlie Ross, Truman's press secretary, and Clark Clifford exercised some moderating influence on him. In May 1946, two railroad brotherhoods rejected a White House demand to cancel a national railroad strike. President Truman angrily jotted down a speech in which he called the union leaders liars and Communists, denounced Congress as weak-kneed, and appealed to the veterans for support. "Let's hang a few traitors and make our country safe for democracy. Come on, boys, let's do the job!" Fortunately, Press Secretary Ross could "bluntly tell" Mr. Truman his speech was wrong. "Clark Clifford . . . given the delicate task of rewriting the presidential prose" toned it down considerably, although the speech still compared the railroad strike to Pearl Harbor and included a threat to draft strikers into the army. But the president "realized that Clifford and Ross had saved him from a serious blunder" and he soon gave Clifford another promotion.[30]

Clifford, whom David E. Lilienthal, director of the Tennessee Valley Authority from 1933, chairman in the period 1941–46, and chairman of the Atomic Energy Commission in 1946–50, called "best man in the White House since I've known about things," was President Truman's special counsel in his first term and briefly in his second term. In the first term, "he sensed he was caught up in nothing less than a full-scale battle for the President's mind." Supported especially by Oscar Chapman, Undersecretary and later Secretary of the Interior, Clifford contended with John W. Snyder, Secretary of the Treasury, and others. In late 1946 the liberals (Clifford and company) began to plot a course of action. According to Clifford's account, "the idea was that 6 or 8 of us would try to come to an understanding among ourselves on what directions we would like the President to take on any given issue. And then, quietly and unobtrusively, each in his own way, we would try to steer the President in that direction." Noting their struggle with the conservative forces, Clifford went on: "It was completely unpublicized, and I don't think Mr. Truman ever realized what was going on."

Among Clifford's successes with Truman were the following: In September 1946, after the conflict between the President and Wallace, Clifford warmly approved firing Wallace. Afterward Clifford and Press Secretary Ross "were able to persuade Truman never to approve a speech until his staff had studied it, and to begin saying 'no comment' at his press conferences when issues were raised about which he was ill-informed." In 1947, Clifford prevailed over others and persuaded Truman to veto the Taft-Hartley labor bill, despite the fact, according to Leon Keyserling, member of the Council of Economic Advisers, that the president was "getting tremendous pressure from his congressional leaders to sign the bill, also from every member of the Cabinet except . . . the Secretary of Labor." With Chapman in May 1948, Clifford "persuaded Truman to override State Department objections and grant immediate recognition to the new state of Israel." This coup involved overriding the redoubtable General Marshall. In November 1947, Clifford prepared a forty-three-page memorandum outlining the strategies he believed President Truman should use to be reelected. The memorandum closed with the declaration that the end was important enough to justify any means that Truman might employ.

When George F. Kennan, head of the planning staff of the Department of State, alerted the United States to the threatening posture of postwar Russian communism and proposed political containment, Truman consulted Clifford, who wrote a seventy-page memorandum urging that it would be highly dangerous to conclude that international peace lay only in "accord," "mutual understanding," or "solidarity" with Russia.

The language of military power is the only language which disciples of power politics understand. The United States must use that language in order that Soviet leaders will realize that our government is determined to uphold the interest of its citizens and the rights of small nations. Compromises and concessions are considered by the Soviets to be the evidence of weakness.

The Clifford document closed by advocating that the United States should "support all democratic countries which are in any way menaced or endangered by the U.S.S.R." Thus Kennan's stress on political containment of Russia was swept aside in favor of military containment.

Nevertheless, Clifford's success with President Truman (as others earlier had enjoyed some success with Franklin D. Roosevelt) lay essentially in encouraging the president to do what he characteristically wanted to do. Whether the conflict was with John L. Lewis, with Thomas E. Dewey, or with Joseph Stalin, when others would urge Truman to compromise, Clifford would counsel him to stand and fight. "No advice could have been better calculated to appeal to Truman's own deepest instincts."

Of Truman's cabinet as an instrument of collective decision-making —as Truman put it early in his term, a body "whose combined judgment the President uses to formulate the fundamental policies of his administration"—it must be said that the vision was not realized. Although Richard F. Fenno, Jr., concluded that Truman consulted more seriously with his cabinet than either Woodrow Wilson or Franklin D. Roosevelt, the most important functions of the cabinet as a collegial body were to provide "a political sounding board" and to improve "administrative coherence." Fenno contrasted the "uninformative Cabinet meeting" with the "business-like manner in which members line up to see the President privately as soon as the meeting is over." And he used Truman's cabinet to illustrate the weakness of that body in settling intra-administration disputes, thus underlining "the essential powerlessness of the Cabinet within the political system . . ."[31]

In regard to individual cabinet members, Truman shortly forced, encouraged, or accepted resignations of the chief Roosevelt holdovers —Stimson after his substantial shift on policy regarding nuclear weapons (discussed in the next chapter), Henry Morgenthau in the Treasury after a brief dispute about the Morgenthau plan for Germany, Harold Ickes after a rupture caused by Ickes's opposition to Truman's nomination of Edwin S. Pauley as Secretary of the Navy, and Commerce Secretary Henry A. Wallace after the latter's provocative speech challenging American foreign policy in September 1946.[32] Shortly afterward came the parting of the ways with Truman's own appointee, Secretary of State James F. Byrnes, and his replacement by General George C. Marshall.[33] All these moves were consistent with Truman's intention—announced early in his first term and provided a retrospective rationale in 1954—to take charge of his administration.[34]

Truman's strategy was eminently successful, as exemplified in his dealings with the assertive James Forrestal, first Secretary of the Navy and later Secretary of Defense. Although Forrestal was somewhat combative on issues, such as labor policy, outside his jurisdiction, he was much more reserved in face-to-face meetings with the president on questions of first importance to Forrestal himself. The prime example is the unification of the services into one Department of Defense, a subject on which Forrestal worked long and hard. But when it came off and he was offered the Defense post, 26 July 1947, Forrestal made only the most oblique and diplomatic efforts to dissuade Truman from appointing Stuart Symington as Secretary of the Air Force. Forrestal's fears were soon confirmed. According to Hanson W. Baldwin, "unification became a joke when the Secretary of the Air Force [went] over the head of the Secretary of Defense and of the President himself."[35]

Dean Acheson, Mr. Truman's Secretary of State in his second term (with previous service as both undersecretary and assistant secretary), gave much thought to presidential-secretarial relationships. First, the secretary must be the President's agent; both parties must understand who is president, and the secretary must not consider himself, or attempt to be, a prime minister. But this "does not mean subserviency on the part of the Secretary" who must "stand squarely up" to the president when the president's interests and those of the country require it. Second, the president must refrain from being his own Secretary of State. In foreign affairs the nation must deal with people and geographical areas beyond its jurisdiction and control. Moreover, what occurs in the foreign field is so complex, voluminous, obscure, and unstable that it defies full comprehension. The president must do his best to comprehend the incomprehensible and then to devise, adopt, and execute appropriate policies. To do this the president needs help but not a surrogate. His secretary must be his "principal adviser" in foreign affairs. "The worst of all courses would be for the President to delegate the functions of understanding to some super staff officer [Henry Kissinger? McGeorge Bundy?] and retain the function of deciding, or apparently deciding, for himself." Finally, in the poisonous Washington atmosphere, it helps to maintain the necessary mutual confidence between president and secretary if "there is a strong admixture of affection between them. . . ."[36]

From Acheson's standpoint, his relationships with Mr. Truman were close to ideal. Humiliated by what he considered Franklin D. Roosevelt's patronizing, Acheson, the patrician, was devoted to Truman, the plebeian, who reciprocated. There was virtually complete accord between president and secretary. Both men wholeheartedly embraced if they did not create the cold war. Generally, the procedure was for Acheson as the president's principal adviser in foreign affairs to seek not only an "understanding of the incomprehensible" but also to formulate foreign policies for presidential approval, which was usually promptly and unequivocally given.

Examples include the restatement of American foreign policy in NSC–68, 25 April 1950. When the Soviet had first exploded an atomic weapon, in November 1949, Truman asked Acheson to review the nation's foreign and military policy. The result was a proposal to reject isolation, appeasement, and preventive war in favor of resolute resistance to Russia backed by sufficient military capability in the United States and her allies. Annual military budgets were estimated to require $50,000,000,000—up from $13.5 billion currently.[37] After the North Korean attack in June 1950, and President Truman's determination to meet force with force, Acheson spelled out the implementation that Truman accepted.[38] After Korea, Acheson reconsidered the question of German participation in European defense and recommended rearming Germany. The president acquiesced.[39]

Nevertheless, when accord between the two was not complete, Acheson found it difficult to "stand squarely up" to the president. One occasion, the prosecution of the Korean war, will be discussed in the following chapter. A second example involved one step in the exceedingly complicated Palestinian question. At the time James F. Byrnes was Secretary of State; but he was not inclined "to project himself into this issue, but rather [tended] to leave . . . it more and more" to Acheson as undersecretary. Truman clearly was "directing policy on Palestine," on which his deep-seated convictions favored opening the country at once to the immigration of 100,000 Jews from eastern Europe. Currently Britain, the mandatory state, was limiting Jewish immigration into Palestine to 1,500 a month.

At the time, Loy Henderson, chief of the Office of Near East and South Asian Affairs in the State Department, gave Secretary Byrnes "some observations, the wisdom of which has been amply borne out by subsequent events." Pointing to the intractable opposition of Arabs and Jews, Henderson urged an effort to get British, Soviet, U.S., and French agreement to a solution and then seek the approval of both Jews and Arabs. Otherwise, one of the powers might blame whatever happened on the others and encourage Arabs and Jews to fight it out. "There is no record that this advice ever reached the President. . . . ," writes Acheson, who states that he took at this time "more of an administrative than an advisory role." With due recognition of the fact that Acheson was only undersecretary, the incident clearly underlines the difficulty of arguing with any president who had made up his mind.[40]

Dwight D. Eisenhower

Just as Admiral Souers, commenting on Truman's relationship to the National Security Council, referred to the difficulty of "delving into the minds of Presidents," so Robert Cutler, Eisenhower's secretary of the NSC, testified:

The President is an active participant in the [National Security] Council discussions. Sometimes issues which are in conflict are decided on by him in the course of the discussion. He has to be very careful not too early in the discussion to intervene. If you are an affirmative person and you intervene early . . . , and you have intelligent Council members, they inevitably tend to feel a wind blowing from one direction or the other.[41]

Malcolm Moos, formerly administrative assistant to President Eisenhower, wrote:

The Church invented the Devil's advocate, Parliament the loyal opposition, and John Stuart Mill told us that truth needs error to show it off. But how often does this function take place in the White

House? Not, surely, as effectively as it should. What the White House needs at all times is an "abominable no man," who can speak daringly of the new and scornfully of the old.[42]

Eisenhower has been both hailed and blamed for his organization of the executive office of the president and his delegation of authority to act. "Being a soldier by profession [wrote Arthur Krock], Eisenhower placed great reliance on the staff system. Thus, some decisions that should have been referred to him . . . were made on the lower levels."[43] According to Louis Koenig:

> For the better part of . . . Eisenhower's two terms, [Sherman] Adams exercised more power than any other presidential assistant in modern times. . . . Indeed, it is demonstrable that his power and impact upon the national destiny have exceeded that of not a few Presidents of the United States.[44]

Patrick Anderson disagreed. Adams's role as assistant to the President had been overestimated because critics failed to realize that Adams held sway only over lesser issues especially in domestic affairs where Eisenhower normally had little interest. In policy fights within the administration there was little evidence that Adams "ever ran counter to what he felt to be Eisenhower's wishes." Indeed, Emmet John Hughes remarked that Eisenhower "could shake even so strong a man as Sherman Adams—sharply asserting a will, an impatience, or a caprice that (as I witnessed more than once) would spin Adams completely around to reverse the decision already fixed in his own mind." Of Adams, Eisenhower himself wrote:

> many wanted to see in him something of a Rasputin. Actually, he was a tireless, able, and devoted assistant. I never saw him by a single word or action try to act as a "power-behind-the-throne" or to assert an authority beyond that expected of him as my principal White House Assistant.[45]

Naturally enough, Eisenhower rejected as "nonsense" the view that he had "conducted the Presidency largely through staff decisions." While he believed in consultation, "staff work doesn't mean that you take a vote of your subordinates and then abide by the majority opinion." On important matters, he added, "you alone must decide."[46]

He drove the point home in denying the ability of Congress to control the presidency by changing the make-up of the National Security Council. Representative Carl Vinson of Georgia, chairman of the

House Armed Services Committee, attempted to force a reorganization of the NSC in 1958 by providing, among other things, that the service secretaries should be statutory members. Vinson, Eisenhower declared, betrayed an error of understanding common to academicians and especially to congressmen.[47]

Assuming that the NSC acts by committee vote, Congress is frequently compelled to add to, or subtract from, its "statutory" membership. While the NSC is authorized by law and is, when correctly employed, a vitally important body, it is only advisory. . . . Its duty is to advise the President but he can use it, ignore it, meet with it personally or not, in whole or in part, and can add, as he sees fit, any number of people to its membership. So Mr. Vinson's proposal . . . was of no significance whatsoever.

If the NSC under Eisenhower did not collectively formulate policy on important issues, neither did Eisenhower's cabinet, in spite of his own assertions and those of members of his administration to the contrary. It is a familiar story. The image of a cabinet with collegial responsibility for decisions hammering out the policies to be pursued by government is unsustained by the evidence. Richard Fenno noted the greater institutionalization of the Eisenhower cabinet, with its regular meetings and written agenda. Nevertheless, the cabinet performed best on noncontroversial issues. Other issues "would not have been brought up to the group, for the Eisenhower Cabinet members are no different than their predecessors in their natural reluctance to throw serious, interdepartmental conflict into the meeting or to subject themselves to sharp cross-examination." And again: "Less than a fist full of the Eisenhower meetings in five years could be called sharply controversial ones." Despite the careful preparation, the typical situation was that cabinet members came without having done their homework. The results were "unpremeditated, if not aimless, discussions."[48]

Emmet John Hughes described: ". . . the remembered faces grouped, week after week, around the long table of the Cabinet room . . . seated in their high-backed leather chairs, gravely fingering their white notebooks . . . , nodding solemnly whenever the President spoke, and murmuring comment or counsel on [a] bewildering array of matters. . . ." And later:

As the Cabinet was a remarkably true mirror to the whole political life of the Eisenhower administration—and all its attitudes and

prejudices, convictions and conflicts—so, inevitably, its surface did
not merely reflect sharp and vivid images. It clouded again and again
with the film of irresolution and vacillation.[49]

Of individual cabinet members, George Humphrey, Secretary of the
Treasury, and John Foster Dulles, Secretary of State, are probably
considered to have been the most influential. Humphrey was the leading adviser on fiscal policy. "In cabinet meetings I always wait for
George Humphrey to speak. I sit back and listen to the others talk
while he isn't saying anything. But I know that when he speaks he
will say just what I am thinking."[50] The key to the relationship lies
in the last sentence. Humphrey articulated Eisenhower's own thoughts,
instincts, convictions, or prejudices. On economic matters Eisenhower
harbored a conservatism that became more patent in his second term.[51]
It may have been grounded on his experience in the war. In 1941, as
he was painfully aware, America was short of every kind of military
material. After Pearl Harbor, the economy mushroomed to produce
the flood of weapons and other material of war that powerfully impressed Eisenhower, as *Crusade in Europe* repeatedly shows. His instincts were, like Humphrey's, to do nothing that would cripple or
interfere with the working of so efficient an economic machine.

Even more than Humphrey, Dulles has been credited with shaping
policy to which Eisenhower acquiesced. Eisenhower heatedly and repeatedly denied that Dulles had had "virtually a free hand in the conduct of the nation's foreign policy."[52] Early in 1953, Dulles had
sought Eisenhower's guidance, and they had agreed that the objective
of American foreign policy should be—what else?—"peace with
justice." Implementation required America to possess overwhelming
military and economic strength that would be deployed to enable the
poor nations of the "free world" to grow strong enough to repel and
rich enough to reject communism. In all their relationships, Dulles was
the soul of propriety. "He would not deliver an important speech or
statement until . . . [Eisenhower] had read, edited, and approved it."[53]
After meetings with Eisenhower, Dulles dictated memoranda and read
them back to his chief on the phone.[54]

Against this view is the opinion of Sherman Adams that the "hard
and uncompromising line" of the United States "toward Soviet Russia and Red China" was more attributable to Dulles than to Eisenhower;[55] the contrast by Arthur Larson of "Eisenhower's bending
every effort to get along with the Russians . . . with Dulles' implacable

hostility toward all Communists,"[56] and Emmet John Hughes's emphasis on Eisenhower's impulsive willingness, after Stalin's death, to talk to the Russians against Dulles's dogged determination not to budge an inch.[57]

On the contrary, Eisenhower became as implacable toward the Russians as anyone. *Crusade in Europe* revealed the early optimism and the quick disillusionment; the intervening years had "shattered the dream."[58] As president, Eisenhower had become convinced that communism represented the ultimate evil and Russia the last word in perversity, whether issues arose in the Far East, in Berlin, in the Near East, or wherever. The Communists "respected nothing but strength." The failure of disarmament could be explained in one sentence, "It was the adamant insistence of the Communists on maintaining a closed society."[59] Eisenhower was fully in accord with the policy of massive retaliation; indeed, as the next chapter will indicate, he repeatedly flexed the American atomic muscle. If Dulles was on the brink, Eisenhower was behind him—Dulles would not have been there otherwise.

John F. Kennedy

In view of the length of treatment accorded Roosevelt, Truman, and Eisenhower, President Kennedy will be dealt with summarily. His term confirms the proposition that one does not argue lightly with presidents. As with Truman and Eisenhower, the account can begin with the National Security Council. Theodore Sorensen wrote that Kennedy used NSC meetings to increase public confidence and to improve the esprit de corps of participants. But such meetings raised a problem if the president himself were to be drawn into debates for, "in the White House, unlike . . . Congress, only one man's vote is decisive." Therefore, in such meetings "a President must carefully weigh his own words. Should he hint too early in the proceedings at the direction, the weight of his authority, the loyalty of his advisers, and their desire to be on the 'winning side' may shut off productive debate. Indeed, his very presence may inhibit candid discussion."[60]

Robert F. Kennedy was even more explicit. Referring to the Cuban missile crisis (of which more will be said in the next chapter), he wrote:

I believe our deliberations proved conclusively how important it is that the President have the recommendations and opinions of more than one individual, of more than one department, and of more than one point of view. Opinion, even fact itself, can best be judged by conflict, by debate. There is an important element missing when there is unanimity of viewpoint. Yet that not only can happen; it frequently does when the recommendations are being given to the President of the United States. His office creates such respect and awe that it has almost a cowering effect on men. Frequently I saw advisers adapt their opinions to what they believed President Kennedy and, later, President Johnson wished to hear.

I once attended a preliminary meeting with a cabinet officer, where we agreed on a recommendation to be made to the President. It came as a slight surprise to me when, a few minutes later, in the meeting with the President himself, the cabinet officer vigorously and fervently expressed the opposite point of view, when, from the discussion, he quite accurately learned that it would be more sympathetically received by the President.[61]

Robert F. Kennedy himself cut off at least one significant effort to argue with the president when he told Arthur Schlesinger, Jr., to raise no more objections about the Bay of Pigs invasion in 1961 but rather to give the president unquestioning support. In addition to Schlesinger, that disastrous enterprise was opposed by Chairman of the Senate Foreign Relations Committee J. William Fulbright, Director Edward R. Murrow of the U. S. Information Agency, and Undersecretary of State Chester Bowles. Apparently Secretary of State Dean Rusk prevented the dissents of Bowles and Murrow from reaching the president, and Dean Acheson ridiculed Fulbright. "Had one senior adviser opposed the adventure," Schlesinger wrote, "I believe that Kennedy would have cancelled it. No one spoke against it."[62]

Patrick Anderson concluded that Kennedy used his staff with "sure instincts"—at least, after the Bay of Pigs. Kennedy "never called staff meetings, knowing they would only bring differences into the open; instead he relied on one to one dealings with each side." He played his staff members one against another, keeping them in their place ("there was never any doubt about who was boss"), and maintaining social distance from them—one of Anderson's informers quoted Freud: the great leader "is often aloof from other men." Perhaps Kennedy's staff, unlike Lyndon Johnson's, was not "often in fear of outbursts of presidential temper";[63] the evidence suggests, however, that they were not immune from it.

The White House staff can help the Secretary [of State] ride herd on his bureaucratic underlings, and can relieve pressure on the State Department by attending the President's immediate, personal needs for information, advice, for documents, sometimes just for someone to be mad at. "The President," says one member of the Kennedy-Johnson NSC operation, "is entitled to have a mattress—people he can kick the hell out of and they won't do anything at all."[64]

Conclusion

Presidents are above argument. The staff members serving them directly are in no position to engage them in debate. As Bill D. Moyers, counselor to President Lyndon B. Johnson, wrote: "You aren't a man in your own right when you are working for a President. To be most effective you have to have an umbilical cord right to his character, nature, and personality."[65] It is not that presidents are surrounded by sycophants (although these are by no means underrepresented); rather, the president is often served by persons of outstanding education and intelligence who realize, nevertheless, that their own purposes will best be fulfilled by his success. The effect is much the same. Cabinet secretaries, more remote from the president, are more independent. But they work their subordinate wills, if contrary to his, by frustrating his orders rather than by meeting him in argument to try to change his mind.

Congressmen and senators are in different but not superior positions. The Senate subcommittee on Watergate, searching for precedents when presidents had appeared or had provided depositions for either congressional committees or courts, could find only four and none in the last century. And yet, as Senator Sam J. Ervin, Jr., said, "You can't cross-examine a piece of paper." Examples of the president's speaking and of legislators answering him on or off the floor of Congress are legion—but these do not create the essential clash of minds, "of right and wrong between whose endless jar justice resides."

The essence of presidential debate requires that the protagonists meet face to face in the presence of others in some formal setting that is perceived as part of the policy-making process. It is not enough for the discussion to take place informally and one-to-one, a situation that, it is alleged, enlarges the opportunity for candor.[66] Even on such occasions effective debate is exceedingly rare. Nor is it enough to have a professional devil's advocate. The relationship of the devil's advocacy to genuine debate is that of a sham battle to a fire fight.

Exceptions—that is, situations when the president in the presence of others, is formally, explicitly, and sharply, even heatedly, opposed by someone who enjoys an independent political base or who is prepared to risk his career—are extremely rare. Eisenhower's term produced two, both with Senate Republican leaders. Early in 1953 in a full cabinet meeting to consider Eisenhower's first budget Senator Robert A. Taft was present, heard the president out in "grim silence," then, losing control of himself and pounding his fist on the table, shouted his dissent at Eisenhower. When Taft finally subsided, the silence was deep and uncomfortable. Eisenhower was flushed with anger. But some began to exchange small talk that allowed the two men to get hold of themselves; and . . . nothing happened. There was no debate. The second occasion was in 1957, when Senator William F. Knowland (R., California, and Republican floor leader) precipitated "the most angry scene [Adams] had seen since . . . Taft . . . exploded in 1953" over the Status of Force Treaties. Eisenhower stood firm.[67]

Franklin D. Roosevelt's time brought forth at least two examples. One occurred in a cabinet meeting on 30 December 1937, with economic indices falling and the bill to enlarge the Supreme Court ending in disaster. Referring to a forthcoming message to Congress and looking straight at Vice-President John Nance Garner, Roosevelt said, "Jack, I am going to reassert leadership." Garner asked whether he had ever given it up. Roosevelt said that he had put it aside temporarily because he was tired.

The Vice President retorted, "You were afraid, Mr. President. . . . Before you went to Florida . . . you were both scared and tired. You were willing to give up on taxation, on holding companies," and he mentioned one or two other subjects. I have never heard anyone talk like this to the President, and the President did not pursue the subject any further.[68]

The other example is probably unparalleled in the annals of the presidency for the kind of language that was hurled at the Chief of State. In Roosevelt's first term he sought economy by cutting budgets. Secretary of War George Dern became alarmed enough at the depth of the proposed cuts to ask for an audience to which he took General Douglas MacArthur, Chief of Staff, and others. As MacArthur recorded it, Dern "grew white and silent" under Roosevelt's tongue-lashing. MacArthur entered the argument only to draw down "the full vials of his sarcasm" on himself.

In my emotional exhaustion I . . . said . . . that when we lost the next war, and an American boy, lying in the mud with an enemy bayonet through his belly and an enemy foot on his dying throat, spat out his last curse, I wanted the name not to be MacArthur, but Roosevelt. The President grew livid. "You must not talk that way to the President!" he roared. He was, of course, right. . . . I said that I was sorry and apologized. . . . I told him that he had my resignation. . . . As I reached the door his voice came with that cool detachment which so reflected his extraordinary self-control, "Don't be foolish, Douglas; you and the budget must get together on this."

Dern had shortly reached my side and I could hear his gleeful tones, "You've saved the Army." But I just vomited on the steps of the White House.[69]

The purpose of this chapter has been to put the problems of the presidency—which may become so overpowering as in the summer of 1973 that they seem intensely and solely connected to the personality of the present incumbent—in an institutional perspective. I want to illuminate the degree of irresponsibility that we the people have created in the presidential office. It is as though we elected him—for a limited term, it is true, but long enough in all conscience for great good or consummate evil to come of it—and said to him, "Mr. President, you are our chosen leader; and whatever ideas you have, whatever snap judgments, whatever comes to the top of your head, these shall be our commands."

At the same time it is not a matter of the quality of mind of the president or of those who surround him. Rather, the intellectual drive that needs the sharp challenge of debate is blunted by agreement. There may be something in political life, if it is only the amount of whiskey consumed, that dulls the intellect and produces what Joseph A. Schumpeter called "a reduced sense of responsibility, a lower level of energy of thought and greater sensitiveness to non-logical influences."[70] Taking over the post of Attorney General in 1973, Elliott Richardson complained of a pervasive "sleaziness" in government. We need to infuse into our politics the challenge, the confrontation, that will force the ideas and their explanations to surface and make them bear the cold and public light of day. Abraham Lincoln may offer guidance. In December 1861 Lincoln asked his Secretary of State William H. Seward to write a note stating the reasons for England's handing over James M. Mason and John Slidell. Seward disagreed and wrote out the reasons for England's not giving them up. Lincoln set out to put his view in writing but did not do so; rather, he permitted Seward's note to become policy. When Seward asked him whether he had framed arguments on the other side, Lincoln replied: "I found that I could not make an argument that would satisfy my own mind. And that proved to me your ground was the right one."[71]

3 Government by Presidential Instinct

Lear: . . .—I will do such
    things,—
What they are, yet I know not, but they
    shall be
The terrors of the earth . . .
        —Shakespeare, *King Lear*

The president occupies a position of unique authority, insulated from debate and enthroned as a democratic monarch whose purposes are all too often uncritically accepted. The consequences are decisions, some of them of great importance, that are shaped by presidential whims or prejudices. A striking example is the contrast between the notions of Franklin D. Roosevelt and Harry S. Truman about dealing with Russia. Roosevelt's irrepressible optimism and his confidence in his ability to cajole or cozen anyone into his way of thinking led to his conciliatory policy toward Russia; but so did his assumption that the two nations must find a way to live in some kind of mutual forbearance. When Truman came to power in 1945, he immediately replaced Roosevelt's conciliatory assumptions with the equally simplistic ideas that the only way to get along with the Russians was to beat them over the head and that the world was ineluctably divided into two camps, the free and the slave. The associates of each president, often the same persons, smoothly accepted the transition—some happier with Roosevelt than with Truman and vice versa—but the main thing is that they went along.

First, this chapter will set forth policies, drawing upon the administrations of Roosevelt through Kennedy, which seem to have been shaped essentially by the presidents themselves and to have been the product of presidential instincts or unexamined assumptions.

Second will be a discussion of the reforms that might force the president to explain his actions, subject to the challenge of a peer, namely, the leader of the opposition.

Franklin D. Roosevelt

Consider Roosevelt's ideas about Russia and China. William P. Gerberding has traced and interpreted the shifts in Roosevelt's conception of the Soviet Union during the Second World War.[1] By June 1941, when Hitler invaded Russia, Roosevelt's "bitter contempt" for the USSR because of the attack on Finland had diminished but not disappeared. By early September, however, Roosevelt was writing the Pope that churches in Russia were open and well-attended, that Russia might yet accept freedom of religion, and that Russia would pursue its aims outside its borders only with propaganda, not arms.

"A variety of circumstances and influences combined to . . . alter and . . . completely overturn" Roosevelt's earlier view of Russia. "Perhaps the most important single factor was Roosevelt's personality. . . . Roosevelt was a 'positive' man, generally optimistic and hopeful, who tended to look on the bright side of events and who believed that men could and would create the conditions for peace and security in the world." Noting the anomaly that Russia was now united with the democracies in a war against fascism, Gerberding conjectured "that Roosevelt simply could not live with this kind of ambiguity, and his resolution of the problem was to develop a view of the Soviet Union which made it appear more attractive than simply a lesser evil than Hitler's Germany."

Listening to those advisers who agreed with him and ignoring the muted warnings of others, Roosevelt showed "virtually no understanding of, or interest in, communist ideology, except in its crude outlines [which] preached the violent overthrow of existing governments and seizure of power by the vanguard of the proletariat." He expected Russia's revolutionary spirit and doctrine to cool and soften, and he seemed incapable of considering that Stalin came to their meetings informed in his thinking and perceptions by Communist doctrine rather than by FDR's own trust, good will, and faith in his persuasive powers. Roosevelt, Gerberding thought, also underestimated Russia's capacity for imperialist expansion after the war; rather, he believed that Russia's aims were essentially limited to "achieving the security which would permit them to live at peace and rebuild their country." Above all, Roosevelt believed in the idealism of the Four Freedoms and in his powers to persuade virtually anyone but Hitler and his kind to accept his views. "A more cynical generation," Gerberding concludes, "can only wish he had been right."

Policy toward China came up even before Roosevelt was inaugurated in 1933 when he had to choose between the Stimson doctrine of qualified intervention in the Far East and "the traditional American concept of neutrality, of disinterestedness, impartiality, and non-participation in foreign quarrels." Roosevelt's advisers, Rexford Guy Tugwell and Raymond Moley, believing that the domestic economic crisis should take precedence, tried hard to convince Roosevelt that it would be a mistake to underwrite the Stimson doctrine. They might as well have held their breath.

Roosevelt put an end to the discussion by looking up and recalling that his ancestors used to trade with China. "I have always had the deepest sympathy for the Chinese," he said. "How could you expect me not to go along with Stimson on Japan?"
    That was all. It was so simple, so incredible, there could be no answer.[2]

For the critical period, 1941 to 1945, I shall draw on Tang Tsou:

President Roosevelt was captivated by a vision of an era of international peace, freedom, and justice based upon the moral principles of the Atlantic Charter and the Declaration of the United Nations, ushered in by the establishment of an international organization and policed by the peace-loving powers.[3]

Believing that no irreconcilable conflicts existed between the United States and the U.S.S.R. or other countries, FDR thought of himself as the future arbiter, conciliator, and teacher, "adjusting the differences between Great Britain, the Soviet Union, and China and educating them in the new ways of international behavior."
    Roosevelt's idealism was exemplified in the Four-Nation Declaration of Moscow, 30 October 1943, among the U.S., the U.K., the U.S.S.R., and China, which declared that "after the termination of hostilities they will not employ their military forces within the territories of other states except for the purposes envisaged in this declaration and after joint consultation." Tang remarks: "The Moscow Declaration vividly revealed America's faith in the capability of general principles couched in ambiguous language to exorcise the conflicts among nations and to restrain the ambitions of an aggressive revolutionary power." FDR and Secretary Hull carried their purpose of making China a great power—so that it could serve with the U.S., the U.K., and the U.S.S.R. as one of "the four policemen"—to a series of international conferences in 1943 in Moscow, Cairo, and Teheran.

By 1945, however, FDR had recognized that China was not ready to join the others in policing the world and shifted his policy.

Thus, Roosevelt tried out the policy of making China a great power for a period of three years, from 1941 to 1944, while experimenting with various military programs. In 1941 and 1942, his chosen means was lend-lease and one of his most influential advisors was Lauchlin Currie, a lend-lease specialist. In 1943, his principal instrument was Chennault's air force. In 1944, he forsook Chennault and experimented with the B-29 Matterhorn Project and the Stilwell approach. After Stilwell's recall and the removal in January, 1945, of the B-29 from the Chinese bases to India, he lost his interest in China and intensified his search for wartime and post-war co-operation in the Far East with the Soviet Union.

Tang Tsou thought that he could explain Roosevelt's actions as reflecting the moral pretensions of the United States exemplified in the Open Door policy originally, later expressed in the Good Neighbor policy toward Latin America, and then shown in the misapplication of the Good Neighbor policy in the rest of the world, including the Far East. It followed from these premises that Roosevelt would assume that China would cooperate in internal reform without any coercion or even pressure on our part. Roosevelt opposed Stilwell's repeated requests to bring pressure upon Chiang Kai-Shek until too late, and then he acquiesced in Chiang's request for Stilwell's recall. In consequence, the United States failed to achieve her ends in China. "It was Chiang, despite the asymmetry of power between Nationalist China and the United States, who used Roosevelt for his purposes instead of the other way around."

Harry S. Truman

Vietnam provides a bridge from Roosevelt to Truman. Intervention in that country had to wait on an instinctive presidential reaction just as the expansion of intervention by future presidents and the escalation into war were, at their critical junctures, the product of presidential idiosyncrasy. President Roosevelt "never made up his mind" whether to support the French effort to reclaim its Indochina colonies. Similarly, in his first administration, Truman "had no clear-cut reaction to the conflict that broke out in 1945 and 1946 between the French and the Vietminh." During these years Washington refused French requests for military assistance but also ignored Ho Chi Minh's appeals to accord Vietnam "the same status as the Philippines." Only in 1949 when the Communists had triumphed in China did the United States dramatically end its ambivalence by announcing military aid to the French in Indochina, beginning with a grant of $10,000,000. "The U.S. thereafter was directly involved in the developing tragedy of Vietnam." By 1954 American military aid paid for 78 percent of the French war effort.[4]

Turning to American policy toward the Soviet Union, I shall cite Gar Alperovitz on Truman:

his view of how to treat with Russia was far different from Roosevelt's. His decision abruptly to cut off Lend-Lease, his show of force over the Trieste dispute, his reconsideration of Roosevelt's Far Eastern agreement, his breach of the Balkans understandings, his refusal to adhere to the Yalta reparations accord—all these acts testify to the great gulf between his view and the view of his predecessor.[5]

Encouraged in his hard line by a memorandum from the Department of State, dated 13 April 1945, the day following Roosevelt's death, Truman took his position in a meeting on 23 April, in which the most significant though by no means the only issue was Soviet policy toward Poland. Russia was insisting on seating the Lublin government as representative of Poland in the forthcoming San Francisco conference designed to shape the United Nations. The State Department called the action a breach of the Yalta agreements that pledged free and democratic elections in Poland. Truman asked for comments. Naval Secretary Forrestal said that the Russians thought the United States would let them take over all of eastern Europe and declared that we had "better have a showdown with them now than later. . . ." He was supported by Ambassador Averell Harriman.

On the other hand, War Secretary Stimson warned that it would be well to find out how far Russia intended to go. "He said he thought that the Russians were perhaps being more realistic than we were about their own security." Admiral Leahy, who had been at Yalta as Roosevelt's military aide, said that the Russians had never intended a free government for Poland. He would have been surprised had the Russians behaved otherwise, and added that their interpretation of Yalta might differ from ours. Stettinius denied the legitimacy of different interpretations of Yalta and asserted that the U.S. must insist on a free and independent Poland. General Marshall cautioned against the risk of breaking with Russia whose assistance in the war against Japan would be extremely valuable.

In the end, the president took the risk, as Assistant Secretary of State Charles (Chip) Bohlen, who was taking notes, recorded. "The President said . . . that he felt our agreements with the Soviet Union so far had been a one-way street and that he could not continue; it was now or never. He intended to go with the plans to San Francisco and if the Russians did not wish to join us they could go to hell . . ."[6]

Consider now the use of the atomic weapon in Hiroshima and Nagasaki as well as the decision to withhold atomic information from Russia and then to override Secretary Henry J. Stimson's proposal for a collaborative approach with Russia in the control of nuclear energy. All show the importance of the president in initiating major policies. True enough, on 26 May 1945, a committee of prominent men, plus their scientific advisers, unanimously recommended the use of the atomic bomb without warning and against a target that would prove its devastating strength. One committee member, Undersecretary of the Navy Ralph E. Bard, reversed his opinion on 27 June and proposed an alternative course of action. His advice ignored, he resigned —a rare occurrence. Others outside the committee demurred at the time. General Dwight D. Eisenhower, who as president was to threaten the use of atomic weapons, recoiled from employment at first. "It wasn't necessary to hit them with that awful thing."

Regardless of the weight of advice, it is hard to believe that President Truman would have done anything else. He stressed that the final decision was his. "The dropping of the bombs [on Hiroshima and Nagasaki] stopped the war, saved millions of lives." And again: "Let there be no mistake about it. I regarded the bomb as a military weapon and never had any doubt that it should be used." And again: "The atomic bomb was no 'great decision,' . . . not any decision that you had to worry about . . ."[7]

Secretary Henry J. Stimson had chaired the committee that recommended the use of the bomb against Japan. He had also urged President Truman to curb his instincts to get tough with Russia long enough for the bomb to be tested so that its influence might be used in negotiations. (J. Robert Oppenheimer recorded "incredible pressure" to ready the atomic bomb before the July Potsdam meeting. According to Winston Churchill, after President Truman received the message at Potsdam that the bomb was a success, "he was a changed man. He told the Russians just where they got off, . . . and generally bossed the whole meeting.") Soon Stimson sensed that things were going wrong. "It had become perfectly clear that the American nuclear monopoly had not made Russia tractable and in fact had fostered dangerous distrust and fear." Late in 1945 General Eisenhower observed in Moscow: "Before the atom bomb was used, I would have said, yes, I was sure that we could keep the peace with Russia. Now I don't know . . . people are frightened and disturbed all over. Everyone feels insecure again."

Stimson made two proposals for controlling atomic energy and thus changing the direction of policy in cabinet meetings on 11–12 September 1945. Although Stimson was supported by some members of the cabinet, the president, with the backing of others, rejected his proposal. Stimson then wrote:

The problem of our satisfactory relations with Russia is not merely connected with but is virtually dominated by the problem of the atomic bomb. Except for the problem of the control of that bomb, those relations, while vitally important, might not be immediately pressing. The establishment of relations of mutual confidence between her and us could afford to await the slow progress of time. But with the discovery of the bomb, it became immediately emergent. *Those relations may be irretrievably embittered by the way in which we approach the solution of the bomb with Russia. For if we fail to approach them and merely continue to negotiate with them, having this weapon rather ostentatiously on our hip, their suspicion and their distrust of our purposes and motives will increase* [Stimson's italics].[8]

Stimson pressed his point further, to no avail, and resigned. When the Big Three met in December 1945, the United States had no plan to offer on the control of atomic energy. When it did finally propose the imposition of controls by stages so that an effective inspection system would be ensured before the manufacture of atomic bombs was stopped and stockpiles were destroyed, the Russians demurred. Ensued an impasse.[9]

Skipping reluctantly over the Truman Doctrine, the Marshall Plan, N.A.T.O., and Palestinian policy, I turn to the Korean war. When South Korea was attacked, according to Professor Louis J. Koenig, President Truman "came quickly and solitarily to a fundamental decision: North Korea's aggression across the 38th parallel must be countered by force. . . . Truman apparently did not even consider the

possibility of a nonviolent response. . . . The President more than anyone else establishes the atmosphere of a discussion. . . ." The decision
itself flouted an assumption "generally embraced by top American
military authorities and sanctioned by Presidents Franklin Roosevelt
and Truman [himself]: United States ground forces . . . should never
engage on the Asian mainland. . . . Least of all should they be
committed to an area like Korea, slight in military value and difficult
to defend."[10] As Truman remembered it later, he had been in Independence, Missouri, when Secretary of State Acheson called to tell
him of the North Korean invasion. Truman remained in Missouri.
Acheson called the following morning to report that the North
Korean attack was in force; ". . . and I said, 'Dean, we've got to stop the
sons-of-bitches, no matter what,' and that's all there is to it!"[11]

According to Ernest R. May, the decision to intervene in Korea was
not based on a calculated policy. "Instead, their minds flew to an axiom
—that any armed aggression anywhere constituted a threat to all
nations everywhere."[12] In addition to contradicting the myth that
such decisions are carefully deliberated, the incident casts doubt on
another favorite White House principle regardless of the identity of
its occupant: The president knows best because he alone has all the
facts or more of them than anyone else.

On sweeping policy decisions, which are, after all, relatively few, a
President makes up his mind on the basis of the same *kind* of
information that is available to the average citizen. . . . When Harry
Truman decided to resist Communist aggression in Korea, he knew
very little more than that the Forty-ninth Parallel [*sic*; 38th?] had been
crossed by Communist troops, a fact that was already in the headlines.[13]

Earlier on, the Korean war aim was restricted to containing the
enemy north of the 38th parallel. After MacArthur's success in the
Inchon landing, the war aim became the unification of Korea, in spite
of its low priority for President Truman.

He wanted to affirm that the UN was not a League of Nations, that
aggression would be met with counter-force, that "police actions"
were well worth their cost. . . . He wanted to avoid "the wrong war,
in the wrong place, at the wrong time" . . . and any "War" if possible.
He wanted NATO strengthened . . . the United States rearmed
without inflation. . . . He also wanted to get on with the Fair Deal,
keep Democrats in office, strengthen his congressional support from
North and West, and calm the waters stirred by men like
Senator [Joseph] McCarthy.

None of these, wrote Richard E. Neustadt, required the unification of Korea; and all took precedence with Truman.[14] But he did not act that way, and he had essentially only himself to blame—at least under our system of presidential government.

It was one thing to leave MacArthur's orders unchanged on November 9; it was quite another to leave them unchanged day by day thereafter while he prepared and began his victory march. . . . In the two-week interval before MacArthur's march, the General, not the President, became the judge and arbiter of White House risks. . . .

By 9 November, the major advisers, both civilian and military, knew that the unification of Korea and the destruction of enemy forces were no longer possible, although they did not conclude until 25 November that the president should change his directives to Mac-Arthur. But who should inform the president?

No one went to Truman because everyone thought someone else should go. . . . When worry grew, the military chiefs deferred to State; let Acheson, as guardian of "policy," ask Truman to reverse MacArthur. But Acheson, already under fire from the Capitol, was treading warily between the Pentagon and that inveterate idealist about generals, Harry Truman. In immediate terms the risk was "military"; if it justified reversing the commander in the field, then the Joint Chiefs must make the judgment and tell Truman. So Acheson is said to have insisted, understandably enough, and there the matter rested.[15]

Dean Acheson wrote:

As I look back, the critical period stands out as the three weeks from October 26 to November 17. Then all the dangers . . . were manifest. We were all deeply apprehensive. We were frank with one another, but not quite frank enough. I was unwilling to urge on the President a military course that his advisers would not propose. They would not propose it because it ran counter to American military tradition of the proper powers of the theater commander since 1864. . . . While everyone acted correctly, no one, I suspect, was ever quite satisfied with himself afterward.

Acheson saw the President five times during the critical period. "I have an unhappy conviction that none of us, myself prominently included, served him as he was entitled to be served."[16]

As Richard E. Neustadt concludes, a president must help himself. Truman's experience suggests that the president would be greatly assisted in that task if he could count on someone to stand before him, argue into his teeth that he is wrong, and force him to examine and defend his own instincts and prejudices.

Dwight D. Eisenhower

"The U.S. never lost a soldier or a foot of ground in my Administration," Eisenhower declared to Patrick Anderson. "We kept the peace. People ask how it happened—by God, it didn't just happen, I'll tell you that."[17]

On occasion Eisenhower pulled the country back from the brink of war. In 1954, prompted by the opposition of Senators Richard Russell and Lyndon B. Johnson and the refusal of the British to approve and join in, he vetoed the rash proposals of Messrs. Dulles, Nixon, and Radford (chairman of the Joint Chiefs of Staff) that the United States go to the aid of the French in Dien Bien Phu.[18] Moreover, he kept General Norstadt and the Joint Chiefs from forcing Russia's hand over Berlin in 1958.[19] And yet Eisenhower's avoidance of major war seems in retrospect to have been largely a matter of luck in which he was often assisted by both friends and enemies. Even in the defense of Dien Bien Phu, Eisenhower seems to have been willing to commit the armed might of the United States, at least on certain conditions.[20] In the intermittent crises over Quemoy and Matsu, he was ready to make an armed response even when he thought it was against military wisdom.[21] In 1960 he was prepared to fight in Laos, with or without allies.[22]

Eisenhower's willingness to employ atomic weapons is in point. At the end of World War II dropping the atomic bomb against the Japanese shocked him. I have already referred to his reaction in 1945. In *Crusade in Europe* Eisenhower recalled telling Secretary of War Stimson his hopes that "we would never have to use such a thing [the atomic bomb] against any enemy. . . ." The United States should not be the first to use "something as horrible and destructive as this new weapon was described to be."[23]

As president, however, Eisenhower placed heavy reliance from the first on nuclear weapons. Very early Eisenhower told the Communists through indirect channels that if they did not promptly agree to a reasonable armistice in Korea, the United States would slough off limits in both weapons and geography.[24] He was convinced that the ultimatum had been decisive in ending the war.[25] At the Bermuda Con-

ference, in December 1953, Eisenhower's announcement that re-
newed attacks in Korea might cause the U.S. to use atomic weapons
against military targets aroused Churchill's fears that Britain might be
wiped out in a nuclear war. Eisenhower said that the United States
would never act rashly but insisted that past limitations on the use of
the bomb would not necessarily be observed.[26]

The heart of the "new look" in American military policy was
reliance on nuclear weapons. Assuming that the United States would
not begin a major war, Eisenhower held that the country needed larger
and more effective forces than it would if it were to strike first in
order to absorb the enemy's attack and then deliver a crushing response. But the reply did not need to be in kind. If Europe were
invaded on the ground, we might strike with other weapons. The new
look stressed "the deterrent and destructive power of improved
nuclear weapons, better means of delivery, and effective air-defense
units." Never again would we permit an enemy to "enjoy a sanctuary
from which he could operate without danger to himself; we would not
allow him to blackmail us. into placing limitations upon the types of
weapons we would employ." In other words, we would use nuclear
weapons in wars like the Korean war.[27]

In the Lebanon landing, 1958, the United States forces included an
"Honest John rocket battery with atomic capability. . . ."[28] In the same
crisis, Eisenhower mobilized other forces in the Near East and told
General Nathan F. Twining to be prepared to employ, subject to
Eisenhower's approval, "*whatever* means might become necessary to
prevent any unfriendly forces from moving into Kuwait."[29] Furthermore, Eisenhower added that the United States might not be willing to
fight on the brush-war periphery but would be prepared "to hold the
Kremlin—or Peking—responsible for their actions. . . ."[30]

Move now from the willingness to use atomic weapons to the
definition of ideological warfare. In *Crusade in Europe* Eisenhower
closed with a distinction between democracy's belief in "individual
liberty, rooted in human dignity . . ." and the Russian embrace of
"dictatorship and collectivism."[31] *The White House Years* are filled
with assertions of Communist evil and Russian perversity.[32] And his
distinction between the Communist totalitarian slave world and "the
Free World" (which he always capitalized) was as sharp and simplistic as Truman's—and as blind to the inclusion in "the free world"
of dictatorships, authoritarian governments, or totalitarian autocracies

so long as they were not Communist. The effects were to help protract the rigid animosities of the cold war. A slight flurry of Eisenhower sentiment portending some willingness to change came at Stalin's death; the results were nil.[33]

Similarly, the Eisenhower intransigence toward the People's Republic of China solidified and extended the mutual enmity with incalculable costs to both countries. Earlier on, Eisenhower had talked about expanding contacts with China and about the value, especially for Japan, of increasing trade with her. But then he changed. By July of 1955 India's ambassador, Krishna Menon, had tried twice to persuade Eisenhower that India might mediate between the People's Republic and the United States. "Both times I had told him bluntly that there was no use ever mentioning the subject as long as Americans were unjustly held as prisoners by the Communists in Red China, to be used as pawns in bargaining."[34]

Whenever the British broached the question of recognizing the People's Republic of China and admitting her to the United Nations, Eisenhower "became angry and peremptory . . . ," responded "in near wrath," and denounced the "Chinese Communists as unfit for human society." By contrast, Dulles, without moving an inch, would argue the questions dispassionately and show understanding of the British position.[35] Allen S. Whiting's report adds an ironic twist.

Responding to a press query, Eisenhower listed several steps Peking would have to take to win a reconsideration of Washington's position both in bilateral relations and in the United Nations. Quietly but consistently, the People's Republic of China reacted, releasing Americans from jail, withdrawing its forces from North Korea and receiving the United Nations Secretary in Peking. The only response from Washington was a harsh restatement of our cold-war view of the Mainland regime by . . . Dulles . . . in June 1957.[36]

John F. Kennedy

I shall point to Kennedy's failure to extract the United States from Vietnam when the opportunity arose in 1963 and his handling of the Cuban missile crisis in 1962.

America's original involvement in Vietnam and the fateful expansions thereof over a period of eighteen years came with little or no debate—as is consistent with the operating theory of a polity that makes great departures in policy on the basis of the instincts and predispositions of the man in charge, the president. When American intervention began the basic assumption was that Communist domination of Southeast Asia would critically endanger "United States security interests." Communist domination was not defined. American security interests were not analyzed. Costs of preventing Communist domination were not estimated. Comparisons of losses and costs were not made. Rather "Indo China's importance to U.S. security interests was taken for granted. Once the policy of intervention was set it was maintained virtually without question until 1967."[37] Once more: this is typical of a polity that makes major departures in foreign and military policy by indulging presidential instincts.

One might expect a succession of presidents at least to bring different presidential instincts into play, but the innovations were not enough to shake the original commitment to intervention in Vietnam. John F. Kennedy cannot be debited with starting the policy, but he increased the few hundred military advisers Eisenhower had in Vietnam to 15,500. More important, he missed an excellent chance to extract the United States in 1963.

The opportunity came just before Ngo Dinh Diem, president of South Vietnam, was replaced by a military coup and then assassinated, along with his brother, Ngo Dinh Nhu, head of the police. These events remain controversial. Whether the United States encouraged the coup and its bloody aftermath, encouraged the coup but not the assassination, merely permitted the coup, or was powerless to prevent the events—whatever the answer to these questions, there seems to have been a way out of the swamp that the president did not take. The occasion arose out of conflicts between President Diem and the Buddhists who protested a decree forbidding display of any but the national flag and flew their own in Hué (May 1963). An altercation between Buddhists and governmental troops led to gunfire in which nine Buddhists were reported killed and more wounded. Protests flared all summer, including the self-immolation of Buddhist monks. On 21 August, the South Vietnamese Special Forces (wearing army uniforms) attacked a number of Buddhist pagodas in Saigon, Hué, and various other cities, beating monks and jailing more than 1,400 persons.

These actions led to feverish activity in Washington; and they were eventually followed by the coup and the assassinations. According to Roger Hilsman, then Assistant Secretary of State for Southeast Asian

Affairs, Diem had "callously broken his word . . . [and] had made no gesture to salvage the dignity of the United States." Soon afterward Nhu "began a campaign of intimidation against Americans."[38] It would be hard to imagine a more golden opportunity to liquidate the American mistake by pulling out of the country.

Kennedy had entertained thoughts of withdrawal. In 1961 both General Douglas MacArthur and General Charles de Gaulle had warned him against involving America in a land war in Vietnam. Late in 1962, when Kennedy was accelerating military participation in Vietnam, Senator Mike Mansfield sharply cautioned him that this would mean Americanization of the war. Kennedy was startled, apparently because someone had had the temerity to argue with him to his face. "I got angry with Mike for disagreeing with our policy so completely. And I got angry with myself because I found myself agreeing with him."[39] In the spring of 1963 Senator Mansfield again criticized American Vietnam policy, "this time in front of the congressional leadership at a White House breakfast, much to the President's annoyance and embarrassment." Nevertheless, the president had the senator in for a talk and told him that he now agreed with him on the need for a complete military withdrawal from Vietnam. He intended to do so after the 1964 election, fearing that earlier action would prompt a conservative outcry wild enough to cause another Joe McCarthy era.[40]

No doubt the ghost of Joseph McCarthy, whom Arthur Krock once called "the feral Senator from Wisconsin," still haunted Washington.[41] But Kennedy must also have reflected on the debacle of the Korean war, which clearly had fed McCarthyism, for both the country and especially for the Democratic party. Moreover, Kennedy had just received a lesson in the profound preference of the public for peace—in the political appeal of the nuclear test ban treaty of 1963; indeed, the lesson was driven home to him in the week of 24 September![42] It would be hard to imagine a better opportunity for ending a bankrupt policy and to do so with a classical example of presidential "teaching."[43]

But it did not happen. Instead, Kennedy maintained American participation and went ahead to issue his highly controversial cablegram on the coup plots on 5 October.[44] In all this period there was no naysayer. There was no voice in his entourage stridently urging him to get out. His staff had the excuse of the anticipated presidential reaction to anyone who might demur. No one wanted to go up against presidential policy and his presumed predilection—and incur his wrath.[45]

During the famous "thirteen days" of the Cuban missile crisis, 15–28 October 1962,

there was a higher probability that more human lives would end suddenly than ever before in history. Had the worst occurred, the death of 100 million Americans, over 100 million Russians, and millions of Europeans as well would make previous natural calamities and inhumanities appear insignificant. Given the probability of disaster —which President Kennedy estimated as "between 1 out of 3 and even"—our escape seems awesome.[46]

On Monday evening, 15 October 1962, analysis of U–2 espionage flights over Cuba discerned "the first rude beginnings of a Soviet medium-range missile base."[47] On Sunday morning, 28 October, came the news that Khrushchev had accepted the Kennedy terms for ending the Cuban missile crisis. "Missiles were being withdrawn. Inspection would be permitted. The confrontation was over."

Between these two dates, a group of about fifteen men called the Executive Committee of the National Security Council (Ex-Com) met almost continuously first to formulate the policy of the blockade of Cuba along with the proposal for an agreement with Russia to end the crisis and then to advise the president on the administration of the policy until the news came that the Russians had accepted the terms.

The Cuban missile crisis shows the value of uninhibited debate in formulating policy. But the circumstances were uniquely favorable. First, the gravity of the choice was supreme. Second, enough time was at hand to permit the rational process to work. Just before his public announcement of the situation and the blockade on 22 October, President Kennedy met for the first time with the entire cabinet, with the entire National Security Council, and with some twenty congressional leaders. The "only sour note of the day" (wrote Sorensen) was the meeting with congressmen.

Reacting to a McNamara-Rusk-McCone picture briefing the same way most of us originally did, many called the blockade irrelevant and indecisively slow, certain to irritate our friends but doing nothing about the missiles. An invasion of the island was urged instead by such powerful and diverse Democratic Senators as Russell and Fulbright (who had strongly opposed the 1961 Cuban invasion).

But the president refused to be moved. He had rejected suggestions of reconvening Congress or requesting a formal declaration of war, "and he had summoned the leaders only when hard evidence and a fixed policy were ready." Later the president said that if the congressional leaders *"had gone through the five-day period we had gone through— in looking at the various alternatives, advantages and disadvantages . . . —they would come out the same way that we did"* (italics supplied).

Third, the discussions were secret. Every participant could speak his mind without fear that his remarks would be played back to him later. The only breach of the kind of confidence needed for the integrity of the discussion was the publication by Charles Bartlet and Stewart Alsop of Adlai Stevenson's conciliatory proposals. Stevenson suggested abandoning Guantanamo (which was considered obsolescent) and withdrawing American missiles from Turkey and Italy in return for the removal of the Russian missiles from Cuba. Everyone attacked him; but in retrospect his proposal greatly contributed to the relatively moderate decision to blockade rather than to launch an air strike or "as one chief advocate of the hard military line put it: 'to go in there and take Cuba away from Castro.' "

Fourth, President Kennedy attended the Thursday night session and again on Saturday afternoon when the group had reached something of a consensus on the blockade but otherwise absented himself. According to Sorensen:

one of the remarkable aspects of those meetings was a sense of complete equality. Protocol mattered little when the nation's life was at stake. Experience mattered little in a crisis which had no precedent. Even rank mattered little when secrecy prevented staff support. We were 15 individuals on our own, representing the President and not different departments. Assistant Secretaries differed vigorously with their Secretaries; I participated much more freely than I ever had in an NSC meeting; and *the absence of the President encouraged everyone to speak his mind.*[48]

Fifth, and probably most important of all and certainly unique, the president could remain absent because he had Robert F. Kennedy sitting in for him. Having been badly hurt by the Bay of Pigs, the president could hardly have stayed aloof if he had not been able to rely on his brother. It was Robert F. Kennedy who passionately blasted the idea of a military strike as "a Pearl Harbor in reverse [that] would blacken the name of the United States in the pages of history." It was Robert F. Kennedy who tacitly indicated to Soviet Ambassador Dobrynin that President Kennedy had been anxious for some time to remove American missiles from Turkey and Italy and that shortly after the crisis the missiles would be gone. It was Robert F. Kennedy who suggested that of the two Khrushchev messages the United States choose the more moderate and conciliatory one to answer. Finally, it was Robert F. Kennedy who objected to the "content and tenor" of the hard-nosed reply drafted by the State Department. President Kennedy then sent Robert Kennedy and Sorensen off to draft the alternative reply that provided the basis for the agreement to end the crisis.

Dean Acheson wrote that President Kennedy was lucky to come off as well as he did. "It does not detract from . . . Kennedy's laurels . . . that he was helped by the luck of Khrushchev's befuddlement and loss of nerve." Acheson was right about luck. The United States was lucky to have a president with the strength to be conciliatory and doubly lucky that the president had a brother to act as his surrogate so that effective debate could explore the issues and shape a policy. How often will these favorable conditions coincide? Had Harry S. Truman been president in October 1962, with Acheson as his chief adviser, it would not be difficult to imagine the American response—whatever the consequences.

Conclusions: The Shape of a Corrective

With illustrations from four presidents I have sought to show that overreliance on presidential initiative is inherent in our political institutions. Examples have been confined to foreign affairs, but they could have been supplemented from the domestic side of policy: for Roosevelt, the bill to enlarge the Supreme Court in 1937 and the effort to purge Democratic candidates for the House and Senate in 1938; for Truman, persistence in pressure on the Federal Reserve Board to continue supporting government bonds at par and the consequent fillip to the inflation of 1950–51, and for Truman also his insistence on the inordinately high agricultural price supports of the Brannan plan of 1949; for Eisenhower, the stubborn fix on conservative economic policies in the late 1950s that deepened the second Eisenhower recession; and for all four, although Kennedy eventually learned better, the death grip on the ideal of a balanced budget even when it made economic nonsense.

Now it may be said that the flaw is not in the overweaning leverage of the president but rather in the cabal that develops in his staff. The summer of Watergate brought forth a defense of Richard M.

Nixon on the ground that he was the innocent beneficiary—or victim —of a perversely loyal staff intent on keeping him ignorant of their machinations. Something similar has been suggested of recent American foreign and military policy with its centerpiece of idiocy in the sustained intervention in Vietnam.[49] Nonsense. Presidents may be frustrated by the inertia that pervades large organization, or they may be undone and even intimidated by the bureaucracy.[50] But any president who does not control his own shop is a dismal and dangerous failure. As these chapters have shown, however, presidents have been in the middle of decisions. Often they have been wrong. They can be blamed. But in our polity not only the presidents but the *presidency* is at fault.

What can be done? James David Barber's illuminating analysis of the faults of certain types of character in presidents leads him to suggest, specifically with regard to "active-negative Nixon," that the president himself and his friends could recognize his tendency to "commit himself irrevocably to some disastrous course of action." A procedure might then be created to provide presidential consultation with his associates *after* he has settled on a course of action.[51] On the contrary, the foregoing analysis has shown that the president's associates are the weakest of all recourses to correct his tendencies toward malevolent actions—even before his mind is fully made up, let alone afterward. For institutional and psychological reasons, his friends and associates are unable to perform this duty.

Persuasive as Professor Barber is on the character of presidents, I prefer George E. Reedy because he enlarges on the tendency of the office itself to demoralize occupants of whatever character. No one, says Reedy, talks to the president "like a Dutch uncle." Rather, the presidency is devised "to remove [its occupant] from all the forces which require most men to rub up against the hard facts of life on a daily basis." There is an "environment of deference, approaching sycophancy. . . ." Councils in the White House "are not debating matches in which ideas emerge from the heated exchanges of participants." Everyone talks to the president and the first idea that strikes his fancy "becomes subconsciously" the thought of "everyone in the room." Meanwhile the president is coddled by the concept of how overburdened he is that serves "to separate the chief executive from the real universe of living, breathing, troubled human beings. It is the basis for encouraging his most outrageous expressions, for pampering his most childish tantrums, for fostering his most arrogant actions." Reedy expressed his doubt that even "Harry S. Truman—the most democratic of contemporary presidents—wore the same size hat when he left the White House as he did the day he entered."[52]

And yet Reedy's solution that the only hope for restraint must "come from the presidential soul and prudence from the presidential mind" is sadly inadequate. It is nullified by his own argument. He has, however, given a clue to the answer by noting that the president has not "been put to the test of defending his position in a public debate. And it is amazing what even the best of minds will discover when forced to answer critical questions."

The necessary thing is to provide an adversary whose questions the president must answer and whose analyses of situations and proposals for policy the president must consider. With all respect to reporters in press conferences, they are incapable of performing this function. Their forte is to get the news. What is needed is an alternative leader who is motivated—and obligated—to ask the questions that arise from his different perspective on the problems of the polity and on the procedures for dealing with them—and who can not only ask a question but set forth a criticism of what the administration is doing together with an alternative course of action.

There is no guarantee that an organized and focused opposition marshaled behind a leader who approximates a peer to the president will save us from ourselves. Salvation escapes human reach, but improvements are possible and a much greater degree of assurance can be had that the vital function of presidential debate will be performed.[53] In addition to the support of logic, the argument for presidential debate gains from the experience of cabinet secretaries who have to prepare for hearings before congressional committees. Although the experience is not wholly comparable to that of a head of state meeting the leader of the opposition, it occurs in a governmental forum and often pits adversaries against each other in a situation requiring thorough preparation by the secretary if he is effectively to defend his policies. The anticipation of adverse questions in congressional hearings obligates the secretary's staff to anticipate the most searching examination and emboldens them to deal with him much more candidly than they would otherwise be wont to do.[54]

There can be no glossing over the proposition that to provide the president with a peer requires a major constitutional revision, as chapter 10 will propose. Under our present system the president can organize his office, exploit his favored access to the public through television, and build his influence by his skill in timing state events. With luck and brains he has the chance to forge a formidable power structure. The same favorable condition obviously does not now exist to encourage the rise of a leader of the opposition. If such a leader arises, he must do so by gathering the presently centrifugal forces in Congress. He will emerge only as the head of a consolidated opposition party, a consummation that defies achievement through the spontaneous self-discipline of the large number of persons involved who are now urged by every institutional compulsion to carve out their individual, discrete, and semi-independent positions of power. The constitutional reforms proposed later are hard medicine, but there is no avoiding something of their magnitude if we are to escape the tragedy that seems imminent for our constitutional democracy in the working of its outmoded structures.

4 The Problem of Bureaucracy

The insolence of office, . . .
—Shakespeare, *Hamlet*

With examples drawn from four presidents, I have argued that presidential initiative without presidential debate is dangerous. Government by whim or by instinct is encouraged. The habit of searching inquiry into the wisdom of major policies is lost at the highest level of government. Now I turn to a novel danger in the conduct of American government, bureaucracy-out-of-control.

The Nature of Bureaucracy

The following exposition accepts Richard E. Neustadt's use of the term bureaucracy to describe combinations among ranking officials of federal agencies, strategically located congressmen, and (commonly) leaders of relevant organized groups—combinations that often gain significant and sometimes dangerous degrees of autonomy in policy areas.[1] The term is used with some regret because it has been applied by publicists and politicians to the public administrative service whose members, it is said, inevitably become arbitrary and arrogant toward the citizenry. I am not offering just another indictment of "bureaucracy" in these sweeping and typically demagogic terms. On the contrary, I have no quarrel with those scholars who have recognized the necessary apparatus of the modern state, have sought to improve the philosophical breadth of those who staff it as well as to increase their efficiency and effectiveness, and have acknowledged that, without good organization and procedures, good government and, indeed, good life are impossible to achieve.[2] Rather, I should largely agree with Joseph A. Schumpeter that successful democratic government requires (among other things) "a well-trained bureaucracy of good standing and tradition. . . ." Such a bureaucracy must be efficient, competent to give advice, and "strong enough to guide and, if need be, to instruct politicians. . . ." To this end bureaucracy "must be a power in its own right" and must have a degree of independence in which its tenure and promotion "depend largely . . . on its own corporate opinion. . . ." This kind of bureaucracy will help to keep democracy from extending "the effective range of political decision . . . too far." Limitations, prudential rather than legal, signify that, *once major questions of policy are decided,* the detailed articulation of policy must be left to experts.[3]

Once major questions of policy are decided—that is the critical point. The United States has seen disturbing bureaucratic encroachment on the central political organs of government in major matters of policy, as will be shown in detail, using the military bureaucracy.

Back to Neustadt, who argues that the great bureaucracies (the linkages of administrative-legislative-private interests) have become a problem new to the American polity, in and after World War II, with the doubling of the federal government's civilian employees and —note this well—the increase of the uniformed officer corps of the armed services by a factor of ten. (In agriculture, the move came earlier —the United States Department of Agriculture's personnel tripled in the 1930s from 30,000 to 90,000, not counting approximately 90,000 members of what were then called the AAA farmer committees. The Bureau of Reclamation and the Army Engineers also were vastly expanded in the same period.)

Increased numbers reflected an enlargement of policy and the growth of government to spell it out and administer it. Growth in numbers is accompanied by the flowering of agency philosophies. Bureaucracy takes on extra drafts of loyalty and added resilience in proportion as its own ideology matures and is fixed in an agency code that can be learned and taught and that becomes a source of justification of official actions in doubtful cases and, more generally, a body of dogma that gives the members (who typically live out their working lives in the agency) something beyond financial remuneration and even the rewards of recognition: a sense of dedication to a worthwhile purpose.[4]

As government takes on new tasks, spells out policies to perform them, and forms and expands the agencies required, the emergent bureaucracies tend to escape general political control of either the president or of Congress. This does not mean that all agencies are always out of the president's reach but rather that some of them get virtually into this position, at least for significant periods. It is enough that they get out of control for sufficient time to have decisive influence on critically important policies. The means of escape are simple. The president's nature is unity; that of Congress, diversity. These two "independent institutions sharing powers" address themselves according to their different natures to the control of bureaucracy, fail, and struggle with each other. Bureaucracy escapes.

To amplify, the president tries to control the bureaucracy by ensuring that the budgetary requests of each agency are judged on their intrinsic merits, are weighed against the demands of other agencies, and are appraised in terms of governmental fiscal and monetary policy. He tries to be the arbiter of important departures in policy, using both the formal device of legislative clearance[5] and also such informal strategies as Franklin D. Roosevelt's "flushing up" theory—the studied use of overlapping assignments to stimulate enough conflicts among administrators to ensure that the President will be informed and will have some things left to him to decide.[6] Another favorite device is to create an effective network of news and rumor gatherers who can give the president early warning of developments and thus get "information in his mind as well as decisions in his hands." For all these purposes the president's staff is critically important.[7] The Bureau of the Budget, renamed by President Nixon as the Office of Management and Budget, is the main formal tool, presiding as it does not only over the formulation of the executive budget but also over the legislative program of the president with which agencies are supposed to make sure that their proposals are in accord, and over the administrative practices of the agencies. As would be expected, the Office of Management and Budget, since its emergence into real significance as an instrument of executive coordination, has been a villain in congressional eyes.

With this formidable apparatus—and it looks even more threatening when viewed from Congress—the president would seem to be in full command. Certainly this is the century of presidential leadership in which the executive has become the chief legislator as well as the chief administrator of a government that has expanded as a regulator, promoter, conditioner, guarantor, and creator of economic and social conditions and values beyond all but the wildest dreams of earlier visionaries.

But the president, though preeminent in getting things started, is often foiled in his effort to coordinate their execution. The great organizations that are formed to carry out the vast reaches of the new policies take on lives of their own. In order to see how this happens, the congressional approach to the control of government must be analyzed.

The congressional approach, to repeat, is the opposite of the president's. Where the president tries to coordinate and synthesize, Congress divides up and disperses, allocating bits and pieces of policy to various committees and subcommittees. "Congress is a collection of committees that come together in a chamber periodically to approve one another's actions."[8] Policies initiated by the president have frequently settled into the bureaucracy, there to be separated from his effective control.

Traditionally, Congress has controlled administrative agencies by chartering them, defining their statutory powers, authorizing their finances, annually providing their appropriations, and investigating them. Congress creates the agency, names it, and spells out its organization, often in some detail. Congress states the purpose of the agency and frequently divides its functions, vesting some of them in bureaus. Again, by creating agencies within existing departments Congress may legalize a degree of autonomy in the agency, thus compromising control by the department—and by the president, as well, acting through the secretary of the department who is—to a degree, at least—the president's man. In addition, Congress authorizes and appropriates funds for the agency, without which its functions would be merely hypothetical. Finally, it investigates.

Often these powers enable Congress to keep agencies under control through limitation on granted powers or through limited and sometimes parsimonious funding.[9] Indeed, the road to bureaucratic eminence seems to be paved with gold. "The perennial issue with the Department of Agriculture is who will control the PMA," a ranking USDA official told me in 1947. Since 1935 that has been salient in the contest for power between the Secretary of Agriculture and the price-support, production control agency that typically has accounted for two-thirds of the department's budget.[10] The Bureau of Reclamation, a water agency, has historically disposed of a quarter to a half of the budget of the Department of the Interior. Among water agencies, the Army Corps of Engineers, with some two-thirds of the funds in this luxuriant field, has had central significance.[11] Among the great spenders the armed services have emerged as the giant, accounting for a quarter to a half of the entire budget, and dwarfing even the wealthiest civilian programs.

Power and expenditure do not form a simple equation. Government disposes of other things besides money, including property rights such as licenses[12] or mineral leases[13] or contracts and including recognition of valuable status.[14] A suspected hoard of sensitive information about the great and near-great may generate much influence.[15] Nevertheless, control of expenditures of large amounts of public money or even administration of the channels through which the money flows provides, I believe, the most significant and durable factor in empowering the administrative partner in the three-way bureaucratic partnership here under discussion.[16]

The accretion of power in the big agencies prompts Congress to look for some new means of control. Congress tries to influence appointments at the assistant secretarial level where the process of administrative policy-making centers. To the annual appropriations, presided over by the appropriations committees of both houses, Congress adds annual authorizations that give the subject-matter committees an opportunity (at the cost of protracting and complicating the act of governance) to review programs each year. Finally, Congress extends "committee clearance," the device by which the Public Works Committees of both houses have achieved a continuing involvement in the detailed administration of the Rivers and Harbors Programs, to other agencies. Wherever contracts are let, loans made, projects started, facilities established, or experiments undertaken—wherever, in short, some specific act is taken to implement general policy, the congressional subject-matter committees involved may try to require the agency to report the action to them or even to get their prior approval before "the dirt begins to fly."

To the extent that congressional committees succeed in preempting detailed administrative decisions, presidential control is superseded. But effective congressional control even with these new devices may be confounded. The major modern agencies often have a geographical and a functional breadth of responsibility that enables them to transcend the jurisdictions of individual subject-matter committees. Sometimes agencies are caught in the cross fire of their many congressional masters; but if the agencies are large enough and have sufficiently shrewd leadership they may be able to play their masters off against each other—appropriations committees against subject-matter committees, subject-matter committees against each other, House against Senate, and Congress against president.

Thus responsibility disintegrates through dissemination, and a natural result is to compound frustration. When officials either in the executive or the legislative feel that the control of administration eludes them, a natural tendency is to blame the other branch. Congress and the president, based as they are on different constituencies, shaped by different cultures, informed by different perspectives, and using different tools of control, look on each other with suspicion. In the ensuing struggle the bureaucracy escapes control from any source.

So runs Neustadt's argument. He concludes by exhorting politicians at both ends of Pennsylvania Avenue to unite in order to reestablish political control. I do not see how such unison can come about except through the strengthening of party ties; therefore, I use Neustadt's analysis as central to my own because it reveals more precisely than any other source I know the malfunctions of present institutions and does so in a way that underlines the case for party government.

Other Views

Neustadt's model has emerged from the accepted tradition of interpretation by political scientists of the governmental process in the United States. E. S. Griffith advanced the theory of "government by whirlpools," which included civil servants, strategically located congressmen, and frequently interest group members. At the center of the whirlpool was a

Congressional-bureaucratic relationship that underlies the reluctance of Congress to give department heads effective control over their bureau chiefs. The first Hoover Commission correctly pointed to this situation as handicapping effective control by the President over much of his administration.

Nevertheless, Griffith viewed the phenomenon with equanimity. As soon as the appetites of congressmen and their constituents were satisfied, the congressmen could look to the public interest. Indeed, his satiation provided "the best hope of the public interest prevailing. . . ."[17] The idea that the public interest gets served after the private interests have had their fill has attracted others, among them the Moses of group political theorists, A. F. Bentley: "And the Lion when he has satisfied his physical need will lie down quite lamb-like, however much louder his roars were than his appetite justified."[18]

But others, like King Lear—"O, reason not the need: . . . allow not nature more than nature needs, man's life's as cheap as beast's . . ."— are differently impressed by the same phenomenon. Pendleton Herring saw the collapse of the public interest under the concerted drive of interested groups, each with its own access to government, each generating pressure and eliciting responses, but without miraculously uniting in a general program to serve the common welfare. "There is no provision . . . for unity and consistence in the interpretation of the public interest. A . . . system of checks and balances between Congress and the President . . . has proved a device for stalemate. . . ." Herring called for "promoting the purpose of the state over and above the medley of interests that compose it." In spite of the failure of political parties to provide the means, the "fundamental need is a governmental institution that will join the disparate economic forces in society behind a unified political program." Herring's impulse was to turn to the president who "has time and again been better able to uphold the public interest than a Congress controlled by blocs and organized minorities." Recognizing that the public could not form a "spontaneous and coherent . . . opinion . . . to solve political problems . . . ," he nevertheless believed that the public could choose between alternatives if they were clearly presented. All this might seem to suggest a redoubled effort to find the social and institutional basis for a strengthening of political parties, but Herring turned to the bureaucracy and especially to the coordinating capabilities that he saw inherent in the Bureau of the Budget, which would be reinforced by a network of committees and councils that trapped both the expertise of government and the special knowledge and capabilities of affected interests.[19]

Fourteen years after Herring, Professor Charles S. Hyneman also wrestled with the problem of bureaucracy, came to similar conclusions about the need for symmetry and coherence in policy, and proposed a Central Council that would unite the politicians at both ends of Pennsylvania Avenue by means of political parties. "The goal of politics [he wrote] is to control the activities of government; the activities of government are carried on by the bureaucracy; whoever controls the bureaucracy controls the activities of government." After discussing presidential and congressional efforts at separated control, Hyneman concludes in favor of a marriage between the two.

It is possible . . . that instead of having central agencies for advice, service, and control that report to the President (like the Bureau of the Budget) or to Congress (like the General Accounting Office), we will want some agencies that report to the leaders of the party in Congress and others that report to the leaders of the opposite party in Congress.

All this presumed, in accord with Herring, that vigorous presidential leadership is essential to bring about both effective and responsible government. But the president's power must never be enough "to force Congress to do his bidding. . . ." The president must be curbed, too, and "there is nothing to control the actions of men except the actions of other men." Marriage, balance, mutual control, and effectiveness would all follow from the creation of a "Central Council made up of leaders of the party that has been given the job of running the government," selected by the president from congressional and administrative leaders, who together would concert policies and bring about their acceptance.[20]

Hyneman provoked Chester I. Barnard to write a highly critical review.[21] Barnard, interpreting Hyneman somewhat differently, scored Hyneman's emphasis on congressional control of bureaucracy, his depreciation of presidential control, and his apparent refusal to discuss administrative responsibility. Interestingly, Barnard concluded in much the same vein as Hyneman's final chapter (the only one that he did not analyze in detail). In the federal government, Barnard found, "the constitutional restrictions on Congress and the exclusively parochial nature of congressional representation are calculated to put a premium upon obstruction and dissent, and to minimize representation of the national interest as a whole." For Barnard, only the president and vice-president have responsibility by and to the country as a whole. Congressmen are too beholden to local and particular interests. Thus Hyneman's Central Council, while it might help, would not be enough. Barnard proposed that 20 to 30 percent of the congressmen and senators be elected at large and for four-year terms, coincidental with the president. This would increase party responsibility, avoid irreconcilable conflict between president and Congress, and promote "a more definite development of the President's political responsibility."

With great uniformity, students of American bureaucracy are led by their analyses to the separation of powers or to "separated institutions sharing powers." Given weak political parties and coalition politics, the separation of powers throws up obstacles to generalizing and integrating political control by either president or Congress and nourishes "bureaucracies," "subsystems," "whirlpools," or "alliances" in which power is hived off and more or less insulated, to be developed and used at the pleasure and in the interests of insiders. Many scholarly interpretations have been critical of bureaucracy as here defined, and some have been alarmed. Some have looked with more equanimity on the development, usually for the reason that bureaucratic drives for power are said to encounter natural obstacles that sufficiently check any tendencies to evil.[22]

Conclusions

The following chapters on the military bureaucracy are presented to persuade readers that bureaucratic power is implicitly dangerous and is not sufficiently curbed by natural checks. If space permitted, illustrations could be added from experience in agricultural price policy[23] and in water policy.[24] Similar examples could be shown in forestry policy,[25] in the administration of public grazing lands by the Bureau of Land Management,[26] in the operation of the Highway Trust Fund,[27] and doubtless in many other areas.[28]

A final and eventually a poignant note came in the effort of Richard M. Nixon, apparently mounted on analyses quite in keeping with the foregoing, to bring bureaucracy under control by attacking precisely those elements that give it the strength to be autonomous. In March 1971, he proposed a sweeping reorganization. Keeping the departments of State, Treasury, Defense, and Justice, he proposed to combine Agriculture, Labor, Commerce, Housing and Urban Development, Transport, Interior, and Health-Education-Welfare into new departments of Natural Resources, Human Resources, Economic Affairs, and Community Development. If successful, this move would have upset the lines between bureaus and congressional committee leaders and shaken the power bases of bureaucracies, at least for a time. When this did not work, Mr. Nixon began his second term by announcing the "New American Revolution" and appointing Robert Ash, who had chaired the 1971 reorganization commission, to head the Office of Management and Budget. Second, he systematically downgraded the cabinet posts and began to create in his own staff—where they would explicitly be out of reach of questioning by congressional committees —supersecretaries who would direct the administration of government. Third, working through his then Chief of Staff, H. R. Haldeman, he moved his own men into ranking or secondary positions in many departments and agencies; and he began to replace assistant secretaries of Administration in the departments—traditionally career civil servants—with his own men direct from the White House who would become agents of presidential control. Fourth, he shunted out a number of the more independent voices in his administration, replacing them with more pliable persons. And, fifth, he moved against Congress and, therefore, against the congressional end of the bureaucratic power triangle by asserting sweeping presidential powers to impound funds and by greatly extending the conception of executive privilege against congressional inquiry.

The poignancy came with the Watergate and related exposures that dashed the machinery designed to bring bureaucracy to heel—whether it ever had much real chance of success, as analysis offered here makes doubtful. But it should also be noted that Mr. Nixon left the military bureaucracy untouched.

5 The Military Bureaucracy: Its Nature

"The courage of one's convictions and the willingness to speak the truth as one sees it for the good of the country are what patriotism really means—far more than flags and bands and national anthems." Letter from a congressman to General David M. Shoup, U. S. Marine Corps, Ret., printed in a foreword to Colonel James A. Donovan, U. S. Marine Corps, Ret., *Militarism, U.S.A.*

Congressman H. Mendel Rivers: "I regret that I have but one Congressional district to give my country to—I mean to give to my country" (laughter and applause).

Military bureaucracy is a classical example of Neustadt's model. Among its characteristics, all mutually reinforcing, are, first, its enormous size and scope as shown by its budget, its property holdings, and its widespread, variegated, and entrenched involvement in the economic, social, and political life of the country (military posts, camps, schools, veterans' hospitals, defense industries, laboratories, proving grounds, missile sites, radar stations, etc.). Second is its age ("the long grey line") and the monopoly of many of the most stirring memories of the nation. And yet the military bureaucracy as a *problem* is new, newer even than bureaucracies in water and agriculture. As a problem it began in the 1940s and 1950s and became greatly aggravated in the 1960s.

Third are organization and internal procedure, including the role of the Joint Chiefs of Staff and of the "planners," the rigorous observance of hierarchy, the transformation of interservice rivalry into logrolling, and new developments in the art of dissimulation. Fourth are ties to Congress. Fifth are beachheads in the executive, especially in the foreign policy establishment. Sixth are group alliances and support —and the promotion of public favor.

Seventh is the powerful ideology inhaled in the sound of ancient guns and fifes and heroes marching; exhaled in fire. Ideology pervades, informs, and inspires all the other characteristics of the military bureaucracy.

Size, Scope, Spread

Senator Paul H. Douglas wrote in 1952: "One approaches the military budget with feelings of awe and fright."[1] Before the Korean war, military budgets and personnel were cut back after peace came.[2] Even World War II's expenditures, peaking at over $80 billion in fiscal year 1946, dropped to $12 billion in 1948. In the Korean war the top was $50 billion, which in the cold war fell only to $40 billion. Under Eisenhower, defense budgets were held at about $45 billion as the military—especially the army—chafed. Then came the myth of the missile-gap and, under JFK, a sharp rise in nuclear strike forces (which prodded the Soviets to increase theirs) and a build-up of regular forces able to fight what were ironically called "limited wars." The military budget rose to $55 billion even before Vietnam.

From 1945 to 1970, the United States spent about $1,100,000,000,-000.00 for military purposes, $150,000,000,000.00 of it in Vietnam.[3] From mid-1965 to mid-1968, defense spending rose at an average rate of 17 percent a year, compared to 13 percent for federal nondefense spending—much of the increase was brought on by inflation propelled by the war and by mistakes in fiscal and monetary policy.[4] In 1968, federal outlays totaled $178.9 billion of which defense took more than $80 billion outright—and probably more than $100,000,000,000 if the defense share of the interest on the national debt, the cost of veterans' programs, and hidden outlays for foreign military assistance were counted. By contrast, the federal government spent about $2 billion each for the war on poverty and for housing, $5.2 billion for education, and $500 million for the food stamp-school lunch-special milk programs.

In 1970 much was said about slashing defense budgets; but actual cuts were small and, early in 1971, the military expenditures started upward again. In the first quarter of 1972 (an election year) defense spending increased at an annual rate of 28 percent. The Pentagon was accounting for 65 percent of the "controllable half" of the federal budget; and its spokesmen were demanding huge increases as their price for permitting the Strategic Arms Limitation Treaty to pass the Senate.

The military owns an empire of 29 million acres within the United States, about the size of the state of New York. In 1968 the value of real and personal property was grossly underestimated at $202.5 billion—a sum larger than the value of all business and residential buildings in the country. The international sector included 2,170 known military bases in 29 countries, which added 2,500,000 acres, mostly leased.

In 1969 there were 3.4 million uniformed men and 1.3 million civilians in the armed forces; 2 million uniformed and 1 million civilian personnel were spread throughout fifty states. Defense contracts, employing 3.8 million workers, were held by 22,000 prime and 10,000 secondary contractors. Happily sharing were small firms, middle-sized firms, and the "industrial giants which swarmed around the Pentagon to get their share of the sweets with no less enthusiasm than their smaller brethren." Defense money was spent in 363 of 435 congressional districts.

Organization, Process, "Planners"

Millions have been impressed by the speed with which the military can snatch them from civilian life, subject them to a few weeks of basic training, shuttle them to Korea or Vietnam, and send them into fire fights. But the same efficiency is not apparent to all. "In a homely manner of speaking," said Vice Admiral Hyman G. Rickover, "the Defense Department is constipated; it must be purged or it will become increasingly torpid." His fire was directed especially at the McNamara Pentagon with its civilian general staff. The General Accounting Office (GAO) has repeatedly scored the profligacy of the Pentagon. In 1969 the GAO found that major weapons' systems were costing at least $20 billion more than their estimates and that no one person in government knew how many such systems there were or their costs. Reporting on the acquisition of fifty weapons' systems in 1970, the GAO complained of a $34 billion gap between estimates and costs. Part of the extravagance was attributed to the "layering" of bureaucracy. Between the general in charge of the army's acquisition and the Army Chief of Staff were eleven clearances that typically took 190 days; the navy had 129 briefings en route to the Chief of Naval Operations.

This talk of military inefficiency can be misleading. On the contrary, the military bureaucracy's rise to commanding influence may well reflect the perfection of its organization under Secretary of Defense Robert McNamara.

In the name of better management and efficiency, the command and operations of the armed services were unified, techniques of computer analysis and control were introduced, and the "military-industrial team" coordinated and strengthened. As a result many of the service inefficiencies once caused by overlapping, duplication, and rivalry have been replaced by a powerful organized war machinery which defies effective democratic and Congressional controls.[5]

Interservice rivalry has failed to prevent the rise of bureaucratic power. Asked early in 1966 whether the military was not becoming a dangerous influence, Senator Eugene McCarthy dismissed the threat. In its wisdom, Congress had created a separate air force, thus ensuring that any one service that waxed too strong would be checked by a combination of the other two.[6] True enough, rivalry among the services may lead to military gamesmanship in which each tries to outdo the others, for example, by getting into action first with the most men.[7] But the more significant effect apparently has been to substitute logrolling for rivalry, with the several services combining to support each other's proposals.[8] This logically leads to the formation of a common front against outsiders. As Colonel James A. Donovan ended his chapter on "Military Gamesmanship":

The propaganda designed to shape public opinion and attitudes, about the progress of the war . . . was created by the four services. Each has its own point of view, but the total result is a united effort to sell the war to the nation.[9]

The conduct even of modern war over great distances demands the devolution of authority. It also promotes the growth and perfection of organization—and the aggrandizement of staff analysts or planners. In the "prewar period . . . [Franklin D.] Roosevelt was the real and not merely the nominal Commander-in-Chief of the armed forces." But war brought changes. Initial disasters destroyed previous strategy. Of necessity, theater commanders (MacArthur, Nimitz, Stilwell) had wide discretion to deal with enemy thrusts. In Washington, the military was drastically reorganized. From 1942 Roosevelt dealt with men who were still his personal military advisers but now also were chiefs of their services in a global war. Between these men (Marshall, King, Arnold) and the field were the planning staffs that gave "directives of higher authority . . . precise and substantive military meaning." Theoretically advisers to the chiefs, the planning staffs, "often took the initiative and produced basic strategic conceptions like the plan of 1942 (Overlord) for an invasion build-up in Britain." Although pressure flowed down as well as up, "the military chiefs to a great extent saw the war through the eyes of their planners."[10]

By the end of World War II, according to President Roosevelt's Chief of Staff, Admiral William D. Leahy, "The Joint Chiefs of Staff [JCS]" were "under no civilian control whatever."[11] The military profession achieved an "unprecedented level of power and prestige." What happened may be shown in the evolution of the JCS. First organized by executive order in the second world war, the JCS acquired a statutory basis in the National Security Act of 1947, which created the Department of Defense, and later went through seven changes, culminating in the Defense Reorganization Act of 1958. The JCS became advisers to the Secretary of Defense but also to the National Security Council and to the president at the same time that they retained the operational command of the armed forces. Commands were to be "unified," but the three major services were maintained (with the Marines and naval aviation specifically mentioned within the Navy Department) and each was to have its own secretary. "Unified direction under civilian control" was to be provided, but the departments were specifically not "merged." So the services were brought together only enough to facilitate collusion, and the Joint Chiefs were told to report through the Secretary of Defense unless they decided to go directly to the president.

In this situation, the driving personality of Robert McNamara and his deep commitment to scientific management, while apparently subjecting the Pentagon to unprecedented civilian direction, may actually have endowed the military with unexampled independence. By 1969 the military

was in fact playing a greater role in determining American policy than at any time since World War II. McNamara became an advocate of the . . . establishment and in a large degree a captive of its programs. He didn't represent political control as much as . . . civilian management that created an immense and powerful bureaucracy which dominates much of government.[12]

Under Nixon the influence of the JCS was reported rising. In part this may have been attributable to a secretive president's penchant for dealing with a few White House advisers and the military directly and, in part, to an early administrative reorganization. Both the secretiveness and the reorganization may have weakened the president *vis-à-vis* the military especially by cutting out appraisal of military proposals by the civilian staff and also by diminishing the authority of the Secretary of Defense. In the Cambodian invasion, the White House reportedly relied on military advisers who unanimously supported military interpretations and the military line on policy.

In 1970 a "blue ribbon" panel, headed by Gilbert N. Fitzhugh, chairman of the board of the Metropolitan Life Insurance Company, reported that profound reforms were needed to restore civilian control of the military. Grouped but not merged, the services had substituted logrolling for rivalry (the report found). The JCS had split on only 0.2 percent of their recommendations in 1966–69. Members of the Joint Chiefs had kept their service identities; and each had enlarged his own staff made up of officers whose career ambitions could be realized only within their own services. Neither the president nor the Secretary of Defense had sufficient staffs to provide independent evaluations of the military.

These developments underwrote the significance of the "planners." Ability, indoctrination, energy, and dedication enabled these colonels and naval commanders to become "the key schemers and military doctrinaires." They analyzed the recommendations of field commanders, prepared position papers, and reduced various statements of objectives to briefs for their superiors who, at the highest level, were the JCS themselves. The problems occupying the JCS were so many and complex that briefings became essential; and the planners who commanded the details often controlled the result. The JCS and the Secretary of Defense "tend to become captives of . . . the planners. . . ."[13]

Among the most important were the oral briefings in which the same groups engaged. These involved both "a formal, stylized presentation and an informal meeting where decisions are arrived at by elaborate compromise. Crucial decisions frequently hinge upon the techniques and skill of the briefing officer and staff planner." Briefings were daily affairs that had no civilian counterpart; and they "contributed no small part to the military's ability to 'snow' the civilians in the Department of Defense and Congress. . . ."

The military administrative process had two other characteristics, both inherent, but both given a special distortion by the nature of the military involvement in Vietnam: the first was the perfection of the ordinary administrative urge to secure absolute and unquestioned support of policies; the second was the ancient art of deception that military men, like politicians, have always valued highly.

On the first point, Secretary McNamara laid it down in 1965 that military witnesses before congress, if asked for personal opinions, were required to give the Pentagon's positions together with the supporting factors. The tensions caused within the military as well as among civilians by the Vietnam war gave this characteristic of professionally exaggerated conformity an unfortunate twist.[14]

Second was a new development in the art of dissimulation. Politicians lie in the hope, often vain, that they will thereby win and not lose votes. Soldiers lie in the hope, often vain, that they will deceive the enemy—and they may become unable to distinguish either the truth or the enemy. Once again, the Vietnam war has perverted this patriotically dishonorable practice. The systematic inflation of the body count is the most notorious example. General Matthew B. Ridgway soberly inquired whether an officer could now tell the truth without risking his career when he had to choose between falsifying the "body count" and jeopardizing his own and others' promotions. This kind of institutionalized prevarication required the unit commander "to repudiate the code Sylvanus Thayer indelibly engraved on the hills of West Point—the code on which the corps of cadets was nurtured—don't lie, cheat, or steal." Ridgway discerned a threat to the honor of the officer corps—"the great reservoir of integrity, moral courage, competence, and subordination to lawful authority."[15]

Military Ties to Congress

In 1937 Alfred Vagts emphasized the controlled, limited, constitutionalized nature of the American military, an interpretation more recently shared by Samuel J. Huntington and Morris Janowitz.[16] These views no longer appear to be valid. The escape of the military bureaucracy from control has become most notable since about 1964;[17] but the basis was laid in the expansion of the establishment in World War II. David Halberstam wrote:

The growth of the sophistication of weapons and the enormous increase in their price had given the Pentagon a quantum jump in power. Its relationship with . . . Congress, always strong, but based in the past in large part on patriotism and relatively minor pork-barrel measures, was now strengthened by a new loyalty based on immense defense contracts, conveniently placed around the homes of the most powerful committee chairmen.[18]

The establishment of congressional strongholds has enabled the military to shake off executive direction. Links to Congress are many; a recent count found 32 senators and 107 congressmen to have reserve commissions. Nevertheless, the ties of crucial importance are to the armed services and the appropriations committees. Other congressmen typically defer to the leadership of these committees and expect deference in their turn on matters of their own "expertise." Within the committees, a small group of insiders tends to monopolize power.

A glimpse of how the process works was provided in the field of agricultural policy by the tribute of Congressman William H. Natcher (D., Ky.) to Congressman Jamie L. Whitten (D., Miss.), chairman of the House subcommittee on agricultural appropriations: "We have an able chairman on this committee, and if that were not the situation, we would be in difficulty every year that we present this [agricultural appropriation] bill." Whitten then noted that perhaps his greatest service to agriculture was getting the late Congressman Clarence Cannon, chairman of the appropriations committee, to put him on the public works subcommittee—"so that the other members realized they couldn't kick agriculture around without having to face me on the other committee."[19]

Congressman Whitten's power extended into the defense area. In a controversy with Congressman Robert L. Leggett (D., Calif.) over price supports for cotton, Whitten noted that Leggett was a member of the armed services committee and added that California "got about half the Federal contracts for defense." Leggett said that it seemed to be a diminishing amount and added, "We are fighting that. . . ." Whitten: "I deal with that on the armed services appropriations." Leggett: "I know."[20]

But even Jamie Whitten felt somewhat outside the charmed military affairs circle. In 1960, he complained that "you can look at some of our key people in the key places in Congress and see how many military establishments there are in their districts."[21]

I am convinced [Whitten told the joint economic committee's defense procurement subcommittee] defense is only one of the factors that enter into our determinations of defense spending. The others are pump priming, spreading the immediate benefits of defense spending, taking care of all the services, giving all defense contractors a fair share, spreading the military bases to include all sections, etc. ... There is no state in the union and hardly a district in a state that doesn't have defense spending, contracting, or a defense establishment. We see the effects in public and Congressional insistence on continuing contracts, or operating military bases, though the need has expired.[22]

The inner circle has been powerful and hawkish—but, in keeping with the theory of bureaucracy, they have *not* effectively controlled the military. The hawkishness and avarice of the late J. Mendel Rivers (D., South Carolina) were well known. His motto was, "Rivers delivers." If he brought home one more defense plant (it was said) Charleston would sink beneath the Atlantic. As a hawk, Rivers urged Truman to drop atomic bombs on North Korea in 1951, Eisenhower to invade Cuba in 1960, and the United States to wipe out the nuclear potential of the People's Republic of China in 1965. (He also praised the John Birch Society and hailed Generalissimo Franco's military forces as the "greatest allies we ever picked up. ...") Rivers was known as a drunkard. Some said that only in the morning was he sober enough to conduct the public's business. Apparently the question of what would have happened had a national crisis emerged in the afternoon was never raised by the men who run Congress. The principle of seniority must be preserved. When Rivers died, he was succeeded, in another example of congressional bondage to seniority, by Felix Edward Hébert (D., Louisiana). No stauncher friend of the military existed in Washington. No doughtier hawk. No one more apt in anointing belligerency with piety (he once asked President Truman to set aside the Sunday before Christmas as a day of prayer for national unity "in the fight against a Godless ideology"). Hébert has actively propagandized Americans on the unquestioned virtues of the military, suggesting that those, whether in or out of Congress, who dare to criticize the military are traitors.

Examples of the special privilege of the little inner circle abound. The Senate foreign relations committee had been assured just before the Cambodian invasion in May 1970 that there would be no invasion —but Senator John C. Stennis of the armed forces committee had been secretly privy to the plans. The Multiple Independently Targeted Re-entry Vehicle (MIRV) program was kept secret for three years except for a handful of men on the armed services committee. When the veil was stripped from the military aid program in 1971, the deputy assistant Secretary of Defense declared that the relevant committees in Congress had known about it all along. Congressman Richard D. McCarthy (D., N. Y.) smoked out the extent of the Chemical and Biological Warfare (CBW) effort and the deployment of its noxious agents (as well as of the accidents that had occurred) and proved that the repeated military denials had been lies; the reply was that the inner congressional circle had always known. John W. Finney wrote that Congressman McCarthy had uncovered what the "Army has managed to keep secret" through "cooperation of senior members of the Appropriations and Armed Services Committees," namely, what the military had spent on CBW.[23]

The cuddling of military officers with the little coterie of well-placed congressional hawks is combined with a contemptuous spurning of other more critical legislators. Thus the military has refused to release research prepared by outside institutes to the Senate foreign relations committee, even though the fruits of such studies may be agreements with foreign countries that purport to commit the United States to war. On 24 July 1969, the *U. S. News and World Report* claimed that at least twenty-four such surreptitious agreements exist.

If the foreign relations committee was ignored, so was the subcommittee on government economy of the joint committee on defense production. Its chairman, Senator William Proxmire, wrote that Congress had become "a pushover for the Pentagon, reinforced as it was by its ties to the Armed Service and Appropriation Committees."

Despite the Proxmire subcommittee's disclosure of monumental waste and the emergence, even in the armed services committees, of some criticisms of the military, the House of Representatives passed an arms funding bill, on 3 October 1969, in precisely the form that the armed services committee had recommended, with approval for all controversial items. On 6 November, the Senate having approved the bill, Congress passed it in virtually the same form, with the debated items intact. John Stennis, chairman of the Senate armed services committee, declared: "No major weapon has been left out of this bill and none has been seriously affected." The joint conference committee struck down almost all restrictive amendments. It retained one permitting the comptroller general (Congress's own watchdog) to study defense profits but required him to get approval of the armed services committees before he subpoenaed contractors' records!

If rival committees are brushed off, the floor of Congress gets even shorter shrift. Not that more time has been needed. Defense appropriations have traditionally been whooped through Congress.[24] In 1969, after months of armed services committee hearings on the authorization bill for $21 billion had filled 2,660 pages, the House of Representatives was allowed two days to prepare for the debate in which each member had 45 seconds of speaking time. If encouragement were necessary, the Pentagon has it in abundance, with 339 officers assigned to legislative liaison with 435 congressmen and 100 senators. The Pentagon's lobbyists "have Congress organized like a Marine Corps landing."[25]

How much power do the congressional insiders wield? They are invaluable to the military in its assertion of independence from the executive. They enable the military to deal contemptuously with the foreign relations committee of the Senate and cavalierly with the floor of Congress. But even they do not exercise control. Two poignant examples are provided by Senator John Stennis, chairman of the armed services committee, and the late Senator Richard B. Russell, chairman of the appropriations committee. Both opposed sending American ground troops to Vietnam in the 1960s; but once "the flag was committed," both turned their formidable talents and influence to the unequivocal support of the Vietnamese adventure.

The ineffectiveness of the armed services and appropriations committees in their overview of the military has been widely attested.[26]

Congress stumbled from one defense appropriations bill to another [wrote Edward A. Kolodjiez], directed only by the crudest and most rudimentary elements of a coherent strategic design.[27]

In 1950, for the first time since the hearings on the navy in 1946, was there a "glimmer of interest in the military and foreign policy considerations underlying the defense budget." The vaunted Carl Vinson, chairman of the House armed services committee, did not come off very well, tending to parrot what the Joint Chiefs of Staff told him, particularly the Chief of Naval Operations. George Mahan, chairman of the military subcommittee of appropriations, did only a little better, being overly concerned with details and economy.

As men died [in 1953] and the world trembled before the prospects of global conflict, Congress through its appropriations groups fiddled with accounting forms and budgetary estimates. . . .

A close relationship appears . . . between Congressional fascination with military hardware and the multiple budgetary categories of the defense bill. [The spread of manufacture of hardware among congressional districts adds to the fascination.] Each year the appropriations committees move in almost ritualistic form through the confusing labyrinth of budgetary classifications.

When criticism comes it tends to stem from special constituency interests—there is much discussion of travel, the size of the National Guard, the use of locally produced milk in Alaska, time-study analyses in shipyards, or the transfer or deactivation of military installations. Small sums are haggled over; billions are approved mechanically. The upshot is that the Defense Department's bureaucracy sets the policy. "Many legislators hold tenaciously to the comfortable assumption . . . that large defense budgets by their very size and awesome complexity produce national safety and success in foreign policy."

Beachheads in the Executive

Given the impressive Pentagon-congressional axis, readers will not be surprised to find the State Department humbled and even the president circumscribed and frustrated. The Pentagon has had an organizational advantage over the Office of Management and Budget (OMB) enjoyed by no other agency. The Pentagon's budget was exempt from the OMB's independent review and report to the president, as applied to other agencies, which then have the right to object to the president. By contrast, the defense budget was reviewed by OMB analysts working alongside Pentagon analysts; and the report was made to the Secretary of Defense who lay it before the president—with the OMB having the right to challenge.[28]

The Nixon administration reportedly stripped Defense of its advantage in the budgetary process.[29] But did it? Noting in 1971 that leaks about the defense budget heralded "another turkey . . . being served up," Joseph Kraft showed how the Pentagon had absorbed nearly all the Vietnam "savings," and more besides. George P. Shultz, director of the Office of Management and Budget, and his deputy "fought hard" to control Pentagon increases for 1972. "But civilians from the President's executive office were no match for the uniformed services, especially after the services got to the President on his visit to the Sixth Fleet . . ."[30]

As the Pentagon has moved on the executive office, it has infiltered and often dominated the State Department. "The country desks at the State Department are often 'in the hip pocket of the Pentagon—lock, stock, and barrel, ideologically owned by the Pentagon.'"[31] In 1965 Lieutenant General Richard G. Stilwell signed a secret military agreement with Thailand that the U.S. Ambassador, Graham Martin, later described as "total and irreversible." Asked whether the pact meant Americans would die, if necessary, to defend the current Thai government, the ambassador replied, "Yes." Thus a secret military pact, undiscussed by Congress, unseen by Congress, unapproved by Congress, has committed the United States to war in Thailand.[32]

Despite the theoretical primacy of the ambassador as representative of the Department of State, Robert Kennedy found the dominant United States figure in some of the countries he had visited "was the representative of the CIA; in several of the Latin American countries, it was the head of our military mission."[33] Former ambassador to El Salvador, Murat W. Williams, recalled that "his" military air mission had "more men . . . than there were fliers in the Salvadoran Air Force." Williams tried to cut the mission's size, was told by the State Department that it was helpless to do anything ("You have annoyed the Pentagon by making the suggestion"), and finally met with a "many-starred general" who was "sent to 'negotiate' " with him. The general agreed to cut the mission from 40 to 38! Understandably Williams concluded: "It is easy to imagine U.S. military missions as 'seconds' to the fighters in that bloody and useless contest in Salvadoran-Honduran forests."[34]

The military's imperial designs on foreign policy are manifest at home in the form of a studied increase in its scope and capacity. The evidence suggests a subtle change in the orientation of foreign policy, a turn away from the classical effort to increase support for, and reduce opposition to, the United States by diplomatic means and turn toward infiltering and taking over governmental operations in foreign countries. The military and especially the army has rapidly increased its ability to run civilian programs. In June 1970, the John F. Kennedy Center for Military Assistance at Fort Bragg, North Carolina, originally established to teach antiguerrilla warfare, graduated "the first class of Army officers trained in the political, social, economic, cultural and linguistic aspects of overseas military activities."

These officers were to be used, according to plans of the Nixon administration, to take over such functions in South Vietnam as "the balancing of the South Vietnamese defense budget, pacification of rural areas, the training of the police, and the care of refugees." All this may be part of a long-range plan. The Pentagon commissioned the Douglas Aircraft Corporation (a curious choice) to make a study, entitled "Pax Americana," designed to show how the United States "can maintain world hegemony in the future." The cost was $89,500.00. Senator Fulbright's request for release of the study was refused.

Supporting Groups and the Public

Responsible positions in defense industries are often manned by retired military officers—721 were counted by Senator Paul H. Douglas in 1959 and 2,072 by Senator William Proxmire ten years later. Although there is little data on them, probably at least as many ranking civilians in the Department of Defense have moved to influential posts in defense industries.[35]

"If retired officers provide a lubricant between the armed forces and the weapons merchants, the many military service–defense industry organizations provide the ties that bind." Defense industry and military establishment "combine to form a powerful public opinion and political pressure lobby."[36] The Air Force Association enrolled some 100,000 members (1970) who were active, reserve, retired, and veterans of the air force. Its board of directors included fourteen employees of defense contractors in 1960 when it enjoyed an income of $1.2 million, including $527,000 from advertising in *Air Force and Space Digest,* which, according to Donovan, supports the "party line" of the association. A "heady mixture of advertising, propaganda, and Air Force doctrine . . . provides its readers and writers a form of . . . hypnosis." The Association of the U. S. Army has nearly 100,000 members. In 1960, the executive vice-president was Lt. General W. L. Weible (ret.) and his board included Donald Douglas, Jr., president of the Douglas Aircraft Co., Frank Pace, formerly Secretary of the Army and chairman of General Dynamics Corporation, as well as Senators Strom Thurmond and John Sparkman. Other organizations include the Navy League, the Marine Corps Association, the American Ordnance Association, and the National Security Industrial Association.

Along with defense businesses, many universities have been linked to the defense establishment.[37] Among the most difficult ties to defend are university contributions to chemical and biological warfare.[38] Some professors have avidly pursued the military research dollar, willing to turn an especially sophisticated trick for an extra megabuck.[39] Nevertheless, university campuses have been important sources of opposition to overreaching militarism. In the early years of the Southeast Asia involvement, a handful of media reporters provided the grist for a few senators and even fewer congressmen to criticize the war. They were strongly complemented by a considerable number of university professors. In the absence of a centralized second party, these scattered critics were all the opposition America could provide.

With few exceptions, notably the United Automobile Workers, organized labor has staunchly supported the militaristic position. In 1966 the AFL-CIO executive council resolved: "Those who would deny our military forces unstinting support are, in effect, aiding the communist enemy of our country."[40] In 1967, President Johnson happily addressed the AFL-CIO convention that resounded with praise for his foreign policies. In 1970, the AFL-CIO just as emphatically endorsed Nixon's foreign and military policy. Any alternative to Vietnamization and the Nixon plan, such as setting a cut-off date for leaving Vietnam, President George Meany characterized a "bugging out." Protests by college students against the invasion of Cambodia in 1970 provoked violent counterdemonstrations by union members, notably the "hard hats" of the building trades. Some workers liked the war because it meant jobs. Some were repelled by the desecration of Old Glory, the waving of Viet Cong flags, and the attack on the military—above all by college students whom they considered the privileged heirs of the good things in life that laborers could get only by long and sweaty work. The hard hat–student clash appeared to some as another rupture in the American consensus. Could the military create a new consensus by appealing to "patriotism"? We are naturally led to a discussion of public opinion.

A bridge to the public is provided by veterans' organizations. More than 26 million veterans comprised 45 percent of the nation's adult males in 1969. About 9 percent of the veterans belonged to the American Legion; about 7 percent to the American Veterans of Foreign Wars; and about 3 percent to other organizations—well over 80 percent belonged to none at all. The average age of veterans was 44.2 years in 1969 (when the average voter was 47 years old); that of veteran organization members is probably much older—more than 13 percent of the World War II veterans belong to the American Legion but only 8 percent of the Korean veterans and a bit more than 7 percent of Vietnam veterans. The legion is strongest in the Middle West and the Great Plains—numbering 55 percent of the eligible North Dakota veterans, 26 percent in Kansas, and 31 percent in Iowa —but only a little more than 5 percent in California.

In most organized groups a few activists do the work, spread the gospel, man the posts, and make the policy.[41] In the American Legion, the ruling elite can squelch opposition; after its committee had investigated and commended UNESCO in 1955, the legion took only 30 seconds to adopt a resolution condemning that agency, prompting *Life* to remark that the convention represented "only the handful of kingmakers who run the national Legion as their private dictatorship."[42] The legion's method of internal voting encourages oligarchy. Except in a few states, individual legionnaires vote only for delegates to county conventions who, in turn, choose delegates for state conventions that elect delegates to the national convention that elects the national commander.[43]

Certainly the American Legion cannot speak for all veterans, nor can veterans be equated with the public; and yet the legion and the Veterans of Foreign Wars offer avenues for the Pentagon and its allies to approach the public. Their national conventions become forums for the fire-eating advocates of overseas military adventures, of an expanded military establishment, and of the increased budgets necessary to support them.

The Pentagon has many other avenues to the public, however. In 1969 the military's elaborate plan to sway the public in favor of the Sentinel antimissile project was disclosed. It provided for briefing "reporters, members of Congress, local governmental leaders and officials, military audiences, scientific, fraternal, and civic groups and organizations. . . ." Speaking appearances were to be arranged, speakers' kits provided, and sympathetic scientists recruited to write articles. The *Washington Post* called it a "mammoth, all-pervasive, overwhelming sales job. . . ."

The CBS film, "The Selling of the Pentagon" (23 February 1971), though criticized as a "propaganda barrage" by the then Vice President Spiro T. Agnew, displays (fairly in my judgment) the military's confidence and its contempt for rules or other impediments to its continuous propaganda campaign.[44] Every year two million news stories and twelve hundred film and television strips, all done at public expense, all lionizing the military, and some of them glamorizing slaughter and brutality, are released from the Kansas City center— enormous amounts of boiler-plate are fed to the country newspapers where strong American Legion posts reciprocate with highly senior congressmen to strengthen the military's political base. These broad-sides are reinforced by teams of paratroopers who tour the country, making exhibition jumps, and by platoons of uniformed and decorated officers who are available, gratis, to address virtually any meeting. The Pentagon pinpoints the nation's influentials, especially small city lawyers, bankers, and businessmen who are taken on military tours, profusely wined and dined, provided attractive uniforms, and per-mitted to fire recoilless rifles and other ordnance and to take over the controls of warplanes. Expensive war shows, involving thousands of troops and great quantities of equipment, are put on for them. When the tour is finished, these gentry become the happy subjects of military newsreels, for general release. In these, they "brag up" their hosts, repeat the ideological litanies, and denounce the likes of Senators J. W. Fulbright and William Proxmire and Governor George W. Romney (how could he have been brainwashed by these wonderful gentle-men?).

I do not imply that the public is necessarily swayed by these tactics; but it may appear to be—and this is often enough to scare congress-men who must build their own organizations virtually by themselves, secure their own finances, and face reelection every two years. Few congressmen feel strong enough to antagonize veterans' organizations, which are rarely effectively balanced by any countervailing groups.

Ideology

A formidable set of universal ideas informs and inspires the military bureaucracy. General David M. Shoup believes that the military-funded "think factories" with their "scientists, analysts, and retired military strategists . . . feed new militaristic philosophies into the Defense Department to help broaden the views of the single-service doctrinaires" and to justify "ever larger, more expensive defense forces . . ." in order to fight "Communist aggression."[45]

"Somewhat like a religion, the basic appeals of anti-communism, national defense, and patriotism provide the foundation for a powerful creed upon which the defense establishment can build, grow, and justify its costs." The creed for this new religion has been supplied most provocatively by such retired generals as Nathan F. Twining, Thomas S. Power, and Curtis LeMay who write that monolithic communism is bent on destroying freedom and especially freedom in America, which has no recourse other than to arm to the teeth and prepare to fight the inevitable holy war.[46]

> The military emphasizes the evil in man and seeks out threats of
> aggression and danger wherever they may be found. To most military
> officers human nature is unchanging and no institutions or wishful
> thinking can result in peaceful civilization. Wars can perhaps be
> prevented or delayed by military power, they can be won only by
> armed strength and, by and large, wars are considered inevitable.
> The standards . . . by which American military strength should be
> measured . . . have been the estimated force which the strongest
> probable enemy could bring against us.[47]

The emergence of the military ideology was heralded by Captain Alfred T. Mahan's, *The Influence of Sea Power Upon History* (1890) in the age of American imperialism. "It was during this period that American military professionals began to evolve and codify their service doctrines. . . ." Between the great wars when the armed forces were reduced and isolated, the "Army and Navy sought reasons to justify their existence and developed professional codes and creeds to guide their exclusive and separate societies."[48]

The full-blown military ideology supplies answers to all questions.[49] Appropriately, it is the particular possession, strength, and responsibility of a relatively small elite within the establishment:

> Actually the influence and importance . . . of the Military and
> Naval Academy graduates have not been based so much upon their
> numbers but rather their ideologies, their attitudes, and their values
> which have always dominated the ethics and set the standards and
> goals of the American military establishment.[50]

The separate services nourish their own myths; but interaction among them helps strengthen a common military ideology. "Each of the armed services teaches somewhat different . . . doctrines . . . , but all of the military have in common the codes of discipline, veneration of tradition, and the demands of *esprit de corps*."[51]

The ability of military officers, the organized impact of both their professional training and their life experiences, and the strength of their motivation combine to give the ideology greater effect. General Shoup wrote ". . . the professional military, as a group, is probably one of the best organized and most influential . . . [on] the American scene."[52] Since 1940, the military has

produced an unending supply of distinguished, capable, articulate and effective leaders. The sheer skill, energy, and dedication of America's military officers make them dominant in almost every government or civic organization they may inhabit, from the Cabinet to the local PTA.

Officers are carefully selected, rigorously trained, and subjected to continuous competition. They are taught "to command large organizations and to plan big operations." They learn how to influence others. "Their education is not, however, liberal or cultural. It stresses the tactics, doctrines, traditions, and codes of the military trade. It produces technicians and disciples, not philosophers." Often they outdo civilians in high governmental councils because "they work harder, think straighter, and keep their eyes on the objective, which is to solve the problem through military action."

The military exemplifies the classic virtues

used to motivate men of high principle: patriotism, duty, and service to the country, honor among fellowmen, courage in the face of danger, loyalty to organization and leaders, self-sacrifice for comrades, leadership, discipline, and physical fitness.

Preferment comes from performing well, "conforming to the expected patterns and pleasing the senior officers." Above all, promotion comes most readily from combat; civilians must understand that "many ambitious military professionals truly yearn for wars . . ."[53]

Conclusion: The Frustration of President and Congress

Charles L. Schultze, former director of the Bureau of the Budget, told the subcommittee on economy in government that the Budget Bureau can thoroughly examine proposed military expenditures "only when the President feels that *he* can effectively question military judgments . . ."[54] In the environment of the cold war, Senator Proxmire wrote, "criticism made one vulnerable to the charge of playing fast and loose with national security . . . *neither the President nor Congress could question military judgments.*"[55]

The president has enormous power including the ability to initiate military actions and even wars. Once a policy is set, however; once an arms race gains momentum; once a war, declared or undeclared, is underway, the control by the president of the bureaucracy often becomes illusory—as the following chapter will show in detail. Part of his difficulty in controlling the military is attributable to his lack of attention to the necessary details because he has so many other claims on his time; but the experience of recent presidents who have attempted to exercise nearly complete control, for example, of individual bombing missions has often been frustrating. The president's problems may be compounded if the position of his Secretary of Defense is weakened. Recently the Fitzhugh panel reported that the "tools available to the Secretary to exercise effective controls of the Department are seriously deficient."

Partly to placate the generals and their allies, the senatorial hawks, President Nixon and Secretary Laird downgraded the office of International Security Affairs, which had been called "the best foreign policy shop in Washington." Then came Cambodia, the by-passing of Laird, and his belated effort to reestablish control. One of Laird's aides described the secretary's problem.

He knew they would take it as far as he would let them, that they would test him to see how far they could go. They're always testing each Secretary to see whether he is running his department. . . .
As the crunch came in Cambodia, it became evident that dealing directly between the White House and the Joint Staff would continue to escalate, unless something was done.

Regarding control by Congress of the military bureaucracy, I have already provided evidence that the most likely source of influence, the leadership of the relevant committees, possesses little real power over many of the most significant actions of the Pentagon. A further example is provided by the fact that effective criticism of the Sentinel —later the Safeguard—anti-ballistic missile system came from the enterprise of a former foreign service officer who was now an aid to Senator Sherman Cooper. It did not come from the vaunted committees so dear to the defenders of the status quo in American politics. The insiders, just as the insiders of Congress who are supposed to watch the CIA,[56] have been derelict in their duty, duped by the military, or both. The facts are that accountability ravels to nothing in the nooks and crannies of the American political system.

More insight into this foreboding phenomenon comes from a more general examination of Congress as an institution in light of the recent rise of the military bureaucracy. Congress-as-a-whole means congressmen as individuals. The organizational strength of a member of the House is largely within Congress and is effective there on national policy in accordance with his leverage of position, his prestige, and his ability. But this strength helps very little in the hustings where he is on his own, must build his own organization, and essentially must fund his own campaigns.[57] Congressmen may have some influence over local bureaucratic actions, congressmen may bullyrag agencies, including the military, to spend more in their districts (or senators, in their states); or they may be able to prevent or long postpone closing local federal facilities that have become redundant by any national criteria except to keep incumbent legislators in office. But if congressmen are critical of military organization, or operations, or policy, or spending, they often court attack as "unpatriotic."

Since *Federalist Papers* No. 10, the classical interpretation has been that the American polity can safely rely on its rich variety of interests and its almost endless local variations of pressures and counter-pressures to obviate the emergence of any one interest as a serious threat. The supposed result is a system of mutual checks and balances so that no majority interest or any other sufficiently powerful interest will arise to work its will, untrammeled, on policy. Historically, the military was kept so weak and dispersed that it constituted no threat to the system. When the military waxed after World War II, it was supposed to check itself through interservice rivalry. But interservice rivalry has become interservice logrolling; and when war breaks out *the several services, however jealous of each other, come together in support of a military solution. The lone congressman, accustomed to dealing with a rather loose, internally divided, and brawling establishment, suddenly finds himself confronting a monolith against which he is powerless.*

6 The Influence of the Military Bureaucracy—and a Corrective

I don't think $80 billion a year is a matter of style . . . this is muscle, this is influence, this is power. It controls everything that goes on in our government to a great extent. It is the primary control.—*Senator J. William Fulbright*, on the influence of the military

The Emergence of Bureaucratic Influence

Until 1964, wrote General David M. Shoup, the Joint Chiefs of Staff (of whom he was one) felt it unnecessary and unwise for America to engage in a ground war in Southeast Asia. Then the personnel changed, and "in a matter of a few months the Johnson administration, encouraged by the aggressive military, hastened into what has become the quagmire of Vietnam."[1] To be sure, earlier examples can be cited. Building on appropriate precedents that voiced the aim and verbalized some of the ideology, the military, "supported by major industrialists, tried as early as World War II to take full charge of the American economy." The effort did not succeed, "due to Franklin D. Roosevelt's resistance, but it didn't entirely fail, either." After the war, concerted efforts were made to control the nation's youth through perpetuation of the draft (without which the Vietnam war—absent a formal declaration of war by Congress—could not have been fought) and to get command of foreign policy. "Today," stated the *Army and Navy Bulletin* of 18 January 1947, "the Army has virtual control of foreign affairs. . . ."[2]

A good case can be made that MacArthur's ill-fated drive to the Yalu in late 1950 was the general's own contribution to policy, although it can also be argued that the essential mistake lay in President Truman's exceeding trust in generals.[3] By the 1960s the military bureaucracy had acquired enough influence to make a stronger bid to take over the direction of policy.

The period between Tonkin Gulf (August 1964) and Pleiky (February 1965), wrote Colonel James A. Donovan, "was . . . intriguing . . . for the student of militarism's influence on national opinion and policy." The Joint Chiefs of Staff convinced the White House that victory would be quick, easy, and cheap.[4] The military took advantage of an intellectual vacuum—no one was asking questions about the political purposes to be served by military action. James C. Thomson, a Far East specialist in the White House during 1961–66, asked one of the many former policymakers who was writing his memoirs how the American interest in Southeast Asia had been defined in 1961 and again in 1964–65.

He told me that the importance of Vietnam and Southeast Asia to America's security was, as far as he could tell from his memory and from the documents, simply "a given," assumed and unquestioned.[5]

Into the vacuum the military rolled with terrible momentum. Officers of the armed forces found the

war a frustrating but fascinating professional challenge. The very size and scope of the American military force has . . . generated unceasing pressures to satisfy such military demands as trying out new weapons and using the war as a military testing ground and laboratory.

The rising brutality and incredible waste and destructiveness of America's war in Southeast Asia was a product of what Philip Geyelin, editor of the *Washington Post,* called the "escalation machine." Colonel Donovan explained:

The overwhelming size of the American Army presence in Vietnam created pressures to view all problems in military terms and to subordinate all else to military demands.

In the words of the British expert in guerrilla warfare, Sir Robert Thompson:

There was a constant tendency in Vietnam to mount large-scale operations which had little purpose or prospect of success, merely to indicate that something aggressive was being done.[6]

General Shoup wrote that the four services were racing against each other to build up combat strength in Vietnam during 1965. If this was done "ostensibly to save South Vietnam from the Viet Cong . . ." it also appeared "to have been motivated at least in part by the same old interservice rivalry. . . ." Prompt punitive action after the Tonkin Gulf incident showed the navy's readiness to bomb North Vietnam. ("It now appears that the Navy actually had attack plans ready even before the alleged incident took place!") There ensued competitive navy–air force contests on bomb tonnage dropped and killed-by-air figures from sorties over North Vietnam. "In fact, it became increasingly apparent that the U. S. bombing effort in both North and South Vietnam has been one of the most wasteful and expensive hoaxes ever to be put over on the American people." The "Army and Marine Corps played a similar game. Prior to the decision to send combat units to South Vietnam in early 1965, both services were striving to increase their involvement."[7]

"The U. S. Army," wrote Colonel Donovan, "determined the operations, tactics, and much of the strategy in the Vietnam war." The army's concept of victory came to dominate—"find the enemy, fix him in position, fight him—and finish him off." Whereas Lieutenant-General James M. Gavin had strongly advised against American ground operations in Vietnam in 1954, had vigorously criticized military strategy there in 1965, and had argued for an "enclave" strategy in 1966, General Earle C. Wheeler, chairman of the JCS, preferred the aggressive tactics of "seek and destroy" and massive bombing. He prevailed.[8]

But these are mainly generalities! What of specifics? Eric Sevareid has written:

The civilian President says no, they shall not mine the harbor of Haiphong; no, they shall not make hot pursuit into Cambodia or Laos; no, they shall not [invade] North Vietnam; and yes, they shall cease the bombing of that country. [The military accepts] all this of necessity. . . .[9]

On some of these specifics some of the time Sevareid was correct. On the cessation of bombing the north, however, disclosures of 1972 and 1973 showed that he was wrong. In this as in many other situations the influence of the military was crucial. Examples began early.

Following the assassination of Diem and before the advent of Thieu, the government in Saigon turned over a number of times, and

the ups and downs . . . that characterize politics in Saigon [were] really all centered around the question of negotiating with the other side. On two chief occasions when South Vietnamese officials began seriously to think about approaching the Viet Cong, they were cut down by—of all things—*elements of the American mission in Saigon.*

The first was the government of General Duong Van Minh that was ousted in January 1964, in a military coup staged by General

Nguyen Khanh, the special protege of the American military commander in Saigon, General Paul Harkins, *who had brought him to Saigon without the American Ambassador's even seeming to know about it.*

The Khanh regime also became disposed to talk to the enemy but

had barely begun soundings when their government was ousted this June [1965], as a result of protest demonstrations set in motion by another American protege, Colonel Pham Quot Thao, who has since been killed in mysterious circumstances.[10]

Tonkin Gulf

An incident in Tonkin Gulf, 2 and 4 August 1964, produced the famous resolution permitting the president to conduct any kind of war he chose in Southeast Asia. Overwhelmingly passed by both houses of Congress with almost no debate, the resolution was officially described as tantamount to a declaration of war in August 1967.[11]

The incident began 2 August 1964, when the United States destroyer *Maddox,* which was equipped with electronic spying equipment, was allegedly attacked by Viet Cong torpedo boats (there is considerable evidence that the *Maddox* fired first). But much activity preceded the occasion. In February 1964, American personnel were assigned to advise, train, and assist South Vietnamese Marine operations against North Vietnam. In July, when the *Maddox* began its patrol, the United States gave eight fast patrol craft to the South Vietnamese to facilitate their attacks on the North. (As an example of military dissembling, Chief of Staff General Wheeler maintained in the hearings that there was no thought of American participation in the northward extension of the war).

Meanwhile, a "scenario" had been prepared, 23 May 1964, beginning with point 1, to "stall off any conference" on Vietnam until "D-Day," through point 4, to get a joint congressional resolution "approving past actions and authorizing whatever is necessary with respect to Vietnam," to point 15, D-Day, "launch first strikes" against North Vietnam (and finally, of course, to call a conference and profess "limited objectives"). Incredibly, Secretary McNamara was to say that he had not heard of the draft resolution.

Meanwhile also, the United States had moved fighter-bombers into Thailand to be ready to bomb North Vietnam heavily and continu-

ously, and it had readied certain army and marine forces for movement. (News of these and similar actions was not published until 24
November 1966, which happened to be Thanksgiving—perhaps in
the hope that having seen one turkey already the public would not be
interested in another.)

The first reported attack on the *Maddox* came on 2 August during a
cruise that was only the third in thirty months by a United States ship
closely approaching the North Vietnamese coast. Moreover, the cruise
followed a few hours after the first coastal bombardment of the North
by the eight patrol craft supplied to the South. Nevertheless, President
Johnson warned the North that the gravest consequences would follow
another attack on the *Maddox,* which, now accompanied by the U.S.
destroyer *Turner Joy,* was being sent back to the same waters. On
3 and 4 August came a second coastal bombardment of the North by
the South—a bombardment of which Secretary McNamara professed
ignorance, although it was jointly planned by our military and the
South Vietnamese. Then came the second "attack" (which very likely
did not occur at all) on the *Maddox* and the *Turner Joy,* whereupon
Johnson ordered retaliatory air strikes against North Vietnamese targets and asked for the famous Tonkin Gulf Resolution.

Clearly, the Tonkin Gulf affair is of first importance. It led to the
presidential carte blanche of the Tonkin Gulf Resolution, so easily and
deviously obtained. Quite aside from the resolution itself, indeed,
before the resolution was passed, it showed the force of uncontrolled
presidential initiative. At crucial turns of events the presidential
instincts or mind-sets apparently were determinative. On 20 March
1964, Lyndon B. Johnson cabled Ambassador Henry Cabot Lodge that
he was determined to knock down "the idea of neutralization [of
Southeast Asia] wherever it rears its ugly head. . . ."[12] On 24 July,
Johnson killed a proposal by President Charles de Gaulle (with Russia and Mainland China concurring) that the Geneva Conference on
Vietnam be reconvened with the rejoinder: "We do not believe in a
conference called to ratify terror."[13] On 4 August, when the evidence
of the second attack was evaporating it was Johnson's will that made
the attack "a political fact, with all of the President's prestige behind
it."[14]

So much for presidential initiative. There were also important
elements of establishmentarian control of foreign and military policy:
the domination thereof of a little group of devoted and experienced

men who would always discover and concur on the best course of action. Anthony Austin called Tonkin Gulf

a stratagem by a small number of officials in control of the Executive branch of the government for exploiting an obscure naval incident in order to execute a secret plan for going to war against North Vietnam . . .[15]

It is no disavowal of the foregoing interpretations to say that they are incomplete. *The phenomenon of bureaucratic influence as defined in these chapters was also evident in Tonkin Gulf, and it is important for Americans to realize how deep the constitutional faults are and therefore how thoroughgoing the corrective reforms may have to be.*

We must recall how the bureaucracy works. Once the president has made the commitment, the bureaucracy (the military, in this example) tends to acquire important influence on subsequent policy determination, using its ties to strategic power centers in Congress (here, the armed services committees) as sources of additional leverage. From the beginning in Vietnam, the president was under military pressure to expand the war.[16] If he failed to go all out, he subjected himself to attacks for needlessly prolonging the war, for being soft on the enemy, or worse.[17] Senator Thruston B. Morton, announcing his shift from hawk to dove in 1967, stated his belief that President Johnson had been "brainwashed" by the military-industrial complex as early as 1961. So had Morton himself. "In early 1965, when the President began to escalate the war, I supported the increased military involvement. I was wrong."[18]

More than brainwashing was involved. At critical junctures, to use its own language, the military interdicted presidential control and assumed the direction of policy. On 2 August 1964, Commodore John J. Herrick, in command of the mission of the *Maddox,* became sufficiently concerned about the possibility of a North Vietnamese ambush that he left his close patrol of the shore and made for the open sea, cabling his superior, Vice-Admiral Roy Lee Johnson, accordingly. Johnson immediately directed him to resume the patrol when he considered it prudent. This critical decision put the *Maddox* back into the situation that had invited the first incident. It was taken, apparently, in the Pacific command, without reference to Washington.[19]

After the 2 August incident, Admiral Thomas H. Moore, commander-in-chief of the Pacific fleet, cabling that it was "in our best interest to assert right of freedom of the seas," directed the resumption of the Tonkin Gulf patrol with two destroyers and extended it two days beyond the previous cutoff time. All this was done on Moore's own motion, subject to Washington reversal (President Johnson liked the two-ships idea so well he announced it as his own). Thus the patrol "kept poking the very center of the hornet's nest. . . ." This position was supported closer to the action, not perhaps where the lookouts searched the whitecaps for the wakes of torpedoes, but at the flag-officer level. With barely concealed anticipation, the rear admiral on the *Ticonderoga* cabled that North Vietnam had "thrown down the gauntlet and now considers itself at war with the United States" whose ships should henceforth expect to "be treated as belligerents. . . ."

A naval ship had been attacked [wrote Anthony Austin] and the President had decided not to retaliate but merely to warn. Wherever navy men gathered, there was a felt need to do something, put the chip on the shoulder, show that the Navy could not be pushed around.[20]

Then came 4 August, the patrol, the confusion in the Pacific dark, the misinterpretation of radar and sonar signals, and the reports, later drastically qualified, of an attack. Herrick had cabled:

Review of action makes many recorded contacts and torpedoes fired appear doubtful. Freak weather effects and overeager sonarman may have accounted for many reports. No actual visual sightings by *Maddox*. Suggest complete evaluation before any further action.

This message should be studied by every American. It was forwarded at 1:25 A.M., Tonkin Gulf time, 5 August (or 1:25 P.M., 4 August, Washington time) by the naval communications station in the Philippines to the Joint Chiefs. *Apparently, it stayed in the Joint Chiefs.* The Senate found it only by dint of much digging, with the help of anonymous tips, and then only in 1968. *Senator Fulbright said that this one message would have kept him from steering the Tonkin Gulf Resolution through to adoption.* It is not clear that this particular message was known even to the Pentagon's congressional cronies. But the power of the Pentagon-congressional axis was much in evidence throughout the period. In later years, whenever Fulbright probed what happened in August 1964, some senators would suggest that he was bordering on treason. Even his colleagues on the foreign relations committee awaited the disclosure of the Herrick cable and the destruction of McNamara's effort to explain it away before siding effectively with Fulbright.[21]

After Tonkin Gulf

Shortly after Tonkin Gulf came the incident at Bien Hoa, the South Vietnamese military airport (which was destined to outgrow Chicago's O'Hare). The White House staff learned that the air force was planning to move a squadron of B-57 bombers from the Philippines to Bien Hoa in South Vietnam. The air force would keep control of these "obsolescent" aircraft but shift their function of training South Vietnamese to Bien Hoa. Michael Forrestal, White House assistant on Vietnam, and William Bundy, assistant Secretary of State for Far Eastern affairs, told Secretary Rusk that the aircraft would become an "irresistible target" for the Viet Cong. Unimpressed, Rusk finally called McNamara, who did not want to intervene because, as Rusk put it, he had "so many issues with the JCS that he would rather finesse this one. . . ." Rusk agreed with McNamara. Nothing was done. On 3 November, Viet Cong mortars killed five Americans, wounded seventy-six, and demolished six aircraft. Ambassador (General) Maxwell Taylor demanded retaliation, but it was postponed until after the election on 5 November in order not to damage Johnson's image anti-Goldwater. "There seems little doubt, however, that the Bien Hoa attack crystallized official U.S. determination for intervention."[22]

Examples continued. Late in 1966 Janusz Lewandowski, the Polish representative on the International Control Commission for Vietnam, served as intermediary in an effort to bring the U. S. and North Vietnam to the conference table. It was literally exploded by American bombs dropped for the first time on Hanoi. The bombing runs—like all such—had been approved at one of President Johnson's Tuesday luncheons and it could be argued that the mechanics of the chain of the command were to blame. The North Vietnamese were told the bombing was a mistake, appeared to believe it, and agreed to reschedule the talks—when on 13 and 14 December Hanoi was bombed again! "At first [wrote Norman Cousins] the United States denied that the bombing had taken place." But Hanoi refused to go on with the talks.

How could a military decision to bomb Hanoi—if it were in fact a military decision *(and what else could the second bombing have been?)*—be allowed to supersede and destroy a decision, made at the highest political level, to bring about negotiations? To what extent do military decisions in the field force the hand of the President? These questions call for discussions and debate.[23]

Meanwhile, President Johnson maintained control of the bombing of the North, over the bitter objections of the Joint Chiefs of Staff; but he bowed to the JCS, and overrode McNamara, in letting the field commander have full discretion on the ground.

The shooting war on the ground thus proceeded with full autonomy, subordinating by its sheer weight (and undermining by its sheer destructiveness) the political efforts aimed at pacification. . . . The preferred military doctrine dictated the strategy and the strategy determined the policy. Though not officially acknowledged, nor even planned that way, military victory became an end in itself.

Westmoreland was a thoroughly decent, moderately intelligent product of the Army system. . . .[24]

But of course!

During all this period, Congress strongly upheld the military bureaucracy. An example is furnished by the decline of Secretary McNamara. Having staunchly supported the war since the beginning, he began to have doubts that led to a "dramatic public split" with the Joint Chiefs of Staff before the Stennis subcommittee of the Senate armed forces committee in 1967. McNamara opposed the Chiefs' proposal further to expand the bombing of North Vietnam. But Senators John C. Stennis and Richard B. Russell "told the President they wouldn't support him on the war if he didn't support the Chiefs on the bombing, and the bombing was expanded."[25] Shortly thereafter McNamara went to the World Bank.

In March 1968 the Vietnam policy was reversed by the conditional bombing restriction north of the 20th parallel. A similar proposal drafted by Secretary McNamara and his aides in the spring of 1967 (and purportedly paralleling State Department proposals for cut-backs) was turned down by President Johnson "after it ran into heavy opposition by the Joint Chiefs of Staff. There were reports at the time that some senior generals would have resigned if it had been carried out." In 1968 the policy was changed in a week-long process showing how "foreign policy is battled out, inch by inch, by negotiation rather than decision." Changes may often have been incremental in the twelve preliminary drafts of President Johnson's speech on 31 March, but the cumulative effect was profound. Johnson announced the bombing restriction and his decision not to run for a second term. One official said that the speech "ended up 180 degrees from where it started."

The president's speech brought great relief to the nation. "The bitterness of months had been lanced in a stroke." But while the world was awaiting Hanoi's response, "Navy jets struck Thanhhos, 210 miles north of the demilitarized zone. . . ." Relief evaporated. Not knowing that Hanoi and the Russians had been told that the restriction would not apply north of the 20th parallel, politicians complained that the public had been misled. "State Department officials privately accused the military commanders of trying to sabotage the President's peace offensive."[26]

When the bombing of the North was completely halted on 1 November 1968, the U. S. military command in South Vietnam instituted a policy of "patrolling more aggressively" and "engaging the enemy far more frequently than before." The tactics were part of what one highly placed U. S. official described as the "total war" strategy of General Creighton W. Abrams. The increased attacks appeared "to explain why both the enemy and the American casualty figures remained consistently high" after the bombing halt. The figures also helped substantiate W. Averell Harriman's claim that the North Vietnamese offensive of February 1969 was "essentially a response to United States actions. . . ."[27]

Vietnam in the Nixon Administration

A major example of the influence of the military bureaucracy in Vietnam has been the "protective reaction strikes" of 1970–72. The United States claimed that North Vietnam had agreed to overflights of unarmed American reconnaissance planes as part of the mysterious "understanding" of 31 October 1968. Some questioned whether Hanoi had ever made the concession. In any event, Secretary Laird announced that the United States would make "protective reaction" strikes to retaliate against attacks on reconnaissance planes.

Questions soon arose whether "protective reaction" was a smoke screen for unprovoked strikes by the military against the North. Confirming evidence surfaced in June 1972 when General John Lavelle was dismissed from the command of air force units in Southeast Asia and retired with the loss of one star, the only four-star general in American history to suffer such demotion. Lavelle was held responsible for conducting some twenty unauthorized raids on military targets in North Vietnam and reporting them as "protective reaction" missions. These raids occurred between 8 November 1971 and 8 March 1972; but subsequent evidence indicated that unauthorized raids had been conducted throughout 1970 and 1971, indeed, that their total had been more than three times the number of "protective reaction" strikes reported by the Pentagon—and that the continued conduct of the raids had been well known in the upper military echelons during the period.

These unauthorized raids may have damaged the credibility of the American negotiating position with Hanoi, and they may also have undermined American protests against Hanoi's infractions of the 1968 "understanding." Once more, the raids called into question the will and ability of the political arm of the government to control the military. At the same time, the affair demonstrated that the problem of control lay not in finding and disciplining an occasional overeager officer but rather in coping with a recalcitrant bureaucracy. As Joseph Kraft put it, General Lavelle had apparently "allowed himself to be made the scapegoat for a massive, sophisticated and systematic stretching of Presidential orders by the military commands in both Washington and Vietnam."[28]

On the day the evidence of the bombing excess transpired, the air force ceased giving detailed briefing accounts of air raids over the North—an action suggesting the desire to conceal further evidence. Moreover, the highest circles in the Pentagon, including the Secretary of Defense himself, tried to muzzle Congressman Otis Pike who had publicly aired the affair; and the government also said that Seymour M. Hersh, the correspondent who broke the Lavelle story, was out to embarrass the government and give aid and comfort to the enemy. To quote Kraft again:

> ... the problem of controlling the military is no mere matter of enforcing discipline on a few Hotspurs. It involves the far more difficult task of bending ... a vast, highly organized and impenetrable

bureaucracy that does not understand or, in its heart, accept the limits

which have been imposed on it by official policy.[29]

Spain

Military determination of policy is not confined to Vietnam.[30] "Influence of Joint Chiefs is Reported Rising," wrote Neil Sheehan[31] in June 1969. Secretary of Defense Melvin R. Laird had "substantially vitiated the effect of the elaborate machinery constructed by former Defense Secretary Robert S. McNamara to impose aggressive civilian management and control over the military. . . ." One of the changes was to reduce the power of the "Office of International Security Affairs, which [was] the Pentagon's Foreign Policy Section. . . ." Under Paul C. Warnke,

the former head of the Office of International Security Affairs, the office had adopted a position paper that expressed considerable skepticism about the military value of the air bases in Spain and recommended that no further commitments be made to retain them.

Under Laird this position "was subsequently reversed at the request of the Joint Chiefs." Not only was the agreement (dating from 1953) extended and Spain given $50 million arms aid grant and a $35 million credit from the U. S. government to purchase weapons in the United States, but the new agreement provided that

a threat to either country and to the joint facilities that each provides for the common defense would be a matter of concern to both countries and each country would take such action as it may consider appropriate.

The Senate foreign relations committee warned that the United States had assumed a "quasi-commitment" to the Franco regime and disclosed that a ranking military officer had assured Franco that "the presence of American armed forces in Spain constitutes a more specific guarantee to Spain than would a written agreement." In June 1969, a Senate foreign relations subcommittee reported that American armed forces had taken part in at least two Spanish military exercises to perfect techniques to quell civil disturbances. In December 1969, Senator Fulbright revealed that the Department of Defense "on its own motion had sent additional jet fighter planes to . . . Spain without informing either the State Department or the Defense Department's Section of Internal Security Affairs."[32]

On 6 August 1970, the U. S.–Spanish accord was extended for five years, over Fulbright's vehement protests, by executive agreement. Fulbright wanted the proposal in the form of a treaty to give the Senate a chance to examine it. The State Department refused—or was ordered by the Pentagon to refuse. On 24 July at a hearing before the Senate foreign relations committee, Undersecretary of State U. Alexis Johnson (who could be counted on to advance the Pentagon's cause within the State Department) and Deputy Defense Secretary David Packard agreed to consider Senator Fulbright's request for full discussion of the proposal. Four days later, David Abshire, assistant Secretary of State for Legislative Affairs, informed Carl Marcy, the senate committee's chief of staff, that plans for signing the Spanish agreement were postponed and that there was no rush about considering the wisdom of a public hearing. Eight days later—five working days—the agreement was signed. Nothing could better illustrate the contemptuous manner in which the administration dealt with the leading congressional committee dealing with foreign policy.[33]

Chemical and Biological Warfare

Chemical and biological warfare (CBW) provides further examples of bureaucratic domination of policy. Beginning with the successful drive in 1925 to prevent the Senate from ratifying the Geneva protocol that renounced chemical and biological warfare, the bureaucracy—after a lag that extended into the 1950s—reasserted itself. Small changes, but with large cumulative effects, were made in policy and were followed in the early 1960s by enormous increases in appropriations. All was done with great secrecy by a handful of congressional insiders, operating under the mutual deference principle in Congress. All occurred apparently without topside review in the White House, the State Department, or even the Pentagon.

In the rise in capabilities of CBW, many implications went unexamined. Relationship to overall policy was not probed. The grave threats of potential enemies (Russians) were dutifully advertised but without convincing evidence. Disclosures of the extent of American commitment came about by accident, resulting in some fatalities to livestock and illness to human beings. Typically, the official reaction was to deny everything. But the truth came out, and the upshot was—supposedly—a presidential reversal of policy together with an order to destroy existing stocks of chemical and biological agents. I say "supposedly" because subsequent evidence made it questionable to what extent the presidential directive was obeyed.

"The history of our nation," wrote Congressman Richard D. McCarthy, "is often the result of decisions that have not been considered by either the public, Congress, or the President."[34] Nevertheless, a handful of his fellow congressmen played significant roles. First among them was Robert L. F. Sikes, a major general in the army's chemical reserve, whose Florida district housed the air force's largest CBW research laboratory and test station, and who was chairman of the defense appropriations subcommittee. Sikes was one of five congressmen cleared for "top secret"—five men whose names were unknown even to Majority leader Carl Albert. Only they were familiar with the funding of the CIA, the Green Berets, CBW, and other secret projects.[35]

At the same time, information was denied to ranking policymakers in the State Department and the Pentagon and, indeed, even to the president of the United States. Speaking of the insiders, the military bureaucracy who secretly controlled the destiny of CBW, James Reston wrote:

So great was their power that even the Secretary of State and the President—though they will probably deny it—didn't really know what the military was doing with nerve gas in Utah and Okinawa. . . .[36]

In the huge military budget, this mere $300-million-a-year program got scant attention. No interdepartmental review had been made since 1961. Budgetary supervision was perfunctory.

Dozens of interviews with past and present Pentagon and Administration officials produced little evidence that any really serious thinking about the strategic, political, or moral implications of CBW had been conducted in the Defense Department or anywhere else. . . .

Many top officials conceded their ignorance, their wonder at why the program had grown so large, or their simple disbelief that any "such a buildup took place."[37]

Naturally enough, the universal and sufficient excuse for the American CBW program has been the Russian threat. When Congressman Richard McCarthy, prompted by his wife (who was stimulated by an NBC report on the Utah sheep kill), sought a briefing from the Pentagon, he was met by considerable deviousness. ("To say that I was disappointed by the briefing would put it mildly.") The briefing officer, Brigadier General James A. Heberler, denied that the Utah sheep were killed by nerve gas and then told the press that the Soviet Union had a CBW capacity seven or eight times that of the United States. The latter assertion proved as ill-founded as the reply about the sheep. "I have been amazed to discover," wrote Congressman McCarthy, "that the U. S. had absolutely no hard evidence of any Russian offensive biological warfare activity."[38]

On 25 November 1969, President Nixon announced that the United States would not use biological weapons and would destroy its stocks. But the history of such presidential assertions, together with some disturbing reports of digressions from the announced policy, constitute grounds for skepticism. In any event, a review of CBW policy strikingly illuminates the power that the military bureaucracy has exercised over the years.

Nuclear Warfare

One important piece of evidence exists that both Russia and the United States are sufficiently convinced of the suicidal nature of nuclear war to show restraint—we are still alive. But the "balance of terror" is subject to constant strain as the militarists in both Russia and the United States prod their countries to achieve enough nuclear power to destroy the other without fear of "unacceptable" losses in retaliation. To make the balance convincing, each country must be able to deliver a disastrous "second strike"—i.e., after having been hit by the other's strategic nuclear warheads. A large supply of missiles may not suffice unless enough of them are protected from surprise destruction to ensure that they will survive a first strike. The mutual conviction that the other country has enough invulnerable missiles to mount a second strike has been a prime deterrent. Roswell L. Gilpatric, formerly Deputy Secretary of Defense, wrote of the Russian-American nuclear arms race: "Starting with Sputnik I, the history of the missile age has been characterized by a series of American reactions to Soviet moves and vice versa."[39] The prime advocates have been the hard-line militarists on both sides. A major question is, Who has acted and who has reacted? Both Donald F. Hornig, formerly science adviser to President Johnson, and Roswell Gilpatric imply that the nuclear arms race has been like a seesaw, with now one and now the other up —and with each, seeing the other up, impelled to rise and excel in his turn.

The truth seems to be, however, that America has consistently been on top. The nuclear age began not with Sputnik but with Hiroshima when America was not only ahead but alone. Recall Eisenhower's remark that before the use of atomic weapons he had thought the U. S. might have peace with Russia. "Now I don't know . . . people are frightened and disturbed all over. Everyone feels insecure again."

We maintained superiority by repeated upward surges in nuclear armaments, often in a frantic effort to forestall imagined Russian threats that never materialized. In 1956 an unfavorable "bomber gap" was predicted and we rushed into production. In 1961 (despite Sputnik) both countries still relied essentially on bombers to deliver nuclear warheads. We had approximately 560 B-52s, 40 supersonic B-58s, and 900 of the older B-47 medium bombers, all with intercontinental range, supported by one thousand tankers for refueling in midair. Russia had 150 Bear-model heavy intercontinental bombers and 700–800 medium bombers plus a much smaller tanker fleet.[40]

In 1960 the "bomber gap" had given way to the "missile gap," an even greater fraud. According to former Budget Director Charles L. Schultze, the "missile gap" was promoted by the military bureaucracy "at a time when there was not a single Soviet ICBM . . . deployed." Only later did we learn that the Russians "actually built only three percent of the missiles predicted by 1963. . . ."[41] In 1969, Former Director of the Arms Control and Disarmament Agency, William C. Foster, reviewed the experience:

in 1961 the Soviets had a small number of ICBM's. We . . . did not know whether they planned to keep things that way or to deploy a greater number; so we went ahead on the assumption that they would deploy a greater number. We undertook a very sizeable build-up of Minute Men and Polaris forces. *We thus ended up with a considerably larger arsenal of missiles and warheads than we actually required.*

But then the Soviets also began an extensive deployment—*probably in response to our efforts. . . .*[42]

The fiasco of 1961 provides one of the best (or the worst) examples of the influence of the military bureaucracy. Secretary of Defense Robert J. McNamara had entered office determined above all else to reduce the capacity to make nuclear war. "He was fighting for the highest needs of mankind, plotting against the bureaucracy." He had to pick his issues carefully and avoid taking on too many (if he had tried "to turn the country around on chemical and biological warfare, for instance, [Senator] Russell surely would have opened hearings"). In this situation, McNamara had to rely heavily on President Kennedy, "his only patron and protector in the savage world in which he was now operating." But the president himself was also suspect. A story went around in "hip Pentagon circles that Kennedy was unreliable, almost soft on 'nukes.' "[43]

McNamara's posture changed as he became aware of the danger to him of the military junta in Congress. Determined to improve the flimsy controls then in use on the atom and, privately, at least, vehemently critical of the idea that tactical nuclear weapons could be used without triggering the holocaust, McNamara, nevertheless, learned to dissemble. He became keenly aware of the direct relationship between the number of nuclear warheads he requested and the barometer of his support by the flag officers and their congressional allies.

This is what happened to the effort to slow down the arms race in 1961. The United States had 450 intercontinental ballistic missiles that the White House concluded, after study, were enough. Kennedy asked McNamara's opinion. McNamara agreed. In effectiveness 450 would be as good as 950. But he was adamant that the administration must request 950. The Joint Chiefs of Staff were asking for 3,000. Therefore, 950 was *"the smallest number we can take up on the hill without getting murdered."*[44]

In 1966 we had about 1,000 ICBMs compared to Russia's 250. The USSR set out to catch up, thereby alarming Senator Richard Russell, the most influential congressional spokesman on military affairs, who declared in floor debate on 24 June 1968:

I today cannot assure the Senate, as I have done year after year, that we are superior to any Soviet threat in the field of strategic missiles, because I do not know that to be the case, and I think there is very grave doubt about it.[45]

Still, in late 1969, the U. S. had 3,854 strategic nuclear warheads to the Russians 2,155—a comparison that many believed to ensure that the U. S. would have a second strike capacity whatever the Russians did. But the military, as always, wanted more. "More" was an ABM system plus MIRV, the latter—at enormous expense and, worse, at the cost of subjecting the balance of terror to strains of the utmost danger —was projected to provide America with 10,264 strategic nuclear warheads, compared to 6,295 for Russia.

Efforts to control nuclear warfare have also been bedeviled by the maintenance of American missiles close to Russia and China. Americans can put themselves in others' shoes by recalling how close we came to the ultimate war in 1962 over the threat of Russian missiles ninety miles from the United States. In 1970, the foreign relations committee's subcommittee on security agreements and commitments abroad declared:

We must assume that the Soviets, as they view our placement of tactical nuclear weapons in countries far closer to their borders than Cuba is to ours, will seek to break out of the nuclear ring that has been drawn around them.

And in the same year the Strategic Arms Limitation talks (SALT) were stalled over a dispute about what constituted strategic offensive weapons. Russia claimed that American planes with the capacity to deliver nuclear warheads were based close enough to her borders to constitute strategic offensive weapons. The United States maintained that the planes were part of NATO, which was purely defensive; therefore, they could not be included in "any agreement to limit strategic arms."

Nevertheless, the SALT talks, initiated by President Johnson, reached agreement on strategic defensive weapons in 1972. The United States, once insistent on overwhelming superiority, professed itself now to be satisfied with "sufficiency" and "parity."[46] Much was made of Russian increases in ICBM launchers—1,550 in mid-1972 against 1,054 for the United States, although America still maintained a slight edge in launching tubes on submarines capable of delivering nuclear weapons and nearly a four to one margin in heavy bombers. The real measure of comparative striking power is not launchers but missiles—and here the United States not only maintained but increased its margin, as the following table shows:[47]

	Strategic Forces Strength			
	(1 November 1971 for the US; mid-1971 for the USSR estimate)		(Mid-1972)	
	(estimate)		(estimate)	
	USSR	US	USSR	US
Weapons	2,100	4,700	2,500	5,700

These arrays of weapons should be evaluated against the conclusion of the Pentagon that one hundred warheads delivered on Russia would kill some 37,000,000 people and destroy 59 percent of the industry. Multiply the warheads eight times and kill 96,000,000 people while destroying 77 percent of the industry. Multiply the warheads 16 times to kill a few million more people—but without destroying more industry.[48] In late 1969 another statement, reportedly stemming from the Pentagon, held that the most successful Russian attack in 1975 would still leave the United States with 200 Minutemen, 300 to 600 Polaris missiles, and several hundred nuclear-armed aircraft.[49]

Whether the SALT agreement of 1972 will prove a genuine step toward limiting the arms race or another hoax is too early to tell, but some of the signs are disturbing, especially when they are read in light of the strength of the military bureaucracy. In 1972 federal military spending jumped to an annual rate of 28 percent in the first quarter. Despite SALT, it became clear that production of nuclear arms in the United States would grow. Why did the Nixon administration advertise marked increases in military spending even before the rosy glow of SALT had dissipated? One answer was that the acquiescence of the Joint Chiefs of Staff was necessary to get the SALT treaty past the Senate. "It is now clear the President and Mr. Laird have virtually promised the chiefs that in exchange for their support of the Moscow agreement, the military can have carte blanche on the offensive weapons not covered by the agreement. . . ."[50]

We have seen the nature of the military bureaucracy and the kind of influence it exercises. What can be done about it?

The Shape of the Corrective

In seeking a cure, it is of first importance to maintain that the problem is manageable. We cannot permit ourselves to be trapped by Secretary McNamara's suggestion that criticism of the Tonkin Gulf affair amounts to an allegation of a

monstrous . . . conspiracy which would include almost, if not all, the entire chain of military command in the Pacific, the Chairman of the Joint Chiefs of Staff, the Joint Chiefs, the Secretary of Defense . . . and the President of the United States.[51]

Whatever judgment history has in store for the individuals involved, the allegation of general conspiracies is as wrong as an effort to "indict a whole nation" or to blame our ills on a "generation of vipers."[52] Rather, I have tried to break down the problem by describing faults in our system that makes for government by presidential whim or idiosyncrasy and, in these chapters, by showing the influence of bureaucracy, carefully defined. Serious as the institutional flaws are, they are still subject to analysis and prescriptive correction.

I have cited many concrete examples of decisions made or unmade apparently as a result of the bureaucracy's influence. Moreover, these decisions could have gone another way; in short, they were—or they might have been—manageable.

What will make these decisions manageable? Only superior political power. Recall the nature of the military bureaucracy as identified by Senator Fulbright:

Most interest groups are counterbalanced by other interest groups, but the defense complex is so much larger than any other that there is no effective counterweight to it except concern as to its impact on the part of some of our citizens and a few of our leaders, none of whom has any material incentives to offer.[53]

Compare Walter Adams, who wrote that the military bureaucracy

includes the armed services, the industrial contractors who produce for them, the labor unions [representing defense workers], the lobbyists who tout their wares in the name of "free enterprise" and "national security," and the legislators who, for . . . pork or patriotism, vote the . . . funds. . . . Given the political reality of such a situation and the economic power of the constituencies . . . , there is little hope that an interaction of special-interest groups will somehow cancel each other out and that there will emerge some compromise which serves the public interest.[54]

As I have shown, even these delineations of the military bureaucracy are insufficient. It is more than a system of alliances or a collection of the most powerful interest groups yet assembled or the most formidable of all lobbies. It is strengthened by history, by tradition, and, above all, by an ideology that is the special possession and responsibility of an elite core. Often it has been able to exploit patriotic appeals to create overwhelming support—or its illusion—in the public.

When Neustadt calls for politicians—meaning the president and Congress—to unite in control of the bureaucracy,[55] he is right, as far as he goes. But the union has to embrace more than "the two ends of [Pennsylvania] Avenue." It must be a union of politicians in Washington with those in the states and localities and of politicians in government with those outside. It must have enough depth, strength, belief, and appeal to match and overmatch the military bureaucracy. What is needed is a political organization heavily staffed, well-financed, rooted in the life of the community's vital centers, solid in the community's historical memories, and organized around a core of people who assume a responsibility for an ideology that will take precedence over the ideology of the military. This organization will uphold the civilian leaders who will insist that the direction of the country shall not be taken over by the "professionals in violence."[56]

In short, what is needed are centralized, organized political parties that enjoy, or can reasonably aspire to gain, majority support. They are the only political instruments capable of meeting and conquering the new bureaucratic politics on its own ground.

This conclusion is substantiated by others, directly or by inference. Harrison Brown, one of the atomic scientists who fought the initial battle for civilian control of atomic energy in 1945–46, confessed in 1970 that the Department of Defense had become "de facto the primary executive body of the Federal Government" and that it came close "to being the primary legislative body as well." Brown concluded that the Pentagon must be brought under control, but his best suggestions were to end the seniority system and to restore foreign policy determination to the Department of State.[57]

The palpable insufficiency of Brown's proposals is characteristic also of those of John Kenneth Galbraith.[58] First, we should elect a president bent on putting the military in its place. Neustadt's theoretical argument indicates, however, and I have verified in some detail, that the president cannot effectively achieve and maintain control of the military. He may win on one or two issues if he invests enough influence, but he must divide his time among so many pressing matters that he cannot keep up the detailed and continuous control necessary to command the military bureaucracy. Second, Galbraith calls for reform of the armed services committees. Agreed! But this will require an attack on the seniority system, on its roots in localism, and even more fundamentally on the folkways of congressional government— a far more sweeping campaign than Galbraith recommends.

Third, Galbraith says that every congressional district (or as many as possible) should have an organization of people alert to the threat of military power. Granted. But the idea that perhaps two hundred and fifty such organizations would come simultaneously into being beggars credulity. Even if, miraculously, they should, history tells us that successful single-purpose reform movements surge, strike their blows, and dissolve. But their targets do not dissolve; rather, they survive—or they reemerge in a new guise. And this will be true of the military, which is greatly resilient.[59]

Bruce M. Russett confirms the description of the military bureaucracy, including the link to congressmen, the ties to defense industry (and particularly to defense payrolls), and the grass-roots support for militaristic legislative views (which correlate with the size of payrolls and employment in the constituencies). Russett advises against trying to control the military by concentrating more power in Congress.

We cannot control the military by giving power to Congress unless we first concentrate power *in* Congress. . . . Power in Congress is too dispersed . . . congressmen ultimately depend for political survival on the approval of their individual constituencies, rather than on a central party organization or a national constituency. . . . There is little basis for firm party discipline. . . .[60]

By clear implication, Russett sees the need for party discipline if power is to be concentrated *within* Congress.[61] Precisely the same lesson can be derived from the analysis by the political scientist whose survey of American military politics is most magisterial, Samuel J. Huntington, who wrote:

The criticisms of the strategic reformers go to the very roots of the governmental system. In many ways they are much more profound than the critics themselves seem to recognize. The defects which they highlight . . . are endemic to the political system.[62]

7 "Greater Resistance to Pressure"

Then everything includes itself in power,
Power into will, will into appetite;
And appetite, an universal wolf,
So doubly seconded with will and power,
Must make perforce an universal prey,
And last eat up himself.
  —Shakespeare, *Troilus and Cressida*

This chapter focuses on organized political groups with bases outside the national government, although they often have ties to federal agencies. Such groups may derive political leverage on legislators from two fulcrums, both reducible or removable by party government.

The first results from the small voting turnouts of offyear elections when organized interests can threaten candidates unless they conform to their single-minded wishes on their favorite issues. Synchronization of presidential and congressional elections would diminish this kind of influence by enlarging electoral participation in all national elections. Centralization of control over congressional nominations would force legislators to choose between the party's position and the groups' demands when the two conflict. The assumption is that the choice would almost always be for the party.

The second fulcrum results from the candidates' need for money to pay exorbitant campaign costs. Reducing the frequency of elections, centralizing party finances, and extending tax reductions for contributions would help politicians resist the demands of heavy donors. Eventually party government should lead to institutional changes that would permit much shorter campaigns and thereby greatly reduce the cost of running for office.

In 1950 the Committee on Political Parties of the American Political Science Association justified its call for reform partly on the "need for a party system with greater resistance to pressure."[1] In 1952 a second prestigious group held that, while opinions differed on the degree, "the weight of high-level political thinking today concedes that well-organized minority pressures have excessive weight in our system."[2]

In a sense, these statements point to a more general treatment of the problem addressed by this book. Bureaucracy is only part of the political universe in which all the familiar concepts—government, the state, sovereignty, administration, adjudication, the regime, and even legitimation, authority, and justice—are seen as resultants of the interplay of groups. Politics has been authoritatively defined in this way, and the results are hailed as benign. "The corrupting element [wrote Theodore J. Lowi] was the myth of the automatic society granted us by an all-encompassing, ideally self-correcting, providentially automatic political process."[3]

Lest "everything includes itself in power" we must concern ourselves with power's forms and consequences.

Another problem is somewhat more delicate. The American system of government encourages corruption, lovingly defended as "honest graft." Legislators, it is proclaimed, cannot be economic eunuchs, and anyway much influence is generated because legislators and constituents share attitudes and ideology: a natural occurrence in, and a justification of, representative government. Granted. But this does not excuse selling favors or using official positions to capitalize on inside information, as impressive numbers of state and local officials are daily found to do. Even on the federal level where appointed officials must list their financial interests and conform to strict standards, a veil is drawn over the financial affairs of legislators and their actions are treated very permissively. At the same time, the prevalence of corruption threatens honest politicians with attacks by innuendo.[4]

The problem of corruption would be much diminished by party government.[5] Under the present system, legislators are expected to trade their bits and pieces of power for votes, recognition, or preference; indeed, this is one of the great virtues alleged for it. In such bargaining there is a thin line between swapping for political profit and trading for personal financial gain. Fewer and cheaper elections conducted within a partisan framework would reduce the incentives legislators now feel to sell their influence, and an arrangement that constrains legislators to support policies concerted by their parties would provide a shield against group demands.

The Public Interest

These arguments assume that a public or general interest exists, and many will deny it or else will define the public interest as the natural reward of the pluralistic virtues of the American political system. No public interest or common good is possible, they say, because any proposal advanced in the name of the common good will always be opposed by some. "Since there is nothing which is best literally for the whole people, group arrays being what they are, the test is useless. . . ."[6] "Assertion of an inclusive 'national' or 'public interest' is [often] effective. . . . In themselves, these claims are part of the data of politics. However, they do not describe any actual or possible situation within a complex modern nation."[7] "In all important matters . . . 'the public interest' would prove an insufficient guide; the experts . . . would . . . have to balance the competing values as best they could, which means that they would have to fall back on their personal tastes or professional biases."[8]

Familiar to political scientists, these assertions may surprise—even shock—other readers. Until recently, arguments that no public interest can exist have often been joined to expressions of wonder that the promise of American life is so lavishly fulfilled. Behind this belief is another, namely, that politics is an illusion. Underlying causes are sovereign and will work their will without need of human assistance or possibility of human countervention.[9]

I agree that conflicts of interest are inevitable, but I prefer Madison's formulation in *Federalist Papers* No. 10, which defines factions as groups that, whether minorities or a majority of the whole, are "united and actuated by some common impulse of passion or of interest, adverse to the rights of other citizens, or to the permanent and aggregate interests of the community." Madison not only affirmed the existence of a public interest but explicitly charged government with securing it:

The regulation of these various and interfering interests forms the principal task of modern legislation and involves the spirit of party and faction in the necessary and ordinary operations of government.

That a public interest in Madison's sense exists can be shown by many examples of which I shall offer three. While no causal relationship between group pressures and political results can be fully demonstrated, the connections in the following examples are credible.

Consider the influence of the American Farm Bureau Federation (AFBF) on the first program aimed at alleviating poverty in American agriculture. What I am about to describe should be weighed against the AFBF's stand from the late 1930s in favor of reciprocal trade and, after 1946, in favor of flexible price supports—both positions being in the public interest and both being maintained against vigorous internal dissent.

Shortly after Pearl Harbor, the president of the AFBF declared in the lobby of a crowded Washington hotel, "We've got the Secretary of Agriculture by the short hairs of his chest, and we can move him this way or we can move him that way!" Not all the exuberance can properly be attributed to bourbon. The AFBF savagely attacked the Farm Security Administration (FSA), and the FSA was cut down. In wielding the axe, Congress was prompted by the malevolence of some of its own members as well as by the urging of organizations other than the Farm Bureau, by FSA mistakes, and by the false but persistent identification of FSA with the abhorrent symbols of communism. But its official historian credited the AFBF with the kill, and the AFBF is certainly entitled to part of the brush.[10]

The only significant effort of national agricultural policy to help poor farmers was the Farm Security Administration.[11] It had a resettlement program, first highly touted, later vehemently attacked, which reached 25,000 families over its checkered decade; an eminently respectable tenant-purchase program that was modestly successful; and a rural rehabilitation program that made loans and some grants to poor farmers. At first much less celebrated than the others, this last program *finally served a million farm families so poor they could not get credit, public or private, elsewhere.* Three-fourths of them eventually paid out. The program was a smashing success. But it involved digging into politically unorganized strata in the tightly controlled, one-party South, and it even offered fairly equitable opportunity for Negroes. It seemed to be a threat to every institution or organization that was screwed satisfactorily into the status quo.[12] And so the FSA had to be brought down.

What difference does it make? Is not the "public interest" a myth? Is not whatever the political process produces inexorably good as well as inevitable? On the contrary. The twenty-five members of the president's National Advisory Commission on Rural Poverty wrote:

> The urban riots of 1967 had their roots in rural poverty. A high proportion of the people crowded into the city slums today came there from rural slums. . . .
> This Nation has been largely oblivious to these 14 million impoverished people left behind in rural America. Our programs for rural America are woefully out of date. . . .

Instead of combating low incomes of rural people, these programs have helped to create wealthy landowners while largely bypassing the rural poor.[13]

Or take petroleum, which has been notorious in American politics at least since the early Standard Oil Company "refined everything in Pennsylvania except the legislature." Oil was said to be in control of the 1920 Republican national nominating convention. Teapot Dome money corrupted one member of Harding's cabinet and forced a second to resign. Of the rich chronology of oil in politics I shall stress only the tax and quota advantages.[14]

Oil's special tax privileges date from the 1920s. Until 1969, when the figure was reduced to 22 percent, oil and gas businesses could deduct 27.5 percent of their gross incomes (but no more than 50 percent of their entire incomes) before paying taxes. This "depletion allowance," plus other tax concessions such as expensing allowances, saved oil and gas companies nineteen times their original investment in average wells, according to the Internal Revenue Service. In 1968 American oil companies paid less than 8 percent of their total income in taxes compared with more than 40 percent for other corporations (unless they, too, could find loopholes). That year taxing oil and gas equally with other corporations would have yielded approximately $2.75 billion more for the national government alone. Some states have similar depletion allowances. California is said to lose $35 million a year in taxes from the depletion allowances for oil and gas.

Tax losses to oil and gas are overshadowed by the loss to the public imposed by the oil import quota system established by presidential order in 1959 and justified, like the depletion allowances, on the grounds of national security. The cost to consumers has been estimated at between $5.2 and $7.2 billion annually. Because of the pricing structure for petroleum products in the country, the incidence differs. Using the $5.2 billion figure, economists have calculated the annual cost to a New York family of four in extra payments for gasoline and heating oil at $102.32, to a Vermont family at $195.92, and to a Wyoming family at $258. Not until April 1973 did the president, spurred by the fuel crisis, announce the end of quotas and their replacement by import licenses with fees.

What difference does it make? The national defense argument in favor of the depletion allowance and quotas was false. Both policies provided incentives to use domestic supplies rather than to rely on cheaper and far more plentiful foreign resources, conserving the domestic stock against emergencies. Nor did these particular benefactions stimulate sufficient exploration. A specific subsidy for that purpose would have been much more sensible.

The energy crisis has changed the perspectives on petroleum policy. But in retrospect the familiar derision by certain social scientists of the concept of the "public interest" was not likely to convince Americans (a) irritated by their tax bills when they thought of the loopholes irrationally provided the oil industry and (b) oppressed by inflation when they thought of what an extra $100–250 (tax free) would have bought each year. Beyond this are other arguments. The rising costs of political campaigns is an extremely serious problem in American politics. From profits swollen by quotas and protected by tax favors, petroleum interests derive heavy income advantages that permit reinvestments in the careers of friendly politicians. Like the executive branch, Congress has included many conservatives and a few liberals who can be counted on to support the industry. The late Sam Rayburn made sure that prospective members of the House ways and means committee were sound on oil and Senate Leader Lyndon B. Johnson did the same for the Senate finance committee. Although total figures on election spending are unavailable, in 1964 large contributions reported by officers and directors of the American Petroleum Institute totaled nearly a fifth *more* than those of officers and directors of the entire National Association of Manufacturers.[15] Enormous sums are spent by the oil and gas industry on lobbying, reports on which are highly misleading—much money spent to influence legislation is labeled "research."

Finally, the public interest should be concerned with political extremes that are patently inimical to constitutional government. A free society must permit such groups to spawn, but it certainly ought to examine those of its laws that give them special favors. Of one of the capitals of the radical right, Willie Morris wrote: "So much of the big Houston money was made overnight by digging a hole in the ground, or passed along intact from quick-rich fathers, that as one Houstonian explains it, 'They've suddenly come into a lot of money, and they're afraid the government is going to take it away from them'."[16] Some 400 radio stations carry the ultra-rightist views of Texas oil billionaire H. L. Hunt to more than five million listeners.[17] The Atlantic–Richfield Oil Company, well-known as an angel of right-wing causes, avoided all federal taxes from 1964 to 1967 and, indeed, actually accumulated a federal tax credit of $629,000 while earning profits of $465 million.[18]

Turn now to gun control.[19] Lee Harvey Oswald bought his rifle through an advertisement in the *American Rifleman,* official journal of the National Rifle Association (NRA). As the fourth anniversary of John F. Kennedy's assassination approached, President Johnson said that many of the two million guns sold annually wind up in the hands of "hardened criminals, snipers, mental defectives, rapists, habitual drunkards, and juveniles." He repeated earlier requests for effective control. But the NRA was pleased to report to its members that all national efforts to pass national legislation since 1963 had been turned back or gutted. Except for one significant bill in New Jersey state, rifle associations had prevented action in state legislatures. In January 1967 the Gallup poll found 73 percent of its sample favoring registration of rifles and shotguns; 83 percent, registration of pistols; 73 percent, ending mail-order buying of guns; and 84 percent, restriction of those who can buy guns.[20]

In 1967 the NRA with 850,000 members was a tightly controlled organization. Its life members, about 10 percent, elected the seventy-five-man board of directors that, in turn, elected the executive committee and executive council. NRA was closely tied to the military. Of its executives, nineteen were active and seventeen retired military officers. NRA members—and only NRA members—enjoyed cut-rate prices on U. S. surplus arms and the use of free rifles and ammunition in the army's civilian marksmanship program directed by the National Board for the Promotion of Rifle Practice (one-third of the board were NRA executives). In 1966, the army lent 38,500 weapons, mostly rifles, to bonded clubs and gave them more than 54 million rounds of ammunition.

In addition to its ties to the ubiquitous Pentagon, NRA has links to the arms industry. One-fourth of its money came from gun manufacturers. NRA boasted $10 million in assets, spent more than $200,000 annually on legislative and public affairs as well as $2 million in publishing the *American Rifleman,* which contains much legislative material and editorials on gun control. But NRA refused to register as a lobbyist and has kept tax-exempt status, despite claims that it can hit Congress with one million letters on 72 hours' notice. Senator Edward Kennedy reported more mail on gun control legislation than on the Viet Nam war.

What difference does it make? Under our electoral system with congressmen and senators facing off-year elections and light voter turnouts, NRA has or—equally important—appears to have great leverage. Many legislators, privately critical of NRA, support it in public. The gun lobby's purge lists have included Senators Wayne Morse (Oregon), Joseph S. Clark (Pennsylvania), Joseph D. Tydings (Maryland), Albert Gore (Tennessee), Charles E. Goodell (New York) and Thomas J. Dodd (Connecticut), all defeated, although the lobby's influence therein could easily be exaggerated. Threatened were Senator Frank Church (Idaho), Mike Mansfield (Montana), Gale W. McGee (Wyoming), Hugh Scott (Pennsylvania), Philip A. Hart (Michigan), and John O. Pastore (Rhode Island), all reelected; several of these went out of their way to placate the gun lobby and to identify with it.[21]

With the exception of a statute of 1968 forbidding the sale of guns to convicted felons and the importation of cheap handguns (but not of the parts thereof for assembly in the United States), Congress has been afraid to regulate the gun trade. Members are properly fearful of a group of trigger-happy voters who will punish them because of their votes on one issue, gun control, regardless of how they stand on a thousand other questions. The results are deadly to the public interest. Nothing has been asserted more loudly than the public interest in control of crime. Guns, especially handguns, feed crime. Between 1962 and 1968, the number of rifles and shotguns in the United States doubled and the number of handguns rose more than 400 percent. Meanwhile, the percentages of crimes committed with firearms sharply increased. Of such crimes committed in large United States cities (1967), 92 percent of the homicides, 86 percent of the aggravated assaults, and 96 percent of the robberies involved handguns. The National Commission on the Causes and Prevention of Violence, chaired by Milton D. Eisenhower, unanimously recommended adoption of a national firearms policy to limit the general availability of handguns.[22] In 1971, Milton Eisenhower deplored the failure of Congress to implement the recommendations of his commission and warned not only of ordinary crime but of the systematic buildup of private arsenals entailing threats of armed insurrection in the United States.[23]

Theoretical Criticisms of Group Politics

Many political scientists have criticized both the organization of government that multiplies the effectiveness of the interests and also the pluralistic theories that defend them. Often they end by recommending both a stronger presidency and party government.[24] Rather than expanding on these congenial arguments,[25] I shall deal with two eminent dissenters.

Theodore J. Lowi combines his rigorous critique of "interest group liberalism" (or of American pluralism) with a denial that the solution lies in stronger presidential leadership in a majoritarian democracy under party government.[26] Unfortunately, his remedy, "juridical democracy," while suggestive, is insufficient in the absence of a fundamental change in the organization of political power in this country.

Lowi argued that Franklin D. Roosevelt's revolution answered the first of two traditional questions about what constitutes acceptable government in the United States "for all time" by removing any effective limits to the scope of governmental power. The second question, how such power could be controlled, was answered in pluralistic theory and practice by "interest group liberalism" that dissolved the idea of due process of law in an ocean of bargaining groups. Distinctions between government and society as well as those between public and private were eliminated. The state and sovereignty were rejected. The very existence of political power and coercion was denied. For all these, pluralism substituted the political process composed of human activity in a flux of group formation, dissolution, and interaction. Whatever the process produced became justice. If groups were labeled "governmental," this was simply by convention. Any controls lay outside the groups and even outside the political process in the historical tides of human phenomena.[27] By dealing only with organized claimants in formulating policy and carrying out programs, the politicians got the sense that power need not mean coercion. "If sovereignty is parcelled out among the groups, then who's out anything?" (pp. 74–77).

Lowi provides examples drawn from policy in agriculture, labor, governmental regulation of business, foreign and military affairs, the war on poverty, urban renewal, housing, civil rights, and the one I use for illustration, welfare. The "old welfare program" of Social Security had substantive, organizational, and legal integrity—achieved through the clear statement of ends, designation of appropriate means, and a lucid and logical relationship between them. Under President Kennedy, interest group liberals tried to improve welfare but succeeded only in replacing part of the earlier structure with "non-law—discretion and bargaining." Ends were generalized, e.g., "to combat poverty." Means became vague; "trainees" were to be given "useful work experience." Organization was left floating—it must embrace "maximum feasible participation," but this glittering vagary was to be achieved either through broad community representation or representation of relevant interests (two different conceptions, both lacking in precision); moreover, organization might be governmental, private and non-profit, or mixed (pp. 236–38).

Among unfortunate consequences of the new welfare programs were the demoralization of the civil rights movement, the frustration of hopes of the poor, the further fragmentization of politics in New York City where fragmentation was already a problem, strengthening control of Chicago's machine politics, already notoriously tight, and underwriting nepotistic politics in Pennsylvania. Meanwhile, the strength of the Negro's moral position was undermined by application of the pluralist notion that "one set of ends is about as good as another" and by the emphasis on access and cash as panaceas (pp. 239–47).

Reluctantly I turn from Lowi's illuminating analysis of what has gone wrong to a discussion of "juridical democracy." The first step, he says, must come from the Supreme Court, which having made "a regime of interest group liberalism can also unmake it" (p. 314). The court should reassert control over delegated legislation, requiring Congress to replace vague laws that tell administrators to find and solve problems with laws that define problems, state the ends to be sought in mitigating or solving them, and set forth the means to achieve the ends. Having created administrative agencies to implement these statutes, Congress should supervise them to ensure that the rules are observed. If programs prove unworkable or public dissatisfaction burgeons, Congress should reexamine the statute, redefine the rules, and restate the administrative structure and obligations. This is the heart of his proposal, although he suggests additional reforms (pp. 297–310).

Lowi is right that reform must begin at the national level where major political questions will continue to rise concerning policy in military and foreign affairs as well as in economic and social questions. Moreover, "juridical democracy" should be helpful if applied to many policy areas such as welfare, poverty, unemployment, and racial equality. But a radically different political organization is needed to sustain the application of "juridical democracy" and to make it work—as is shown by Lowi's own illustrations.

In 1965, Lowi notes, the Office of Education moved to withhold $30 million from the Chicago Board of Education pending an investigation of alleged violations of civil rights law. There was no indication that the law was ambiguous; in fact Lowi cited civil rights legislation as an exception to the general decline of legal clarity under the influence of interest group liberalism. But the Office of Education ran afoul of Mayor Daley, who controlled the Illinois delegation to the Democratic convention, appeared chiefly responsible for the leverage of Illinois in the electoral college, and enjoyed the loyalty of the Chicago congressional delegation. Daley proved "too much for the combined strength of the Office of Education and the Presidency of the United States" (p. 212).

Mayor Daley's power could not be overcome by "juridical democracy"—the major elements of which were already present in this example—unless it could be enforced politically. Daley would be vulnerable only to something like a loss of his electoral base or a political defeat such as occurred in the election of November 1972 when he lost control of the vital office of state's attorney.

The same proposition applies to other Lowi arguments. Does he propose to control bureaucracy by "issuing it orders along with powers" (pp. 312–13)? Then such orders must issue from spokesmen who have a political base large enough to overshadow that of the bureaucracy and who command political levers superior to those in its hands.

A similar argument applies to foreign policy, where Lowi concludes that American democracy can be made safe for the world only if it achieves the ability to plan. The villain, he says correctly, is not the public, Congress, its committees, the president, or any other such visible culprit but rather "the outmoded system itself and the out-moded beliefs that support it."

Again, Lowi is right that citizens and legislators alike need proper and practicable roles in foreign policy-making, that the military must be brought once more under political control, and that presidential leadership must be strengthened but also subjected much more than now to critical examination. It is not clear, however, that any of these ends would be achieved by Lowi's reforms. Rather, their realization requires a different political structure from that which now exists.[28]

A Workable and Advisable Corrective?

Would presidential leadership reinforced and constrained by stronger, more centralized, and disciplined parties provide a workable and advisable corrective to the evils Lowi delineates, including the excessive weight enjoyed in America by minority pressures? Lowi's rejection of party government is based on a belief that it will not work, a question to which chapter 9 is addressed. Edward C. Banfield, on the contrary, argues that party government would do more harm than good. "With the President in full control of Congress," he wrote, "log-rolling would cease or virtually cease. . . ." The president would not have to buy the support of congressmen to get legislation passed; "the traders who now sell their bits and pieces of power to the highest bidders would go out of business." Interest groups would be less enterprising.

Policy-making would fall into the hands of "technical experts within the majority party, the White House, and the executive departments." Government would overemphasize principle at the expense of interests; would pursue the will-o'-the wisp of the public interest; and the experts would do badly "what is now done reasonably well by the political process."

The president's power would derive from different sources. "Instead of relying on logrolling and patronage . . . , he would have to rely upon direct appeals to the electorate." Personality politics, the arts of presidential advertisement, and appeals to ideology would all increase. In place of bargaining over favors to individuals (supposedly congressmen), which gives the president "dependable and cheap" control, he would be forced to maintain his power by "the uncertain and costly expedient of offering to whole classes of people—the farmer, the aged, the homeowner, and so on—advantages that they could have only at each other's expense."[29]

Many of the evils Banfield projects under party government have already appeared in the present American polity with its weak parties —overemphasis on the personality of the president, arbitrary government by technicians covertly ensconced in the bureaucracy, and demagogic appeals to large groups of voters such as farmers, labor, highway users, and veterans. It is misleading, in addition, to argue that it is cheaper to buy off individuals than groups. Individuals bargain on behalf of groups in our system, and the costs are often higher. But Banfield also holds that active participation of private interests in public business is weak or nonexistent under party government. Is this true in Britain, the country he has in mind, where party government and management by experts are both supposedly accentuated?[30]

The Relevance of the British Experience

On the contrary, British government, historically and contemporaneously, has been and remains extremely sensitive to group interests. A leading American authority on the subject, Samuel H. Beer, wrote in 1956:

If we had some way of measuring political power, we could quite possibly demonstrate that at the present time pressure groups are more powerful in Britain than in the United States.[31]

In 1965, Beer wrote:

So far has the climate of opinion come to accept these practices, that today it is a rare and serious charge that a Government has made policy without consulting the organized interests involved.[32]

An authority on British political parties, R. T. McKenzie, emphasized in 1958 the "powerful role played by interest groups in Britain. There can be no question that their activities and their influence have increased in recent decades." He had "no doubt that pressure groups, taken together, are a far more important channel of communication than parties for the transmission of political ideas from the mass of the citizenry to their rulers."[33]

In this view, the centralization of British government and political parties stimulates both the centralization and the extension of interest groups at the same time that it enhances their political role. The concentration of power combined with the weakening of individual members of Parliament simplifies the tasks of what Beer calls the producer interests by enabling them to deal with administrative agencies rather than Parliament. All this might be thought to support part of Banfield's criticism, namely, that policy-making shifts from the politicians to the "technical experts." But Beer repeats the classic British interpretation that the experts are responsible to and led by politicians—"if you can bring over the Minister and the Chancellor of the Exchequer you have nothing much else to worry about."[34]

British and American Agricultural Policy

Indeed, the strength of British pressure groups under party government raises a possibility quite the opposite of Banfield's charge that group interests will atrophy under party government. Is party government no more resistant to private pressure than government by separated institutions sharing powers? J. Roland Pennock concludes from a comparison of "Agricultural Subsidies in England and the United States"[35] that English government may be even more vulnerable than the American to group pressures. The uncompromising nature of British party competition

may make leaders extremely sensitive to the demands of pressure groups, and party discipline may be used to suppress elements in the party that would like to resist the demands of those groups.

The result of the competition of Labour and Conservative parties for the farm vote, he concludes, has been farm subsidies two or three times as large as their American counterpart.

Pennock carefully documented his argument, and yet I think that he is wrong on several counts. I question his statement that British subsidies per farm were two or three times as large as American subsidies. I estimate that American subsidies were at least as large during the period Pennock used, 1954–61, and were rather sharply larger in subsequent years, partly because American farm numbers declined more rapidly than the British while comparative American farm subsidy outlays increased somewhat.[36]

Second, Pennock did not sufficiently recognize the possibility that British agriculture may have had a short-term political windfall. By the end of the 1950s, in the judgment of Peter Self and Herbert Storing, the three conditions that had given British agriculture unusual political leverage were weakening. The "national need for additional agricultural production, which indirectly enhanced the farmers' political standing," had "passed, at least for the time being." Moreover, the "cult of the farmers' vote" as an especially strategic bloc in the electorate was "probably passing because of Labour's difficulty in wooing the farmers successfully and because of deeper shifts in the political balance which may make the agricultural vote of much less account." Finally, the advantage of the strong and politically neutral National Farmers Union had declined as the government sought to loosen the ties of partnership.[37]

Third, agriculture has had special political advantages in many constitutional democracies, rooted partly in overrepresentation, partly in the prestige of land ownership, and partly in ancestral connections to the farm. After World War I, with its terrible hunger on both sides, many western European nations turned to agricultural protection. Mussolini's "battle of the wheat" was not distinctive. *"Le blé est un élément sacré pour nos latins,"* remarked a diplomat. Indeed, as successful political claimants of governmental support for prices and incomes, British and American farmers arrived relatively late. The inference is that other interests than the agricultural provide better comparisons for the effectiveness of group pressures in England and the United States.

Non-Farm Groups in Great Britain

British agriculture enjoyed considerable leverage in the budget. Of the English system, however, Allen Potter wrote: "Budgeting is the Government's business." Budgetary operations, whether fiscal or economic, "are not subject to the ordinary practice of [group] consultation. . . ." When the Minister of Health was asked why British doctors had not been consulted about proposed changes in prescription charges, he replied that on such budget questions, "they have never been consulted before a decision of the Government has been made." The Minister of Housing and Local Development told representatives of local authority associations that it had been impracticable to consult them before announcing the decision to restrict their capital expenditures because this had been "a major decision of policy. . . ." The Treasury answered the Opposition in 1954 regarding the failure adequately to consult the cotton industry before entering into the Japanese trade agreement that "it had never been the practice of any Government to consult whole industries before relaxing quotas imposed for balance of payments purposes."[38]

Potter underlined the special position enjoyed by agriculture (along with certain other groups) by referring to the request of the British Legion for consultation on pension rates since teachers, wage earners, civil servants, farmers, and policemen all had "their machinery for discussing their affairs with authority." The answer was that the Government was in no sense contracting with the veterans.

Groups that from experience with their American counterparts one would expect to be formidable politically if British groups are really "more powerful than in the United States" actually appear to be less effective. Some evidence suggests this to be true of the veterans, the public roads lobby, and the medical profession.[39] A number of authorities on English government hold this view. Acknowledging that sharing in policy development by English pressure groups may be normal and healthy, R. T. McKenzie noted that it might unduly fractionalize policy. On occasion, however, governments "stand out boldly against the claim of pressure groups on the ground that to give way would be to betray the national interest."[40]

Concluding his analysis of the "lobby" (as he called the English pressure groups) and the public, Samuel E. Finer emphasized

the different roles played by the Lobby, notably the interest groups, in the American and British systems. The British Lobby is *domesticated.* . . . It acts much more soberly and responsibly.

And in summing up his discussion of the "Lobby and the Public Interest," Finer declared:

The combined influence of our institutions, our procedures and our shared values greatly corrects and counterbalances the Lobby. The Lobby is not generally a corrupting influence in public life; it does *not* generally engender erratic or grossly inconsistent policies. It does not, to any marked extent, lead to the oppression of minorities— even of majorities![41]

In 1958, a group of American political scientists, deliberating on an outline of research for the study of pressure groups, concluded that federalism and the separation of powers created decentralized parties and legislative bodies "less able to aggregate interests and protect themselves against interest penetration than Cabinet-dominated parliaments. . . ." In the United Kingdom particularly, "a disciplined parliamentary party system . . . protects the legislative process from effective interest group penetration. . . .

"A disciplined party system and a powerful executive force [*sic*] interest groups to direct their energies to the upper levels of the executive and the bureaucracy *where only moderate claims, well-supported with technical information, become possible.*"[42]

Deeper Issues

A respectable consensus among professionals seems to hold that party government, as represented by Great Britain, neither reduces groups to impotence nor unduly empowers them; rather, it strikes a commendable balance between the demands of group representation and the superior claims of the general or public interest. The potential significance for America is great: party government should substantially reduce the clout enjoyed by American pressure groups—especially business groups—that has become scandalous in Washington, in many state capitols, and in local government.[43] More profound concerns emerge in the collectivist age. One is the threat of anarchy. Samuel E. Finer expressed his fear that Great Britain had "reached the very position so devoutly wished for by Calhoun, the American sectionalist . . . *viz.*, government by a 'concurrent majority.'" The result was as much anathema to Samuel E. Finer in England as it was to Elmer E. Schattschneider and Grant McConnell in America. Like them he called for strengthening "first the power and second the authority of the numerical majority of the nation. . . ."[44]

Finer was most alarmed by the potential relationships between government and the same economic groups, especially organized labor, that Banfield considered the greatest danger to the polity. Banfield feared that party government would become an orgy of competitive appeals for the support of such groups as labor, the farmers, the veterans, and welfare clients. Thus there would be undue interference in the economy, with government attempting to solve through awkward, inefficient, and expensive public programs the kinds of problems that, left alone, the economy would largely solve; in those marginal areas where market forces proved inadequate, specific correctives would be provided—and there should also be stronger law-and-order programs to protect society from its enemies.[45] This analysis may show some inconsistency with Banfield's contention that political logrolling is generally benign. As I read him, however, his views have evolved, first, from strong advocacy of central governmental planning, then to admiration for pluralistic politics that would produce felicitous social choices, and more recently to a greater appreciation of the Friedmanesque virtues of *laissez-faire* economics (with some supplements).[46] Finer, by contrast, held a belief more like the earlier Banfield, namely, that there is no alternative to comprehensive governmental planning and that the severest threat comes from great groups like organized labor that may refuse to abide by governmental decisions, thus condemning the polity to group-based anarchy.

Anarchy is not the only dimension of the more profound issues. Another question is, Can government cope with the demands created by "modernity"? Today governments everywhere must plan the conditions of the economy and, increasingly, the specifics. Insofar as possible, governments should let economic decisions remain in private hands and allow market forces to work—if for no other reason than to prevent the administrative burden of the state, already enormous, from becoming crushing. But the sphere of *laissez faire* is now definitely limited. By planning the conditions of the economy I refer to the unavoidable demands on modern government to maintain (1) reasonably full employment, (2) a degree of price stability (some control of inflation, endemic virtually everywhere), (3) a steady rate of economic growth, and (4) a satisfactory foreign exchange position.[47] All these activities require effective fiscal and monetary (especially monetary) policy.[48] Specifics that must be planned and provided include (1) Social Security and welfare programs (involving transfer payments from some parts of the population to others), (2) support for science,[49] (3) insurance that the growth of money incomes will fall within the limits imposed by increases in productivity,[50] and (4) supervision of private markets to reduce the ill effects of monopoly. To these rather recent requisites of modern government have been added ultramodern imperatives: balancing the claims of economic growth at high employment with the protection of the environment and the development of an effective energy policy.

The modern demands on government everywhere have encouraged a degree of political centralization and of executive power that may be dangerous to the survival of constitutionalism. Party government in a two-party system seems to offer the best hope of providing competent government that will still be subject to effective controls. In light of these observations I return to the examination of the British polity.

Party Government and Great Britain's Collectivist State

Samuel E. Beer found the various compulsions growing out of modernity emerging in the "collectivist age," which is manifest in "the managed economy" and "the welfare state."[51] Governments must manage the economy in ways that will enhance the welfare of the people. In management, the executives of government must deal with "producer groups" whose advice, acquiescence, and approval are necessary for public policies to work. But there are also "consumer groups" composed of persons "whose welfare is affected in the same way by . . . governmental action"; they are exemplified by pensioners, taxpayers, people on relief, and housewives buying food. Whereas producer groups are mobilized by the executive, consumer groups wield their influence through voting, thus forcing their attention on political parties and Parliament.

In 1965 Beer praised the role of British party government in the collectivist age. The parties sought to learn what important groups wanted and give it to them (or enough to get elected). But they also provided the make-weight by which government could hold the line against the importunacies of organized groups (they protected the member of Parliament by furnishing him the solid deck of party discipline in contrast to his counterpart, the American congressman, who is forced to shoot the political rapids individually in his own canoe); and they educated the public.

Party does not merely aggregate the opinions of groups, it goes a long way toward creating those opinions by fixing the framework of public thinking about public policy and the voters' sense of alternatives and possibilities.[52]

Part of Beer's optimism in 1965 rose from his conclusion that the Labour and Conservative parties, while converging to a marked degree, still remained distinct enough to offer "contrasting conceptions of the public good" and to define and carry out programs accordingly. Such differences are vital, Beer held, to give voters a real choice. In my judgment, differences between the parties are required much more because of the nature of the great economic problems of modern states—such as arbitrating among full employment, the control of inflation, and the protection of the environment—that require different approaches at different times and may need definite political pushes, now in favor of more employment, now in favor of inflation control, now inducing growth, now forcing growth into patterns that will protect the environment. If the parties become alike, their essential gift of providing alternatives and of educating voters thereon will be lost.[53] But, to repeat, Beer's conclusion in 1965 was full of praise for British party government:

It is when we look at the situation in the light of what once prevailed—or what prevails in other parties such as those of the United States—that we properly appreciate the degree of cohesion achieved.[54]

By 1969 Beer doubted whether party government could cope with British problems.[55] He saw a weakening in the psychological sense of class divisions that had supported two opposing parties (although in the end he concluded that the most fundamental meaning of class "rests on differences of power," which tend to remain and to form a basis "for the old class habits"). He was also dismayed at the tendency of British parties to converge until they so nearly agreed on policy that government became too immobilized to deal with vexing economic issues, especially the control of inflation.

Since 1970 the Conservative government of Edward Heath has demonstrated that British parties can present markedly different alternative approaches of policy, from Great Britain's entry into the Common Market to her effort to control inflation. Nevertheless, in 1972, Beer was even gloomier in his appraisal.[56] The class basis of British parties, the historic divisions on class lines within the general embrace of Great Britain's "fundamental oneness," had crumbled further under the thrust of modernity (but then again he held that "ancient and essentially political distinction between classes founded upon domination and subjection will surely persist . . ."). Beer deplored the decline of competence of party government:

The solidarity of support for the parties has been weakened. A new volatility deprives Government of the time and toleration needed to develop new lines of policy and put them into effect.

Inference for America

One cannot claim that party government will inevitably solve the troubles of the American polity in the waning years of this rudderless century. Nevertheless, one can argue stoutly that party government—if it can be attained—provides the best hope that our government will be able to meet its problems. Strong parties will improve governmental resistance to private pressures, increase the coherence of related policies, and encourage government to concert its policies on the great economic issues. In a two-party system, party government will foster an opposition that will not only criticize government but also develop systematic alternative approaches to the leading public questions. Strong parties offer the best guarantee that American government will be able to meet modern demands and still be subject to effective political controls.

These are arguments of principle. One can be more specific. The power of organized labor is widely held to be a major threat to the efforts to control inflation. America has suffered less from inflation than most countries, chiefly because of the size of its internal market, the strength of its economy, the productivity of its agriculture, the extent and variety of its natural resources (including fuel), and perhaps the persistence of the work ethic. Wage gains have been reasonably related to increases in labor productivity. But in the four years 1968–71 hourly wages rose an average of 7 percent a year—nearly double the rate of the four years 1960–63—while increases in output per man-hour were cut in half.[57] These statistics are understandable to any citizen who has had to have his plumbing, his car, or his television set fixed, or his house painted, or his goods moved. But what we have seen is only the beginning. Signs are ominous of a long period of chronic inflation, led by fuel and food prices.

Now it will be said that Great Britain's inflation is worse than ours; therefore, why advocate party government for America? The answers are, first, that Great Britain's difficulties have been much greater because of a weaker industrial economy, a comparative scarcity of natural resources, and, perhaps, an earlier decline of the work ethic. Second, Great Britain's task of subjecting organized labor to general political control is harder than ours because nearly half of the British gainfully employed are organized in trade unions compared to less than 28 percent in the United States.[58] Moreover, labor union membership in America has been concentrated, 68 percent of it in the eleven most populous states in 1970, a fact that has historically weakened labor in Congress but has added to its leverage with the rise of the presidency since these have been the most critical states in deciding close presidential elections. Third, if the British succeed in controlling wage-push inflation they will do it, in Finer's terms, by increasing the authority and power of the numerical majority—through stronger party government. Fourth, has America another alternative? Is not the prospective issue with labor much the same as it has recently become with the military bureaucracy, namely, Which is to dominate—the particular sector's interest or the public interest? We have seen the ability of the much smaller farm bloc to whipsaw the American polity for forty years. It may well become labor's turn—and there were signs in 1973 that big labor, represented by the Teamsters, and big agriculture, represented by the Farm Bureau, were moving toward a political embrace. As with the military bureaucracy, so with labor, the best hope to achieve political control on behalf of the public lies in the creation of strong parties.

One can also be more specific with regard to Banfield's fear that party government will multiply demagogic appeals to the great social groups. The threat to the effectiveness with which government can meet the challenge of modernity is real; but its identification with party government is tragically funny. We have seen many examples of the demagogic appeal in electoral campaigns, notably by candidates for executive office, mayoralities, governorships, and, most significantly, the presidency. How often they have sought to arouse the devils in our nature! Recall Truman's diatribes against the 80th Congress for sticking a pitchfork in the back of the farmer and the subsequent travesty of his farm program; Eisenhower's self-righteous loftiness in 1952 and Richard Nixon's characteristic slurs against the patriotism of the Democrats—followed by eight years of dogged persistence in the cold war against "monolithic communism"; Lyndon Johnson's voyage to victory on a sea of lies in 1964; Richard Nixon's phony promise of a South Asian settlement in 1968; and, finally, Nixon's expert manipulation of the racial issue in 1972.

The 1972 presidential campaign provided a classical example of the demagogic appeal. Beginning in 1970, Nixon wooed the South on the racial issue. A series of federal court decisions ordering busing was a priceless gift to him. On 3 August 1971, he disowned his own HEW's plan for desegregating the Austin schools and declared his opposition "to busing simply for the sake of busing." Conveniently, the courts kept the raw nerve exposed; and the president repeatedly seized the chance to play on human hates, insecurities, and fears in urban area after urban-area reporters found the busing issue uppermost in the mind of many troubled people. In November 1972 Nixon's huge majority was swollen by 33 percent of those who called themselves Democrats—compared to only 12 percent who had shifted from Humphrey to Nixon in 1968 (Gallup). Half of the shifting 33 percent were resentful of gains by blacks (Yankelovich). The *New York Times's* report on the election called race the key issue, "the dirty little secret which is neither little nor secret but central to current politics."[59]

And so we have the spectacle of the election, the control and direction of government, and conceivably the destiny of the nation dominated by a wild shift of a part of the electorate—a fraction, but still large enough to turn a modest majority into a "landslide." But the support was ephemeral. Sobered especially by rising food prices, Nixon's super majority melted. By August 1973 Gallup reported only 31 percent of his sample to believe that the president was doing a good job—by far the steepest decline in the history of this fateful question.[60]

If the people have a political right to anything, they have a right to a form of government that will give them the chance to do the task for which they are uniquely fit—to create a government. They can also have a sense of ongoing participation in government if they are members of an effective and reasonably steadfast majority—or of a minority with a good chance of becoming a majority. These things they can get through party government, along with some strong defenses against the lies and the blandishments of unscrupulous demagogues.

8 The Travail of Public Opinion

The people are not "fine"—the people are not picturesque—
the people— . . .
Why goddam it! Zachariah Joyner roared—I'll tell you what the
people are! . . . The people . . . the *people!* . . . Why, goddam
it, sir, the people are the *people!*

Thomas Wolfe, *The Hills Beyond*

In the summer of Watergate, 1973, public morale in America was low. Distrust of politicians was rife. On the daily television the White House "horrors" and those of the Committee to Reelect the President replaced the artificial traumas of the soap operas, but without the promise of a happy ending. Other scandals added their weight: the concealment of Cambodian bombing since 1969, the apparent leverage of money in politics (higher price supports for dairy products that followed lavish campaign contributions, the I.T.T.'s financial commitment seemingly connected to a favorable antitrust action, questionable circumstances of the federal grain sale to Russia), the unexplained elements in the president's acquisition of San Clemente, and a host of other unseemly or illegal actions or of public perfidy or of the government's contempt for constitutional guarantees when working its will on citizens. Moreover, what transpired in Washington had all too many parallels in the actions, shady or criminal, proven or alleged, of state and local officials. Beneath all these was the remaining bitterness from the Vietnam war, the worries over inflation, the persistent tensions among ethnic groups, and the unremitting stress of racial friction. A profound sense of uneasiness was abroad as most Americans knew from themselves and confirmed in talks with their friends and neighbors.

A Deep-seated Malaise—but Curable

The ills of 1973 had been long a-building. They were symptoms of deep, structural faults in the American Constitution and its operational theory, faults that must be diagnosed before a cure can be devised. The fault lies first in the sovereign role assigned to the public, which is continuously cited by politicians and pollsters as the solver of all problems—for public opinion is "the great source of power, the master of servants who tremble before it."[1] The public is given impossible tasks. Not only is the public unfit for these tasks; its members can rarely find out who does them in our labyrinthine government wherein irresponsibility becomes "an article of faith."[2]

In its frustration, the public looks to the only source it can, the president. He alone is the "People's Choice."[3] There is something mystical and terrible about political power even when it is vested in "the people." Sensing that they cannot wield it, the people look to one who can, and they want to see power somehow in human terms, vested in some person like themselves, who breathes, bleeds, feels pain and joy, and is both a magnet for and a source of empathy—and yet who is also themselves writ large, ennobled, worthily embodying the "awful majesty of the American people," which in the person of George Washington was enough to unman even Gouverneur Morris.

The bond between president and public has led to a great perversion in government. To understand that, one must look again at the president. Forced to share power with an independent legislature and to negotiate policies across the gaps created by federalism, the president must find his essential support in the public. The president is unrivaled as a representative of the nation as a whole, of the public good or the public interest—or he should be, for only he has a national constituency. And the people collectively and individually are likewise enjoined to seek the public good, the "Common Cause," to use John Gardner's term. So how can this excellent bond between president and people be perverted?

The answer lies in paradoxes. The first paradox arises out of the ambivalence of the people who are public-spirited individually and collectively in our mythology but who are encouraged by our political institutions, especially by our systems of electing legislative representatives, to form into groups that strive to get all they can for themselves (asked what Labor wanted, Samuel Gompers replied simply, "More!"). The group drives are facilitated in Congress, and so we have (as examples) silver, or railroad, or bankers', or oil, or wheat, or cotton senators and congressmen. And the result has been acclaimed;

out of rampant selfishness a hidden hand shapes the public good. Only the people do not quite believe it. It is against common sense. The appeal of the president lies in no small measure in his apparent ability to rise above the "scuffle of local interests" in Congress.

But then comes the second paradox. The people, so benevolent individually and collectively in our folklore, want above all to lead private lives. The paradox is that in spite of moral injunctions and good intentions, they often become conscious of the government's actions only when public events press on their private lives, when they fear the loss of jobs, of sons at war, of savings through inflation, of status through unwanted associations, of their lives through violence. Only when such gut issues are active can the president get the public's ear and try to teach the people something that will increase their support for him. His temptation is strong to manipulate the gut issues by playing on their hopes, their fears, their hatreds, or their patriotism.

The sickness is serious and deepseated. The remedy lies in redefining the public's role in government and in designing political institutions accordingly. Instead of saying that the people are sovereign in the sense of deciding all issues, our theory and practice should recognize the strength and weakness of the public. The public cannot properly decide issues. Our ubiquitous referenda items are decided by the public only equivocally: typically, only a few of the public vote on referenda; moreover, the issues have already been largely decided in the wording of the question, something "the people" obviously cannot do. To say that the people are unfit to decide issues is to prepare the way for acclaiming them in their one role of ultimate importance. Only the public can legitimately make and unmake governments.

At the same time, we remain convinced by the logic of the *Federalist Papers* and by the lessons of history that governments are prone to abuse power. So the government must also be redefined as a necessary thing, legitimized by winning an election, speaking with the authority of a majority, but nevertheless limited by our recognition of its fallibility, limited in its term, limited in its scope and procedures, and not only limited but checked and somewhat controlled by an opposition, an opposition that is also visible, with its leadership embodied in one person officially ensconced in Congress—and an opposition that, as much as the government itself, is created and legitimized by the people.

Let me spell out these arguments.

Impossible Demands on the Public

In 1973 scores of millions of Americans heard repeatedly that they were the "jury" of Watergate, that the senators were only bringing out the facts on which they would have to judge. But how could they judge such things as use immunity, constructive knowledge of criminal events, the nature and limitations of subpoenas, executive privilege, the separation of powers (whose meaning constitutional lawyers and political scientists have been arguing for two hundred years), the nature of national security and its use in justifying presidential secrecy, etc., etc.? What the public could decide is whether the Nixon administration was worthy of its confidence, but in the event of a negative answer there was no recourse until the next election forty months away.

It was an old story. In 1913 President Wilson complained about the tariff lobby:

It is of serious interest to the country that the people at large should have no lobby and be voiceless in these matters, while great bodies of astute men seek to create an artificial opinion and to overcome the interests of the public for their private profit.... *Only public opinion can check and destroy it.*[4]

More poignant was Wilson's desperate and unavailing appeal to public opinion on behalf of the treaty ending the first World War and providing for America's membership in the League of Nations. "I ask nothing better than to lay my case before the American people."[5]

Nothing comes more easily to presidents than an appeal to the public with whom they naturally identify. Theodore Roosevelt's "bully pulpit," Franklin D. Roosevelt's fireside chats, Eisenhower's familiar phrase, "I want it stopped; America wants it stopped"—all these are vivid examples, as was Harry Truman's conviction that he was there to see to it that the "country was run for the benefit of all the people and not for just the special crew who has the inside track," or as Lyndon Johnson's pocket full of polls reporting that the people were with him on Vietnam.

Faced with national problems that defy handling by division among virtually independent committees, legislators show the same awe of the popular will. Congress could rise up and deal with the Pentagon only if "the public would back them up. Real change in public opinion is the only way ..." (Senator Proxmire). Efforts to "tighten up our internal security" have been in vain because "the public has not yet responded sufficiently for Congress to . . . act" (Senator Mundt).

Presidents and public figures vie in attributing omniscience and omnipotence to the public. "The American People want the Germans to live . . . but do not want them to have a higher standard of living than other states, such as the Soviet Republic" (Franklin D. Roosevelt). The American public "would probably support a . . . credit of three billion dollars [to Britain] if a satisfactory . . . commercial policy could be reached" (Undersecretary of State Will Clayton). And this from Thomas B. Watson, Jr., president of IBM, who was discoursing on the priorities between civil rights and national security:

I honestly believe . . . that the people of the United States are sensible enough so that they in their own minds will put one above the other in the correct order and will devote their attentions to the most important.[6]

One of the most striking examples of the crucial role imputed to public opinion was produced by the Senate hearings in 1951, after President Truman had fired General MacArthur for insubordination. The public had not been a factor in their argument,[7] but MacArthur's homecoming created a furor. Welcoming crowds in New York and elsewhere broke all records. In the twelve days after MacArthur's dismissal, the White House received 27,363 letters and telegrams compared to the 1,996 stimulated by Franklin D. Roosevelt's plan to enlarge the Supreme Court in 1937. Congress was flooded with mail, much of it viciously abusive of Truman.[8] Some thought that the public response came to the verge of violence against the government.[9]

Then came the hearings on MacArthur's discharge—and a public parade of America's military secrets such as the grand strategy of the country, its estimates of its own potentialities, and the details of what it knew and did not know of the strength of the enemy. "Before God," declared Senator Charles W. Tobey, "the picture makes me stand aghast."

But why was all this information published? The answer is very simple.

These were the facts that would be needed for judgment, not only by the Senators but by the public—from whom, in reality, both sides were asking a verdict.[10]

In 1951 the public rapidly lost interest![11] In 1973, however, as the mire deepened in the Watergate, the interest of the public seemed to become increasingly intense and morbid.

Why the Demands on the Public Are Impossible

In 1927 John Dewey denounced the "superstitious belief that there is a public concerned to determine the formation and execution of general policies."[12] In 1973 the truth of his remark was undiminished. For such a public to exist, three conditions would be required. First, the public must be a "general" one, including the bulk of the people, if it is to speak with authority. Second, the public must know enough about issues to have opinions on what should be done; and its belief in its opinions must convince politicians that the public's demands will be clearly reflected in how the public votes. Third, the public must have some way to act or to threaten action in order to make the weight of its opinion felt. None of these conditions commonly obtain, and the effective combination of all three of them is extremely rare. Let us follow the argument.

Special—Not General—Publics

John Dewey's influential definition described the public as composed of people who perceive that the actions of others have consequences that they want to avoid, modify, or reinforce. In short, some people want to regulate the acts of others in order to control their effects; but regulation implies some entity that can make and enforce rules, hence, a government. To acquire legitimacy as a formulator and enforcer of laws, a government must not exist merely ad hoc to enforce this or that set of rules but rather must make and enforce rules for a collective or a community. In Dewey's ideal community the public would weigh the consequences not just of some particular acts but of all acts together, recognizing an overriding value in the existence of the community itself, so that the regulations to control certain acts would be assimilated and accommodated to a general set of regulations devised to command general respect.

Alas! Dewey lamented that small communities in which simple life and few numbers made possible common understanding and agreement had evolved into large and complex societies. The search for the community then led to the discovery of the state, a very different entity, and the "eclipse" of the public.[13]

Overlooking Dewey's lament, many political analysts have accepted the primacy of particular publics. "Public opinion . . . is strictly speaking specific to a particular set of conditions."[14] The interests that act and the publics that form in consequence yield a "public opinion that is precise, limited, driven home. . . ."[15] What is more, political practitioners increasingly concentrate on analyzing the electorate into its component groups or publics, for each of which a campaign can be tailored.[16] If a larger group, such as a general electorate, is the target, accent is on creating an attractive image of the candidate that, it is hoped, the people will buy with their votes, as an embodiment of those qualities they admire, or aspire to, in themselves. "Ideally the candidate . . . will be pleasant, not abrasive; have a clear, but not too specific, personality; be self-assured, even cocky, but not pretentious; be articulate, but not erudite or glib; be courageous but also cautious; and appear handsome, but not too pretty."[17]

In all this there can be appeals to specific groups on specific issues and general psychological appeals—all on the part of candidates who merchandise themselves as individuals, as our electoral system requires. But it is difficult to see how the voter can emerge from the polls confident that he has created either a government or an opposition. In the same way the voter's sense of belonging to, and helping to maintain, Dewey's community is unachieved. The public is, indeed, eclipsed.

What the Public Knows and How Strongly the Public Feels

The adage of an old country newspaper editor was "never underestimate either the ignorance or the intelligence of the people." People generally are very poorly informed about public issues—a fact of first importance not only to the understanding of the nature and role of public opinion but also to the question of the feasibility of party government (chap. 9). Even when they think they know, their information is often wrong. Wide discussion may increase the number of persons who have heard about an issue without significantly spreading sound information on it. In consequence, even the most sophisticated efforts to delineate opinion often yield confusing results—". . . for wisdom cries out in the streets, and no man regards it."

Lloyd A. Free and Hadley Cantril declared that "more than one-third of the United States population is perhaps too uninformed politically to participate in the democratic process," noting that Gallup had found less than half the voters able to name their own congressman in 1966.[18] They were using such simple tests as whether people recognized Lyndon Johnson to be a "liberal" and Barry Goldwater a "conservative" in 1964.

When we move from personalities to the kinds of issues the public is called on to decide, ignorance is often even more dense. The Bricker amendment, which would have radically changed the conduct of American foreign policy, was widely debated in the 1950s. No less an authority than Edward S. Corwin referred to Bricker's "war on the Constitution. . . ."[19] In 1953 a public-opinion poll indicated that only 19 percent of the public had ever heard or read of the amendment.[20] Of the 19 percent who had heard of it, 9 percent were for it, 7 percent were against it, and 3 percent had no opinion.

In 1947 the Taft-Hartley Act, which organized labor promptly labeled a "slave labor law," was passed. It figured prominently in electoral campaigns in 1948 and 1950. In 1952, the Survey Research Center reported that 30 percent of a national sample had never heard of the law, 25 percent did not know what should be done about it, and 16 percent thought that it should be changed but were completely vague on which direction. In 1953, contrarily, Gallup found that 60 percent of his sample declared they had not followed the debate on Taft-Hartley; but 19 percent said that they would change or amend it against 10 percent for the Survey Research Center.[21] Turning to agriculture, the central policy question for decades has been the level of farm price support, expressed as percentages of "parity." In 1952, however, a survey of Michigan farmers found only 8 percent to have a "good understanding" of the relationship between price supports and parity.[22]

Often people who think they know about public issues are wrong. In the 1952 survey of Michigan farmers, 14 percent thought they understood the relationship between price supports and parity but "gave answers entirely wrong." In 1964, after J. Edgar Hoover had stated that the civil rights movement had not been infiltrated by Communists, Free and Cantril found 44 percent of its sample asserting the opposite, 33 percent (whether they knew it or not) agreeing with Hoover, and only 20 percent saying what virtually all should have said, namely, that they did not know.[23]

Nor is education of the public, even of the "special publics" that are "specific to a particular set of conditions," very effective. The Michigan farmers had long been targets of educational programs on price supports conducted by one of the country's most highly developed agricultural extension services. Labor unions had made great efforts to inform their members about Taft-Hartley. As for the more general public, consider the John Birch Society. A clandestine organization of the far right, the society was formed in 1958 by Robert Welch whose fantasies included the charge that President Eisenhower was "a dedicated, conscious agent of the Communist conspiracy." In April 1961 Gallup reported that 31 million Americans had read or heard of the society; of these 44 percent had an unfavorable opinion of it, 9 percent were favorable, and the rest uncertain.

Ensued much public denunciation of the society by "virtually the entire religious, civic, and political Establishment of the nation"; and in February 1962, Gallup tried again. Now 56 million had heard of it. Opinions were 43 percent unfavorable, 8 favorable, and 49 percent did not know where they stood.[24] But what had those who had heard of the society learned? In July 1964, of a nationwide sample 65 percent had heard of the John Birch Society. Of these, 24 percent identified it with the far right, 16 percent with the far left, 7 percent with neither, and 53 percent said that they did not know.[25]

The Difficulty of Ascertaining How Strongly the Public Feels

Skipping over the guesswork involved in interpreting opinion polls with conflicting results, I shall give only one illustration of the problem of estimating the intensity of public feeling. The anticommunism that Americans often profess to pollsters, although usually under prompting and frequently with contradictions,[26] seemed to be running high in 1952. China had gone Communist in 1949 in "an uproar of hateful philippics. . . ." For five years, from early 1950, "Washington officialdom and professional and intellectual circles throughout the country were in an uproar over communism, with fresh accusations every week."[27] In 1952 the Republicans pitched their successful campaign on the issues of communism, Korea, and corruption. Yet the careful study by the Michigan Survey Research Center of the 1952 presidential vote disclosed that only 3 percent of the sample

mentioned the argument that the Democratic administration had been "soft on communism" and was "infiltrated with Communists," in spite of the fact that this argument was very prominent among the campaign stimuli to which the voters were subjects.[28]

Relationship Between Opinion and Action

Politicians strive to know in advance, or be able to make a reasonably accurate guess, what action the public will take. Short of passive resistance, general strikes, mass violence and, ultimately, revolt, the public has one means of action, namely, the vote. How to find out what is on their minds that will affect their votes? "Man is the only animal that makes a speech before he acts."[29] "Public opinion is what people are willing to say out loud. . . ."[30] "And thus anyone was saying as he looked at his neighbor."[31] All these wise statements suggest that there is a relationship between intent and action and that the intent may be consciously expressed before the act.

This leads to the underlying concept of social psychology, the concept of attitude that Gordon W. Allport authoritatively defined as "a mental and neural state of readiness" to act. "Without such a concept, social psychologists could not work in the fields of public opinion, national character, or institutional behavior. . . ."[32] This is the underpinning of the vast enterprise of attitude surveys. The results illuminate some of the major orientations of the public; but they commonly fall short of delineating an unmistakable public will on the concrete issues that plague government. The obligation on the public remains impossible in spite of the polls.[33]

To be sure, politicians know—and the pollsters have added precision to their knowledge—that voters are deeply concerned about their economic well-being and about war, usually in that order. The stain on the image of the Republicans as the party of the Depression has been virtually indelible. In spite of the bellicosity of many of its leaders, the Democratic party's martial image has been more like the Cheshire cat. The Republican "party of virtue" appears to be handicapped against the Democratic "party of Santa Claus."[34] The polls report up to twice as many voters' identifying themselves as Democrats than as Republicans. A "social issue" was much advertised in 1970—concern over race, crime, dissent, drugs, pollution, smut—but it seemed to fall behind the economic issue in importance when the voters actually voted (chap. 9).

V. O. Key has shown a plausible relationship between voters' policy preferences and the way they mark their ballots. Comparing succeeding elections (1940 and 1944, 1944 and 1948, and so on), Key sought to explain the shift in the vote for president by correlating responses to Gallup's policy-probing with the votes of people who switched parties in the given four-year period and of new voters. He found a striking correlation between policy preferences and voting decisions. *On examination, however, what Key found was not very illuminating about specific issues that confront politicians*—Taft-Hartley, basing-point regulation, 90 percent of parity, reciprocal trade, foreign aid appropriations, and the like. Rather than specifics, the mass of new voters and switchers seemed to be affected in 1948 by their views on whether the government had done well for the farmers and whether it was strict enough (or too strict) with labor unions. In 1952, a rising sympathy for business and a decline of sympathy for labor was of some significance; much more telling was the widespread antipathy to the Korean war. One-third of the 1948 Democrats disapproved of Truman's performance and about one-half of them declared their intention of voting for Eisenhower.[35]

No one was more aware of the politician's difficulty in interpreting public opinion than V. O. Key. He began his book, *Public Opinion and American Democracy*, by defining public opinion as "those opinions held by private persons which government finds it prudent to heed." Conceding the difficulty of research on the subject, he wrote:

If one is to know what opinions governments heed, one must know the inner thoughts of . . . officials. It is even more difficult to know what opinions prudent governments should heed for the success of their policies or even for their survival.

And in his concluding chapter, he noted:

The data tells us almost nothing about the dynamic relations between the upper layer of activists and mass opinion. The missing piece of our puzzle is this elite element of the opinion system.[36]

First among those who must search relentlessly for "the missing piece of the puzzle" are presidents. For their efficacy depends heavily on their standing with the public.

Presidential Prestige and Presidential Teaching

As is orthodox among political scientists, I assume the need of a strong
and unified presidency. Unity is not enough unless the president builds
a power base. However untrammeled his initiative has been in foreign
affairs, domestically his formal powers are frequently frustrated.[37] If
he is to emerge as the leader of a government that, for a limited time
and normally subject to the constraints of the Bill of Rights, is to be
able to govern, the president must supplement his formal powers with
effective political power or influence.

According to Richard E. Neustadt, the president requires a reputation among the "Washingtonians"—the operators who must go along
if policy is to prevail—for skill and vigor in conducting his office.
He also needs prestige with the public.[38] Reputation is important.
Prestige is essential. A president may falter, make mistakes, lack con-
sistency, or lapse into inaction; but if he stands high enough with the
public he will look formidable to the Washingtonians. Let his public
esteem fall sharply and whatever his arts of governance he will lack
the leeway that is essential in making and upholding difficult choices.

To enjoy public prestige it is good for presidents to have the look
of Eisenhower or of Roosevelt, but they may also help themselves by
teaching the public advantageously.[39] The public are perverse pupils.
Usually ignorant about issues and indifferent to all but the most por-
tentous events, the people turn their attention to government only
when they begin to hurt or to feel threatened.

How is presidential teaching evaluated? By far the most important
clue has been provided by Gallup's question, repeated monthly since
1945 (except during presidential campaigns), "Do you approve
or disapprove of the way [the incumbent] is handling his job as President?" The results of this poll are "very widely read" and are "widely
taken to approximate reality. . . ."

Neustadt dwelt on the patterns developed by the Gallup questions
for Presidents Truman and Eisenhower. Truman's rating of 85 percent
favorable for the first few months after his succession to Roosevelt
remains the highest recorded by any president; it fell to 36 percent in
autumn, 1946, with the beef shortage, rose into the 50s in 1947 with
the Marshall Plan, declined during the election year of 1948, rose again
to 69 percent in January 1949, then fell. Ensued the great change on
which Neustadt dwells. During 1950 Truman's approval percentage
ranged between 46 and 37 percent. Thenceforth, to the end of his term

it ranged between 32 and 23 percent. Neustadt compares this with Eisenhower who fell below 60 percent in only one month of his first term but who, in most of 1958, ranged between 52 and 56 percent (falling to 49 percent in one month).

In both these cases popular approval tumbled at a time when governmental action (or inaction) was associated with extraordinary disturbance in the private lives of millions of Americans.

A similar development marked Lyndon B. Johnson's 1965–69 term. Maintaining an average approval of more than 60 percent in 1965 and more than 50 percent until autumn, 1966, he then fell below 50, never to recover: from autumn, 1966 to autumn, 1967, he hovered around 45 percent, dropped below 40 percent, recovered, fell, recovered once more, then fell from 45 percent in May to below 40 percent for the remainder of his term. Neustadt's judgment of Truman finds an excellent parallel.

What happened between 1950 and 1951? [between 1966 and 1967–68?] Above all else, inflation and taxation and lost lives in "Truman's [Johnson's] War," which had become interminable war with the Chinese [North Vietnamese].

The average popular approval of presidential jobhandling for mid-1945 to January 1969 is 58 percent.[40] This figure is swelled not only by the unusually high ratings of Eisenhower but also because "a large number of citizens . . . are inclined to support the country's leadership no matter what it does."[41] The fact that two of the four presidents who served in this period fell sharply below 50 percent and eventually even below 40 percent and tended to remain there (Truman even lower) marks a serious danger for the country if a president needs high prestige in order to have the leeway to make difficult political choices that may confront the country at any time.

Neustadt makes a case for presidential pedagogy as an ameliorating factor, even against odds implicit in the tendency for presidential prestige to decline, so long as the incumbent has the skill to help himself. John E. Mueller's statistical analysis of 292 occasions when Gallup asked his question between 1945 and 1969 is much more pessimistic.[42]

All presidents began their terms with high job ratings. With the exception of Eisenhower in his first term, when he gained 2.5 percentage points annually and in his second term, when his slight loss was statistically insignificant, all presidents declined, Truman at an annual average of 11–12 percentage points, Johnson at about 9, Kennedy at about 6.[43] Mueller explains the general decline as the result of the changes in the "coalition of minorities" that supported the president. The theory is that presidential actions will alienate more and more minorities. Except for Eisenhower whose performance on this variable rose, Mueller's implication is that presidential teaching would have little effect on the tendency to decline. *All presidents except Eisenhower tended to fall from their own starting level at their own rate, regardless.* Another variable, labeled economic prosperity, was similarly deterministic: presidents lost about 3 percentage points (or again, all observed presidents but Eisenhower) for every decline of 1 percentage point in employment from what it was when their terms began. Once they lost Gallupian popularity on this variable, a gain in employment failed to restore it. There was nothing much a president could do to help himself in the ratings if unemployment rose.

Mueller also considered the influence of the Korean and Vietnam wars on presidential popularity. While Truman lost some 18 points directly attributable to Korea, the Vietnam war had "no independent impact on . . . Johnson's popularity at all." With the drive to the Yalu in late 1950, the entrance of the Chinese, the retreat, and the mounting casualties, Truman's popularity took an extra large drop *over and above the rate* determined for his decline that Mueller had already labeled "the coalition of minorities variable." But when American intervention in another Asian ground war became publicly evident in 1965, Johnson's popularity decline did not accelerate. Hence whatever downward effect the war had on Johnson's ratings was "tapped by other variables in the equation, especially the coalition of minorities variable"—that, therefore, becomes a kind of catch-all to explain any presidential popularity losses except the one connected with unemployment.

Mueller introduced one more variable, however, called "rally round the flag" to explain the fillip given to presidential ratings by international events if they involve the president and are specific, dramatic, and sharply focused. In 1945–69, he found 34 rally points. A few were initiated by other powers, e.g., Sputnik, the Berlin Wall, the Tet offensive; some were happenings, such as the U-2 episode. But many followed directly presidential initiatives, e.g., entry into the Korean war, the Lebanon landing, the Dominican invasion, and such international conferences as Potsdam, Geneva, Camp David, and Glassboro.

This brings us back to presidential teaching but with a rather dangerous twist. Since presidential teaching, according to Neustadt, becomes possible only when the indifferent public is suddenly listening because of visceral pain, the implication would already be strong that presidents must attempt to manipulate the gut issues for their benefit. The dangerous twist in the "rally round the flag" concept is its invitation to manipulate one of the strongest—or, at least, *seemingly* the strongest—issues of all: patriotism.

The danger is made explicit by a generalization about public opinion that is widely believed. Mueller holds that "a large number of citizens . . . are inclined to support the government no matter what it does." Sidney Verba and associates found that "the President's support increases no matter what he does—increase the war or talk of negotiations—so long as he does something."[44]

The tendency to uphold the government places a premium on action; it would also seem to deny the proposition that public opinion may be a "dike" constraining the government, especially in the short run. But it is also reported that the rise in public support in response to vigorous action tends to be temporary. What more logical then than to act again?

A leader . . . adopts a position. He then finds support for that position among the public. . . . He then uses that finding to justify . . . his position. This may not be an inaccurate summary of the use of polls [on public support of the Vietnam war] by . . . President [Johnson].[45]

The next step is to take another action, in whatever direction, and measure the applause once more.

The danger appears in the motivation to take risks, to expand military actions, and to continue to do so, egged on by the fillips given to public support. Or the danger might run in the other direction: to fail to see a real threat to national survival and to take countermeasures in time. The fact that the stigma of "appeasement" was misapplied in the 1950s and 1960s does not mean that there can never be a willingness to give so much ground that the safety of the country is jeopardized.[46] V. O. Key referred to opinion "that the government finds it prudent to heed"; but if favorable opinion can be bought by a series of actions—either reckless adventures or heedless surrenders—the president may be tempted to fling away prudence.

This is the fault inherent in the present relationship between the president and a public unorganized in governing parties. It has become manifest in the train of military activities overseas and it has been more than suggested in connection with the "social issue" in domestic politics, particularly with regard to "law and order," and "crime in the streets," and "busing"—all with strong racial overtones.

The danger is further underlined by certain characteristics of public opinion as it seems to be developing in the 1970s.

The Public in Disarray

Public disillusionment with politics was profound in 1973. Perhaps this was only the bottom of a trough. But it may have marked a grave malaise in the polity itself. Apparently the phenomenon was no new thing. George C. Gallup reported in 1968 that the public was confused, disillusioned, and cynical.[47] In 1971 Louis Harris told the nation's newspaper publishers that it was a mistake to think of America as "cooling," rather it was "heated up more than two years ago," although those dissatisfied were determined to gain their ends by peaceful means; however, "if we do not learn to attack our common problems instead of each other, we could be doomed as a nation."[48] "Always in the past [wrote Samuel Lubell in 1970], I have been optimistic about this country's political system. But as my research and interviewing went from one conflict to another, I became alarmed."[49]

A Gallup survey of Americans in two hundred communities (February 1971) found less than 25 percent who believed that "things in this country are generally going in the right direction," a figure Gallup considered "remarkable" in light of the public's tendency to give optimistic answers.[50] At about the same time another national sample, again polled by Gallup for Potomac Associates, Inc., reported 47 percent (and a majority of those with opinions) to believe that unrest is likely to lead to a "real breakdown in this country."

> Traditional optimism about the nation's progress has faltered. The average American feels that the United States has slid backward over the past five years.[51]

Thomas E. Cronin disagrees, citing a 1969 poll. Contrary to the "radical [*sic*] interpretations of current American politics that politicians cannot be trusted," most adult Americans (64 percent) trust the president to do what is good for the people and smaller majorities trust governors, senators, and the Supreme Court.[52]

Abstract questions about trust and confidence in political leaders may merely activate optimistic reflexes. Free and Cantril found 67 percent of their 1964 sample believing in the basic goodness and trust-worthiness of their fellowmen.[53] By contrast, when Americans are thinking of specific politicians, the answers may be different. *President Johnson's Gallup rating was declining to its low of 35 percent at the same time Cronin's poll was taken.* Nearly contemporaneously, Louis Harris was reporting that "Congress Is Losing Public Confidence";[54] and for many people the question whether political leaders could be believed provoked either anger or hilarity.

How close have we come to Hobbes's "warre . . . of every man, against every man"? "For WARRE, consisteth not in Battell onely, or the act of fighting; but in a tract of time, wherein the Will to Contend by Battell is sufficiently known: and therefore the notion of Time is to be considered in the nature of Warre. . . ."[55] For whatever it is worth, one of five American men was recently reported to believe that some degree of violence is needed to bring about social change in the United States.[56]

Antagonism among groups, above all between racial groups, is a clear and present danger. Racial conflict is too obvious to need comment. Tensions also arise between the core cities and the suburbs that, with 76 millions in 1971, exceeded the core cities for the first time and looked forward to electing more congressmen than the cities in 1972. The flight from the city has been found to breed an indifference to its problems—except for a determination to keep them from following the migrants to the suburbs.

Meanwhile, the scores of millions remaining in the core cities, living between the worst slums and the suburbs, have been called the "Forgotten Americans," the "Middle Americans," the "Real Majority," the "Silent Majority," or "The Ethnics." They are white, usually non-WASP, with high-school educations or less. Often both husband and wife work. With his $8,000 to $10,000 a year, the man considers himself "affluent," but he also feels—apparently much more than he did ten or fifteen years ago—that his chance for a significantly better job a decade hence is negligible. Believing that he has paid his own way, he cherishes hard work and self-reliance. His dismay is compounded by the evidence that education, for thirty years an open sesame to better jobs at least for his children, has lost much of its magic.[57] Despite his virtues, of which he is naturally highly conscious, he feels that he gets the back of the politician's hand.[58]

Moreover, he and his family are alienated from the "establishment," which is sometimes blamed for surrendering the "captive nations" of Eastern Europe, for knuckling under to the Communists, and, perhaps above all, for "changing the rules." Their fathers and they themselves have had to work long and hard to get ahead; the children of the upper crust enjoy unearned favors. The ethnics fought bravely in wars that the beautiful people now deride as mistakes or worse. They uphold the virtues of sobriety and decency—in a sea of smut, libertinism, and depravity.[59]

Perhaps all this mutual hate is exaggerated. Much of the evidence is based on reported "attitudes" that may make people appear to be more simplistic, more rigid, and more repressive than they really are. Studying *Middle America*, Robert Coles found many of the invidious sentiments so abundantly reported. But he also found uncertainty, diffidence, reflectiveness, and changefulness, as expressed by the wife of a gas station owner: "I don't know what my views are. I change my mind every other day. I really do."

> She was asking anyone who wanted some knowledge of her (and millions like her) . . . to think about one fact that is to her unutterable, yet comes across in her manner, her way of doing things and talking and responding to others: that is, the fact of her own dignity, her humanity, hence her complexity.[60]

Coles suggests that pollsters, politicians, and political scientists unintentionally falsify the true feelings of the public by oversimplifying them. Nevertheless, *the artifacts produced by the pollsters may become the reality representing "public opinion" in the political equations of power and decision.* Recall the tendency of the public to support (or, which amounts to the same thing, to be reported as supporting) governmental action. Reflect also on the reported willingness of the public to stifle dissent, especially criticism of the government.[61] Are these the opinions that future governments "will find it prudent to heed"? Is a sovereign "opinion" emerging that will strengthen tendencies, already discernible to some, leading to an authoritarian government?[62]

This might be the price of our misunderstanding of the nature of public opinion in our operative political ideas—and of the impossible burdens placed on public opinion in our political institutions.

The Public in Party Government

Party government should improve the health of public opinion. It would foster a better theoretical idea of the public's role. Instead of loading the public with the shattering task of resolving the specific issues of government, the new theory would hold that the public would exercise its power and discharge its duties essentially by those magnificent actions for which it uniquely qualifies—the election at once of a government and an opposition.

The achievement of party government would help put majority rule in perspective. We would be able to escape the terrible assumptions of absolute legitimacy that are implicit in majoritarianism when it represents the "voice of the people." The appeal to the "silent majority" or to the "real majority" is an appeal to an absolute sovereign. A decision by a majority *party,* on the other hand, is much more clearly seen as based on a temporary predominance in numbers that is continually and properly opposed by an organized minority of nearly equal size.[63] Public opinion would then be subject to the limitations urged by John Dewey when he defined it as "judgment which is formed and entertained by those who constitute the public . . . about public affairs."[64] Public judgments are estimates rather than conclusions derived either from inexorable logic or from divine revelation.

Under party government, moreover, the president may be further empowered to wield the unified and decisive leadership the times seem to require; yet the dangers of presidential hyperbole arising out of his present unhealthy relationship to public opinion should be diminished. Structuring public opinion through strong political parties should not only reduce the inflation of support that accrues to a government in response to its actions. It should also give the public points of reference in making reactions to policy. The parties would take their positions. Both the governing party and the opposition would listen to their legislative members' reports on the moods of the electorate. And the electorate, instead of constantly facing the task of making up its individual minds on the complex and awful problems facing modern government, would have encompassing reference groups in its parties.[65]

Let me emphasize that this is a vision of the future and not the way that parties act now.

When it comes to policy preferences on the Vietnamese war, the average citizen can receive relatively little guidance from the ordinary reference groups that help him pattern his attitudes. And perhaps the most serious lack is in relation to party affiliation—the citizen looking for guidance *among his fellow partisans* will find little.[66]

Republicans and Democrats were internally divided on Vietnam as they are on many other issues. Parties are not at present vehicles for concerting opinions as much as they are for collecting them. Citizens cannot now expect anything but conflicting cues from their fellow partisans.

The situation should be different if we can attain organized, centralized, and focused parties—as is suggested by the rapidity with which polled opinion shifts in response to changes in leadership. To illustrate, the public was regularly polled to see whether it supported the bombing of North Vietnam or would like a bombing halt. In autumn, 1967, large majorities continued to support the government's bombing policy. Approval rose with the Tet offensive; one February poll reported 70 percent for bombing and only 16 percent against. Then came the New Hampshire primary, 12 March, and on 28 March President Johnson announced a partial bombing halt. In April the poll findings were completely reversed: 64 percent now approved of the president's decision to stop the bombing.[67]

The Chicken or the Egg?

One of the most provocative students of American parties has raised a serious objection that party government, while highly desirable, is unobtainable unless it follows a fundamental change in values. If this means that a large number of people must be convinced that the faults of the present system require a change, it is undeniable. But Walter Dean Burnham seems to mean more than this. A democratic solution to our problems, he says, will

require an entirely new structure of parties and of mass behavior, one in which political parties would be instrumentalities of democratic collective purpose. *But this in turn seems inconceivable without a preexisting revolution in social values.*[68]

Which comes first, the chicken or the egg? Actually there is much evidence that institutional changes can precede and very probably influence changes in values. Tocqueville was so convinced of the possibility of regulating democracy by the aid of laws that he "assigned a role to political science . . . perhaps even more architectonic than the claim made on its behalf by Aristotle. . . ."[69] To give some examples: when the feudal lords obeyed the summons to parliaments of the early Norman kings, they called themselves the *barones,* the men; but by the thirteenth century they thought of themselves as a group, the *baronagium,* that came virtually to represent England.[70] Even the conservative Sir Henry Maine dwelt on legal fictions as means by which courts adapted laws to changing situations:[71] "Substantive law is secreted in the interstices of procedure." More telling is the marked shift in English values *from* the deference that Bagehot thought cemented the community *to* the sentiments supporting political parties that performed the same function: changes in the party system preceded and shaped the new values.[72] In America the separation of powers gave rise to institutions that produced a political process that perverted Lockean individualism into solipsism.[73] In America also institutional reasons compelling presidents to curry popular support cause actions designed to get the public to "rally around the flag." The stress has often shifted from the wisdom of policies to their effect on the presidential image.[74]

For good or ill, institutional changes can be employed to change values.

9   The Feasibility of Party Government

You know . . . a congressman can do pretty much what he decides to do and he doesn't have to bother too much about criticism. I've seen plenty of cases since I've been here where a guy will hold one economic or political position and get along all right; and then he'll die or resign and a guy comes in who holds quite a different economic or political position and he gets along all right too—*Congressman Herman Peter Eberharter**

Many of America's political ills would be helped if not cured by party government. A majority party would then dominate the executive and legislative departments. It would play the prime role in concerting and enacting policies, its unity permitting its principal officers to oversee and if necessary overwhelm the bureaucracy to make sure that the will of the government is executed. To these ends the party should have preponderant control of the votes of its legislative members, secured by a veto over nominations of candidates who refuse to support its policies. Bargaining and compromising would not end, but in their conclusive stages they would be transferred from legislative committees to the caucus of the governing party. A minority party, similarly organized and empowered, should monopolize the opposition; not only would it be in excellent position to criticize the government but it would also be constrained by the expectations of the press and the attentive public to prepare alternative policies.

Party government is needed, first, to empower the nation to deal with the numerous and complex problems that require a comprehensive and coordinated approach. Second, it is vital to confront the government with an opposition capable of threatening it with defeat at the election; power is always subject to abuse and must be checked by power. Third, periodic elections will permit voters to create the gov-

* The headnote is drawn from Lewis Anthony Dexter, "The Representative and His District," in Robert L. Peabody and Nelson W. Polsby, eds., *New Perspectives on the House of Representatives* (2d ed.; Chicago, Rand McNally, 1969), pp. 4–5.

ernment and, equally important, the opposition; that is the essential of democratic control, the guaranteed opportunity to the people to reject the government. Fourth, in criticizing the government, the opposition must show that it comprehends the problems well enough to offer solutions of its own. This is the essence of responsibility, and it is required by the exceeding difficulty of the problems modern governments must face. This is by far the most important reason for the opposition's program; the customary reason that the mandate theory requires a clear-cut choice in programs for the electorate is not only distinctly minor, it is also misleading—more on this later. Fifth, it follows that the governing and opposing parties should be both alike and different: alike in their acceptance of a common constitution, but sufficiently unlike to make for alternative programs with real differences.

Assuming the desirability of party government, America is blessed by having two major parties that institutional reasons create and nourish. The election of a single president restricts the contestants to two—the proper number to compete for a unique prize. Moreover, the same principle, the election of a single candidate in each constituency, is repeated in the choice of federal senators, congressmen, state governors, mayors, and most state legislators. The two-party division is reinforced by the persistence of voter identification. "No element of the political lives of Americans is more impressive than their party loyalties."[1] The conditions favorable for party government are further strengthened by the strong penchant for presidents, the central figures in the American system, to govern through parties if they possibly can.[2]

Divided Government: The Problem of the Solid South

Party government will flourish best when each of two parties is capable of winning both the presidential and congressional elections. Habituation is vital to the education of politicians in the art of governance,[3] and those who rule should be chastened by the knowledge that the next election may turn them out. The wisdom dates from Aristotle: in a free government, "men learn to command by first learning to obey. . . ." And "a good citizen . . . ought also to know in what manner free men ought to govern, as well as be governed. . . ."[4]

During much of our history one party has been dominant, but the second party has had a chance to win a majority and take over the government. After the seesaw of 1875–97 when the same party controlled both the presidency and both houses of Congress in only four years, the Republicans enjoyed superiority until the coming of the New Deal; but the Democrats were able to win Congress in 1910–20 and to fill the presidency for two terms. Since 1930 the weakness of the Republicans handicaps the achievement of party government. The Solid South—the major legacy in the country's rich inheritance of racial politics—has been the graveyard of Republican hopes. Although Republicans have been able to win the presidency and, after 1938, to hold their own in congressional elections outside the South, they have controlled Congress in only four years, 1947–48 and 1953–54.

The South has over 100 House seats. A pattern whereby Democrats continue to win all or nearly all of them and to compete strongly in Republican areas (even dominating in some traditional Republican areas) is one that guarantees their numerical control of the House of Representatives.[5]

What is the outlook for the Republicans in the eleven southern states? In the Eisenhower landslide of 1952 the GOP won only 6 of 106 southern congressional seats and polled at least 40 percent in only 6 others. In 1968, it won 26 southern seats and polled 40 percent or more in 14 others. Two things suggest that these still insufficient gains may grow. The most important arises from migration. The black population in the South, 32 percent in 1920, down to 20 percent in 1960, is projected at 15 percent in 1980—a figure that will begin to approach the national average.[6] Race may be declining as an issue in southern politics. In 1970, Georgia, South Carolina, Florida, Tennessee, and Arkansas all elected "moderate" Democratic governors, each of whom promised an end to the old racial ways in his inaugural. This is by no means to suggest that discrimination against blacks is over. The situation remains grim in much of the South as elsewhere. But race as a *political* issue may be declining.

Second, a trend of some importance may be the increasing Republican orientation of the southern, urban white-collar class.[7] In the last region to industrialize, southerners may behave like northern industrialists of the 1920s and 1930s—militantly anti-union, largely opposed to governmental intervention in the economy, and generally conservative.[8] If race ceases to be the dominant issue, the accent on economic differences may rise and encourage the emergence of class politics.[9]

Quite apart from developments that suggest a decline in Democratic control of southern congressional delegations, the reforms proposed in chapter 10 would eliminate divided government. Between 1868 and 1970 divided governments ruled in thirty-two years. Synchronization of presidential and congressional elections would have reduced this figure to fourteen years. In addition, the bonus of some fifty congressmen elected at large, proposed in chapter 10 for the party winning the presidency, will provide a working majority in any event.

The Problem of a Stable Majority

Many political scientists would welcome party government; but some, including those anxious for the change, point to serious difficulties. The first is that the necessary constitutional revisions are virtually impossible to achieve. This I cannot accept. If a strong enough case can be made to convince a large number of reflective people that party government deserves serious consideration, the conditions that now appear to prevent its adoption will themselves be changed.

The second argument provides the primary focus of this chapter. It holds that even if party government could be fashioned, it would not work because it requires a stable majority and in America this is impossible. Central to this argument is the proposition that a governing party would rule legitimately only because it has won an electoral mandate. That is, the parties must develop coherent and complete but contrasting programs so that the electorate has a clear-cut choice. The people would then decide not only who shall rule but would give their mandate to one bill of particulars. Now comes the fatal blow: The American people (it is said) are so divided in their interests, in their desires, and in what they expect from government that they cannot agree on a program of specifics. If a majority forms on one issue it will disappear on another as various groups defect. Hence, majorities must be ad hoc: they cannot be composed of politicians who adhere to one party and insist in reconciling the different interests and concerting a program for government within it.

The Mischievous Mandate Theory

Unfortunately, the 1950 Report of the American Political Science Association's Committee on Political Parties (CPP),[10] which has been the salient document in the controversy, relied heavily on the mandate theory. For example, *"we proceed on the proposition that popular government . . . requires political parties which provide the electorate with a proper range of choice between alternatives of action."* Among the reasons

for the widespread lack of respect for party platforms is that they have seldom been used by the parties to get a mandate from the people. By and large, *alternatives between the parties are defined so badly that it is often difficult to determine what the election has decided even in broadest terms.*[11]

The CPP thus invited the counterattack. Criticizing the political conceptions of "the amateur Democrats" as they apply to political parties, James Q. Wilson cited their conspicuous parallels to the CPP and other advocates of party reform. He attributed to them the idea that

a programmatic party would offer a real policy alternative to the opposition party. A vote for the party would be as much, or more, a deliberate vote for a set of clear and specific proposals, linked by a common point of view or philosophy of government, as it would be a vote for a set of leaders.[12]

Similarly, Edward C. Banfield wrote that party government advocates have criticized the American party system on a number of grounds, including: "Parties do not offer the electorate a choice in terms of fundamental principles; their platforms are very similar and mean next to nothing. . . ."[13]

According to Nelson W. Polsby and Aaron Wildavsky, party reformers suggest that democratic government requires political parties that 1) make policy commitments to the electorate, 2) are willing and able to carry them out when in office, 3) develop alternatives to government policies when out of office, and 4) differ sufficiently between themselves "to provide the electorate with a proper range of choice between alternatives of action."[14]

Why is it impossible for the voters to give a mandate to the winning party? As already suggested, the accepted answer is that America is too heterogeneous to produce stable majorities. In a country

so huge, containing such diverse climates and economic interests and social habits and racial and religious backgrounds, most politics will be parochial, most politicians will have small horizons, seeking the good of the state or the district rather than the Union. . . .

The government, Herbert Agar continued,

must water down the selfish demands of religions, races, classes, business associations, into a national policy which will alienate no major group and will contain at least a small plum for everybody. This is the price of unity in a continent-wide federation.[15]

Richard E. Neustadt, a consistent if guarded advocate of party government, agreed that its achievement is for the present, at least, virtually impossible. Our parties "are unlikely to be altered fundamentally as voter coalitions differently aligned for different offices in different places."[16] And again: "What matters is that . . . our politics will be made out of issues *with disparate local impacts. . . .*"

The objection rests on more than institutional obstacles, according to Austin Ranney and Willmoore Kendall:[17]

What prevents legislative action by longer-lived majorities is *not* our formal constitutional machinery but the whole complex of the people's attitudes and the character that those attitudes impose on our politics.

Winning electoral majorities, they say, are

composed of a number of interest groups, each of which holds many beliefs and values in common with the groups in the minority *and* many conflicting beliefs and values . . . among its own members. . . .

What is wrong with these indictments? One defect comes out most clearly in the Ranney-Kendall argument that the attitudes of voters are sovereign or, to put it another way, that public attitudes are independent variables whereas institutions like political parties are dependent variables. This is a similar fallacy to the one discerned in Walter Dean Burnham's argument at the end of chapter 8. Of course, attitudes shape institutions; but institutions also profoundly influence attitudes. The framers of the American Constitution laid the groundwork for political institutions that fragmented the electorate and multiplied "issues with a disparate local impact." *Attitudes supporting heterogeneity were greatly reinforced.* Small wonder that a welter of local interests should form and become politically entrenched. By the same token, a centralizing change in American political institutions will nourish a different set of attitudes, and these, in turn, will encourage and support party government.[18] Evidence will be presented suggesting that attitudes congenial to party government are latent and only await the appearance of favorable institutional conditions to flourish.

A far more important objection strikes at the mandate theory itself. For that theory places an impossible burden on the people, subjects government to a regimen of popular control that cannot be fulfilled, and invites attempts to impose an excess of participatory democracy on the operations of government. As with the jejune theory of public opinion all too often accepted in America, the mandate theory ends by frustrating the citizens and fragmenting government. It does not describe a workable and psychologically viable relationship between governors and populace. Happily, the remedy is a simple one. All that is needed is to substitute for the mandate theory of elections the proposition that elections are acts in which the voters create a government and an opposition.[19]

Issues with a Disparate Local Impact?

I shall concede that *one* issue, race, has been sufficient in the past, and may remain so in the immediate future, to prevent the achievement of party government. Agar was wrong in suggesting that the price of union was the recognition and accommodation of a myriad of local differences and Neustadt in stressing issues (in the plural) with a disparate local impact. What prevented a stable majority in the country was southern determination to put race at the top of every agenda— and to insist that the American political community could exist only so long as national policy honored the southern prerogative of "keeping the Negro in his place."[20]

If this is correct, then the real issue clearly transcends the question of party government. The American assertion of equality may ring hollow forever. We may be condemned to prolong the betrayal of our political ideas by perpetuating the discrimination especially against blacks but also, to different degrees, against other nonwhites. Perhaps party government would merely continue the policy of repression that has prevailed under the system of separated institutions sharing powers. The movement of blacks out of the South will not only make party government feasible. Under *either* system, this migration will force the admission that racial prejudice is countrywide and not the monopoly of any section. Under party government the acknowledgment may merely be somewhat less escapable. For policy will then be focused with an unwonted clarity; and the citizen will be more conscious of his link to the government he has created—he will feel more sharply that he shares responsibility for its acts. Nor will it be so easy to blame one's shortcomings on the seniority system or on the House rules committee or on the Senate judiciary committee. The "struggle for the soul of America"[21] will become an ineluctable part of every conscience.

Other than race, I shall argue that the numerous and shifting interests that are supposed to prevent the emergence of stable majorities have either weakened or would sufficiently decline in significance, given appropriate institutional encouragement, so that party government would be supportable. I anticipate a vigorous rebuttal based on the evidence in congressional roll-call votes of the power of constituency influence. To be sure, in explaining such votes, party membership has been the most significant identifiable determinant.[22] Nevertheless, writes Lewis A. Froman, Jr., if "party is the most important predictor of roll-call behavior, . . . constituency factors explain most of the deviation from party votes."[23]

No doubt constituency influence can be peremptory. In 1972 nearly any congressman who espoused busing aimed at integrating schools would invite defeat in November. Note, however, that this is not "many issues" but one (or a bundle rolled into one) and that it does not have a "disparate local impact"—rather, it has an identical meaning in all districts not dominated by the black vote. Systematic political discrimination is becoming nationalized.

On most other questions, however, the actual threat of punishment by the constituency is greatly exaggerated.[24] Even with the electoral process loaded in favor of local and special interests, the few studies that we have suggest that alienated interests would have little power to punish a congressman who goes against their demands, providing that he showed ordinary acumen in nursing his constituency in other ways. Under the constitutional reforms proposed in chapter 10, which would greatly reduce the loading in favor of special interests, the power of constituency influence—or, more exactly, the appearance of power—would be significantly lessened.

Let me illustrate. Many assertions that the multiplication of "issues with disparate local impacts" will prevent stable majorities capable of party government fail to cite particulars.[25] One classic analysis is an exception.[26] In 1924 A. N. Holcombe suggested that the differentiated alignment of voters on issues required governmental policies to be formulated and supported by shifting coalitions rather than by stable parties. The *Literary Digest* had polled its readers on two issues then agitating the country, prohibition of intoxicating liquor and the federal provision of bonuses for veterans of World War I. The ballot count disclosed that a majority of voters in fourteen states were comparatively dry and pro-bonus; in sixteen were comparatively dry and anti-bonus; in eleven were wet and anti-bonus; and in seven were wet and pro-bonus. Holcombe concluded that these two issues alone would generate four political parties of the policy-oriented variety.

But his argument was not necessarily sound. In only nine years the Eighteenth Amendment was repealed overwhelmingly and with great speed; prohibition disappeared as a national issue. On prohibition as on many others it is impossible to tell whether the differences in attitudes reported by the early opinion polls were actually translatable into solid votes in the ballot box. But on the bonus issue a test was made. The American Legion persuaded the House of Representatives to override presidential vetoes of veterans' bonus bills before the elections of 1922, 1924, 1928, 1930, 1934, and 1936. The electoral fate of congressmen who voted to sustain the president proved to be associated mainly with whether their party gained or lost seats in the subsequent election, not on how they had voted on the bonus veto.

The figures suggest [wrote V. O. Key, Jr.] that votes are more apt to be influenced by the voters' evaluation of a party in general rather than by their evaluation of the voting record of a particular individual.[27]

Key's study of the relationship between congressional votes on the bonus and electoral choice at the polls suggests that party government would work. This position is supported by the very few studies that attempt to deal specifically with the relationship between congressional actions and the behavior of the voters.

Reciprocal Trade Legislation

A major study of American policy on foreign trade concludes that congressmen have a great deal of discretion in deciding their stands on controversial issues that affect their districts. The subject was tariff legislation from the Reciprocal Trade Act in 1953 to the passage of the Trade Expansion Act in 1962. Eight communities, selected on the assumption that they would all have active interests in the debate over reciprocal trade legislation, were probed on constituent-congressional relationships. Interviewees presumed to be deeply motivated on the matter (both pro and con reciprocal trade) were selected.

Nevertheless, in every community that we studied foreign-trade policy was less important than one or more other issues. For some individuals, it might have been vital, but it was never so for the community as a whole. This is, in part, why we found so little horizontal communication. The handful of men who were deeply concerned would have found it difficult to arouse a similar degree of interest among others.[28]

In consequence, whether the authors were studying communities or Congress itself, they were

impressed with the latitude which congressmen have in representing their districts. A congressman must respond in what appears to be a serious and constructive way to the problems of his constituents, but he is free to be a leader instead of led in deciding what response is appropriate to the problem.[29]

The meaning for party government is clear. Study of the relationship between congressmen and constituencies touching one of the most celebrated areas of political controversy suggests that congressmen could function effectively and with reasonable political safety if they were members of centralized, policy-making political parties. They would then be in even stronger position to exercise leadership.

True enough, the authors noted that congressmen sometimes exaggerated the effects of the "relatively few voices, well exercised [which] sometimes created the impression of unified community sentiment. . . ." Congressmen react, "not to actual opinion, but to their image of what opinion could become if not forestalled by action on their part." Congressmen can take care of small and personal or individual grievances and probably the wisest of them do—such things as requests for information, complaints about the lack of response from the bureaucracy, petitions for assistance to someone in the family who was in the armed services or is in need of a passport or some other response from government.[30] The congressman who nourishes his constituency on small grievances can better resist pressures on issues like the tariff. Nevertheless, "the fact remains that men often feel the pressures of supposed public opinion when there are only a few stray voices."

Reforms proposed in chapter 10 would greatly reduce the tendency of congressmen to overestimate local pressures.

The authors remarked that some other issues such as the Saint Lawrence Seaway or urban development might be much more sharply defined geographically and thus might activate communities as communities or congressional districts as congressional districts better than the Reciprocal Trade Agreement legislation did—thus providing clearer examples of powerful district influence on congressional votes. In one such policy area this expectation was not fulfilled.

Agricultural Price Policy

Agricultural price politics has turned on the magic idea of parity that was understood as justice for farmers and was worked out statistically to provide farmers with prices for crops they sold that bore the same happy ratio to prices they paid, both for consumption goods and for inputs for their farming operations, which obtained in the golden age of agriculture, 1910–14. In the 1930s full parity was recognized as requiring prices high enough to cause serious overproduction. The Agricultural Adjustment Act of 1938 therefore provided price supports at 52 to 75 percent of parity, but just before World War II Congress raised supports to 85 percent of parity (90 percent for tobacco) and in the war itself to 90 percent of parity. A wartime statute provided for supports at 90 percent for two calendar years after hostilities had been declared to cease.

In 1947–48 there was much agitation to develop a new farm policy, in recognition of the end of the legal basis for 90 percent supports on 1 January 1949 and the reversion to the 52 to 75 percent supports of the 1938 Act. Everyone agreed that the 1938 level of supports was now too low, but controversy arose over whether to provide a continuation of high price supports or to move toward flexible supports at a different level. The issue crystallized as a partisan one, between Republican flexible price supports at 75 to 90 percent of parity or Democrat supports at 90 percent of parity or higher. Beginning in 1948 Congress annually extended 90 percent supports.

In 1952 when such supports were extended for two additional years, all eight congressmen from Iowa, all Republicans, were present; and all voted for 90 percent supports, incidentally in the face of opposition from the Iowa Farm Bureau with 125,000 members. Then in 1954, under administration prodding, the policy was changed with a modest movement toward flexible price supports. On the critical roll call, the same eight Iowa congressmen again were present, but now three congressmen voted for the administration's position, namely, flexible price supports. A somewhat similar situation existed in Illinois.

As a result of this pair of votes, 1952 and 1954, it was possible to study the effect on voting for incumbent congressmen in the 1954 and subsequent elections; and the study could be based on precincts that were similar in social and economic characteristics (the same type of farming, approximately the same size of farms, the same tenurial arrangements, the same range of farm incomes) and were separated from each other only by congressional district dividing lines.

It would be difficult to imagine an issue that more clearly enjoined congressmen to vote for what was apparently advantageous to his farming constituents, namely, higher price supports; and surely most farm congressmen so read the situation. Yet Thomas B. Gilpatrick's study of two hundred selected and paired precincts found that "price support policy, although much discussed as an issue, showed no noticeable differential effects in rural voting in Iowa and Illinois" in 1954.

Although Republicans lost ground generally and continued to lose more in 1956, there is little indication that they would have fared worse if all had voted consistently for flexible support policy in 1954. In Iowa, those men favoring a flexible support position stayed about even with their high support colleagues, while in Illinois, those voting for flexible supports made comparatively better showing than their high support colleagues.[31]

Gilpatrick concluded:

What we have said about lobbies already indicates our view of the role of Congress. Congressmen have a great deal more freedom than is ordinarily attributed to them. The complexities of procedure, the chance of obfuscation, the limited attention constituents pay to any one issue, and the presence of countervailing forces all leave the Congressmen relatively free on most issues.[32]

Support from the Survey Research Center

Happily, the findings of the Survey Research Center of the University of Michigan strengthen the case that congressmen are already growing in independence from constituency pressures and would be able to sustain party government with its requirement of stable majorities.

In order to threaten congressmen for flouting their wishes, constituents would have to know in some detail how congressmen vote. In its study of the 1958 congressional campaign, the Survey Research Center got more than 6,000 comments about parties from its sample;[33] less than 12 percent "by the most generous count had to do with contemporary legislative issues."[34] Moreover, in explaining why they had voted as they did in 1958, only 7 percent gave reasons that had anything to do with the behavior of congressmen on current issues (aid to education, farm policy, foreign aid, medical care, labor laws, etc.).

Most striking was how little information the electorate had. Of 1,700 interviewed during the 1958 election (referring only to those who lived in districts where the House seat was contested in 1958), 59 percent said that they had neither read nor heard anything about either candidate for Congress, and less than one in five felt that they knew something about both candidates (the incumbent candidate was by far better known). Even those who "knew something" were extremely general in their comments—"He is a good man, he is experienced, he knows the problems, he has done a good job, and the like." Less than one-thirtieth of what constituents had to say about congressmen comprised references to current legislative issues. Indeed, when asked whether the Democrats or Republicans had controlled Congress in 1956–58, one-third had no idea and an additional fifth gave control to the Republicans. Nor does one know how many of the 47 percent who correctly named the Democrats were guessing.

The relationship between congressmen and ordinary citizens is attenuated further by population growth and shifts. The Survey Research Center describes a range of congressional districts from those in which voters share virtually no sense of community (great metropolitan areas) to districts that comprise a natural community consisting of a single medium-sized city and its environs. In between are districts that comprise a great number of small communities as well as surrounding open country.

"In all but the metropolitan districts the salience of the candidate for the voter differs markedly according to whether candidate and voter live in the same community." As expected, many more persons were aware of candidates living in the same community as the voter than of candidates living in other communities.[35]

The striking fact is that even in 1958 over 60 percent of the incumbent candidates lived in *other* communities than voters; and, as urbanization increases and populations grow, this percentage will rise. The trend is toward a more impersonal relationship between voter and congressman. Once more the argument for party government is supported on psychological grounds. For most voters the chance to make a government (or an opposition) by voting for governing parties will provide more comprehensible links to government than the present ones, which continue to weaken anyway. The Survey Research Center's findings thus underscore the workability of party government.[36]

Tendencies Toward Crystallization of Party Differences

The force of the argument based on "issues with a disparate local impact" is further decreased by the evidence that voters perceive more differences between parties than formerly. This is the basis of the earlier assertion that attitudes favorable to party government may be latent and ready to crystallize under favorable circumstances. As recently as 1950, the American electorate was perhaps less ready for party government because it failed to perceive a difference between the parties. Gerald M. Pomper's argument, which supports the need for party government and the growing possibility that, if achievable, it would be viable, relies heavily on the rise in perception of differences between the parties. By 1968, a majority of the electorate had come to agree that the parties differed and that the Democratic party was more liberal on six important issues—aid to education, medical care, job guarantees, fair employment, school integration, and foreign aid. Moreover, intraparty agreement on issues was growing at the same time that differences between the Republicans and Democrats were more sharply perceived. The electorate seemed to be dividing into two major groups that would presumably help support party government.[37]

Theodore J. Lowi provides a contrary analysis—but one that I can answer.[38] In support of his argument that the nature of the American social system prevents the emergence of parties with both a constituent and a policy-making function, Lowi relied chiefly on evidence from opinion polls purporting to show that the electorate divides on many issues in ways that do not coincide with party divisions. When he added enough issues together, however, Lowi found that *internal* party differences became minimal while differences *between* the parties sharply increased.[39] When enough issues are added, responsible parties by Lowi's definition could operate in Congress as well as the present irresponsible parties. If the voters are given the luxury of separate choice on each issue, of course, they may fragmentize so that any effective and cohesive government becomes impossible. But, as I shall now suggest, the tendency of campaigns is to concentrate attention on one or two major issues.

Concentration of Campaign Issues

Richard J. Scammon and Ben J. Wattenberg forcefully argue that campaigns reduce issues to one or two, especially the "Economic Issue" and the "Social Issue."[40] On the Social Issue, the views of "middle Americans" are of great importance. The average voter, forty-seven years old, a white Protestant with a middle income and a high-school education who works with his hands, is for law and order; against crime, violence, and dissent (especially campus dissent); suspicious of blacks who, he thinks, have tried to get too much too quickly; and wants to wipe out dope and smut. In short, he is of one mind on the bundle that makes up the Social Issue. He is in the center, and politicians of both parties had better heed him. But when they do, they neutralize the Social Issue as a partisan matter; and what remains is largely the Economic Issue—one that promotes class divisions.

This argument, which has been very influential, emphasizes the conditions that make for party government. Great stress is laid on a bifurcation of the electorate, partly because of the concentration on the presidential race in which usually two contestants vie for a single position of power; partly because the remaining emphasis is on mayoralty races. The electorate is alike in its views of presidents and mayors as people in charge of running things. Psychologically, this means that the public knows that governments must govern if there is to be law and order and if serious economic threats are to be met by concerted programs. This interpretation agrees with the view of the electorate's function as essentially making and unmaking governments rather than issuing detailed mandates.

Interest in government tends to concentrate on one or two very general domestic issues. Foreign policy occasionally erupts. Recently ecology has bred its messiahs to whom all politicians confess their conversion (which may be wordily honored and little else) and hence it declines as an *issue*. What remains are the Social Issue, which began to surface in 1964 (Barry Goldwater's speech to the 1964 Republican

convention in San Francisco) and crystallized in 1968, and the im-
mortal Economic Issue, concerned with inflation, taxes, incomes,
Social Security, and employment.

Thus the multiplication of issues "with a disparate local impact"
dissolves into one issue (Economic) or two issues (Social and Economic) or perhaps three (including Foreign Policy). Such issues are
powerful solvents of societal divisions. Acknowledging ethnic, religious, income, status, and occupational differences, Scammon and
Wattenberg write that the Social Issue cuts across *all* classes and
groups. The voter is reduced to choosing which of two contenders will
handle best one or two overriding issues. If true, the case for party
government is further established.

But not quite completely. For the Social Issue has contended with
the Economic Issue in the minds of voters. On the Social Issue in 1968
voters were moved toward Nixon (tough on crime, violence, dissent)
or Wallace (tougher still). On the Economic Issue many of the same
tormented voters tended for reasons of history and party identity to
favor Humphrey. The labor union leaders' accent on wages and employment brought most of their straying members back to Humphrey
and "showed that the old Economic Issue, passionately and effectively
voiced, could blunt much of the appeal of the Social Issue for millions
of working-class Americans."[41] But not all erstwhile Democrats returned, and if Wallace had not run, those who went for him, say
Scammon and Wattenberg, would have divided seven for Nixon to
three for Humphrey.

Even so, politics is reduced largely to two issues and two parties.
And the Social Issue may be neutralized.[42] Politicians of both parties
vie to become its own true champion, which required nice judgment in
achieving the right pitch of stridency and the proper protrusion of the
eyeballs when denouncing evil: Wallace apparently overdid it toward
the end of the 1968 campaign, or perhaps voters wanted to leave him
anyway and gave as their reason that he was "too extreme." What remained was that the Economic Issue "ever potent . . . always holds a
high priority. . . ." This issue is "perennial. . . ." If times get hard
enough, obviously so if a depression occurs or even a lasting and major
recession, the Economic Issue "could wipe out the Social Issue as a
major issue."[43]

And so parties move to the center but they have to move on issues in a world in which the "most common and durable source of faction" is still "the various and unequal division of property"—in short, the Economic Issue. As much as politicians of either party might like to, they cannot depend on the Social Issue alone: if the other party succeeds in staying with them in the center ring on *that* issue and has the more appealing sirens on the Economic Issue, it will win. "The Grand Old Party must also move on the bread and butter issues."

Concentration of Issues—Or Is It Inclusion?

A further refinement may be necessary. The Economic Issue may not be one but many. David R. Mayhew calls the Democrats the party of "inclusive compromise" that gives enough favors to enough groups to ensure election. Founded on the proposition "that each segment of the party relied on and deserved the support of the other segments," the Democratic party, say its protagonists, develops programs that thus accumulate into the national interest.[44] In his study of roll-call votes from 1947 to 1962, Mayhew dwelt especially on the representation of interests associated with farmers, workers, the cities, and the West. Most congressmen came from districts classifiable in one of these, except for a few Republican congressmen from small towns in the North and East. A sharp difference emerged between the two parties. Whereas the Democrats (with some qualifications)[45] were inclined to support each others' interests (especially Democratic northern city congressmen supporting farm and western interests), Republican congressmen not directly interested tended to represent taxpayers and to eschew the claims of inclusive politics or Santa Clausmanship.

It was not always so. In the Republican heyday before 1930, the GOP was the party of "inclusive" compromise, finding "a little plum for everyone" in the form of a protective tariff. The difference was that the burden of payment was placed on consumers instead of taxpayers. But the Democrats of that era were saddled with belief in the principles of free trade, and they "were in the role of naysayers."[46]

The emergent picture is somber. The Republican formula for inclusiveness in the 1920s perpetrated the tariff monstrosities culminating in Smoot-Hawley that helped precipitate and deepen the worldwide Depression that caused untold human misery and helped to loose powerful political forces in the world, some of them exceedingly vicious. In more recent years the dominant Democrats have been dedicated to lavish spending without sufficient regard for the worth of the objectives or the distortions in priorities that have resulted.[47]

What are the implications for the argument on the feasibility of party government? Nothing in Mayhew's analysis suggests that party government is impossible. The question is whether party government will equip the polity better to cope with some of the excesses of "inclusive" politics. It should be clear by the analysis of bureaucracy that we have succumbed to rhythms of public spending often with unfortunate results. Our political system can be faulted for making economic policy by the simple addition of enough subventions to enough interests to win elections. In fiscal and monetary policy, moreover, the separation of powers provides governmental institutions that have frequently lacked the integrative genius required by modern conditions.[48] In short, we need to take a hard look at the prevailing theory that political parties perform their function adequately as long as they aggregate interests—without asking ourselves how they do it. On this highly significant issue. I suggest that party government should do better.

Conclusion

Once the South becomes reasonably competitive between the two major parties, the social, economic, and psychological conditions should support party government. Evidence for this conclusion required, first, an examination of the shortcomings of the mandate theory and a proposal to exchange it for a theory that the function of the election is to create a government that can govern and an opposition that can oppose. Second, the inability of the heterogeneous American polity to produce stable majorities was examined and found wanting. Except for race, the evidence suggests that the multitude of "issues with a disparate local impact" tend to disappear or to be reduced to a very few that are manageable within the framework of party government's requirement of stable majorities.

No doubt most of those who believe party government in the United States would be unable to work even if we can get it will still leave the argument by the same door that they entered (although I hope to have shaken the compasses of some of them). As for the rest, I trust my argument will satisfy the criterion of the college student of geometry who, as Arthur Darby Nock related, was asked after an examination if he had proved his props. "Proved!" he exclaimed, "Proved? I don't know. But I think that I rendered them extremely plausible."

10 Reform

For there are two main obstacles to the knowledge of things,
Modesty that casts a mist before the understanding, and
Fear that, having fanci'd a danger, disswades us from the
attempt. But Folly sufficiently frees us, and few there are that
rightly understand of what great advantage it is to blush at
nothing and attempt everything.—Erasmus, *In Praise of Folly*

The Intention

I am less sure of the proposals for reform than I am of the previous
analysis. To make basic criticisms of present institutions implies a conception of a better alternative, one that I have called presidential
leadership and party government. The change will require major
surgery. One cannot stop short of bold and decisive departures. And
yet a guiding principle should be to write the new Constitution in a
way that permits considerable leeway. The ideal is to create conditions
so that the conduct of government itself will be ruled largely by conventions rather than by fixed laws. It will be better to let the precise
means of replacing presidents or leaders of the opposition develop by
convention than to stipulate them in advance; the same is true for the
means of enforcing party discipline and even for the use, devoutly to be
wished, of dissolution as the sovereign means by which governments
end and new governments are created. The principle of constitutional
discretion is not altogether new with us; the present Constitution contains nothing that establishes political parties, congressional committees, the rule of seniority in Congress, or senatorial courtesy.

The proposals lie within the premises of constitutional democracy.
"Constitutional" means "limited." With us the limits notably include
those protections to citizens incorporated in the Bill of Rights as interpreted by the Supreme Court. Far from disturbing these limits, the
proposed change should strengthen them, partly because the new Constitution should create a political system with a greater capability of
providing political answers to political questions, thus diminishing
the tendency to pull the Supreme Court into the "political thicket."
Other limits include the way that governments are established, em-

powered, checked, and changed. Provisions of the present Constitution bearing on these matters would be amended but always in ways that will retain and strengthen the principle of limited government.

"Democracy" means that the people at large have a strong voice in their own governance, realized with us in the rights of petition and of the ballot. Proposals should strengthen and improve the electoral function by clarifying to voters their indispensable roles in the creation of governments and oppositions. In addition, our constitutional democracy, I assume, contains a "constituent group" of persons who not only revere the Constitution but who study it, know a good deal about how it works, understand its fundamental values, and are determined to preserve its principles.[1] The fact that one cannot denote the size of this group or precisely identify its membership does not diminish its importance. This book hopes to help convince members of the constituent group that fundamental constitutional change is necessary, is within the spirit of the Constitution, and will work.[2] One must assume that membership in the constituent group implies an enlightened distinction between the principles of constitutional democracy and any particular set of rules designed to achieve it. The experience of the other most populous constitutional democracies is in point. France has radically changed her Constitution since 1958. Germany and Japan became constitutional democracies after World War II. India was born as a constitutional democracy. Even Great Britain executed a major constitutional change between 1860 and 1890 and followed it up by drastically reducing the powers of the House of Lords in 1911 and 1949.[3] Only the United States persists with constitutional forms essentially as they were devised nearly two hundred years ago.

Proposals for Reform

1. Presidents, senators, and congressmen should all be elected on the same date for four-year terms. The date would be fixed at four years from the inauguration of the last government but with the provision that the government, by law, could change the date and call an election.

2. The House of Representatives (hereafter, the House) should be elected from single-member districts as now but should be supplemented by approximately one hundred fifty members elected at large. Each party should nominate one hundred candidates. The party winning the presidency should elect the entire slate. The losing party

should elect a maximum of fifty at-large candidates, diminished by whatever number is required to give the winning party a majority of five in the House. At-large candidates would be nominated by committees of forty-one in each party, composed, for the incumbent president's party, of the president, the ten ranking members of his cabinet (rank being determined by the party), and thirty congressmen nominated by the House members of the president's party who are not in the cabinet and who are elected from single-member districts. The opposition party's nominating committee for at-large House members should be composed in the same way, substituting the leader of the opposition for the president and the ten ranking members of the shadow cabinet for the cabinet members. Methods of nominating single-district House candidates should not be stipulated except for the proviso that the same committee that nominates at-large candidates should have the right to reject local nominees on the ground that they have refused to accept party discipline.

3. Presidential candidates should be nominated by committees of the parties composed of all House members from single-member districts as well as all candidates for election in such districts. In the event of presidential disability, either physical or political, the nominating committee of his party should be empowered to suspend him temporarily or to discharge him, but in either event it should be required to replace him. The office of vice-president should be abolished.

4. The Senate should be deprived of its power to approve treaties and presidential nominations. Bills would continue to be examined in the Senate but if the Senate rejects a bill that has passed the House twice in the same form, sixty days having elapsed between the first and second passage, the bill would go to the president.

5. The president's veto would be retained but could be overridden by an adverse majority vote in the House; the Senate could force the House to reconsider but could be overridden by the House after sixty days.

6. That part of Article I, Section 6, Clause 2 of the Constitution that prevents members of Congress from serving in other offices of the United States should be repealed, but the proscription should be retained on the federal judiciary.

7. The runner-up in the election of the president should be designated leader of the opposition and provided a seat in the House with privileged membership on all committees and privileged access to the

floor. The opposition leader should have an official residence, adequate offices, and funds for staff, for travel and transportation, and for other expenses essential to the vigorous operation of his office. Like the president, the leader of the opposition would be removable by the presidential nominating committee of his party, with the power of removal matched by the obligation to replace.

8. Presidential elections should be by national ticket with the winning party identified by securing a national plurality of voters.

9. All parts of the present Constitution in conflict with the foregoing proposals should be repealed or modified to conform to them. The Twenty-second Amendment should also be repealed.

Discussion of Proposals

Coterminous elections of president and Congress would go far to strengthen the voters' feelings, now systematically diminished by the separation of powers and the methods of nominating and electing federal officials, that they are sharing in the creation of the government and the opposition. The voters should thereby have a sense of participation in the awesome and necessary task of governing the nation. Voters would be linked to the government or to the opposition by bonds of partisan feeling.[4] Enabling the national parties to veto the nominations of persistent mavericks in Congress would both strengthen parties and also educate the voters to the governing function of parties—that the winning party is elected to govern and the individual congressman is supposed to share in concerting policies necessary to govern rather than to make a career of independence.[5]

The electoral system should both empower the president and subject him to new controls. He would be empowered by winning a national election with an assured congressional majority whose members would have strong incentives to support the administration's position. At one stroke, this move would revolutionize the organization of Congress. Seniority and senatorial courtesy would disappear. The "whirlpools" in which bureaucrats and strategically located congressmen develop virtual autonomy in various agencies would be overridden by the steady flow of political power within the governing party. But if all these developments increased presidential influence, there would also be new controls. Control of the president should derive from the fact that he would now be the choice of a majority rather than of "the people"; he and the country would be continually reminded of that fact by the presence of an opposition headed by a leader who commands resources second only to the president's to publicize his party's position and to dramatize his leadership. Moreover, while the president would continue to enjoy preeminence, he should now be viewed as the leader of a team in which the necessarily collegial approach demanded of governments by modern conditions is orchestrated. The team would be largely composed of politicians like himself who retain their congressional offices but are no longer prevented from sharing in the government; many of them would exhibit their ambition to succeed the president someday, and this should also teach the public that the president is the first person in a government rather than a lone leader of nearly imperial dimensions.

In addition to strengthening the government against the bureaucracy, the changes would increase its ability to resist private pressures for the following reasons. First, House members would know that they were elected for four-year terms coterminous with the president, that their own electoral fate and that of their presidential candidate (who must win if their party is to control the government) will commonly be closely tied to the electorate's appraisal of the performance of the parties as wholes. Second, the electoral turnout will be uniformly high —the midterm drop of 20 to 30 percent in the total vote for congressmen would disappear[6]—and this fact will decrease the leverage organized interests have on candidates by threatening to punish them at the polls when the vote is light; such interests would be submerged in the tide of voters who, less specifically informed about candidates, are more inclined to vote their approval or disapproval of the government. Third, knowing that their use of the party label will be denied if they persistently oppose the party's legislative policies, House candidates will perceive their political survival and political future to be bound up much more with the success of the national party than (as now) with their own ability to build a local political organization and to nurse local interests. Fourth, the new rules should diminish the expenditures in campaigns by cancelling off-year elections and later on, it is hoped, by leading to a substitution of elections following dissolutions for fixed calendar elections. In addition to strengthening the national orientation of voters and putting more muscle in the national parties, this last step would greatly shorten campaigns and thereby slash campaign expenditures.

Party government and short electoral campaigns will enable us to smother the viper of corruption that threatens to poison this country. In the United States it has well been said "elective offices can be purchased; . . . votes of Federal, state and local officials are bought and sold every day; . . . access of the people to their government is blocked by a Chinese Wall of money."[7] There was a time when similar corruption flourished in Britain. But it came to an end. "Thus, Old Corruption was cleaned up by a combination of methods. . . . Above all, a highly organized party which claims for its leading members the responsibility of Government has to proclaim all the political virtues and dare not practice secret vices."[8]

The addition of at-large House members has been suggested by others in order to increase the national point of view of Congress.[9] I propose to manipulate the device to ensure that we will have party government.[10] In this way the party capturing the presidency will also control Congress. Under the suggested formula, the Republicans would have been allotted one hundred congressmen-at-large in 1968 and the Democrats forty-three; the Republicans would then have had two hundred ninety congressmen and the Democrats two hundred eighty-five. In 1972, the Republicans would have been allotted one hundred congressmen-at-large and the Democrats forty-five; the Republicans would then have had two hundred ninety-two congressmen and the Democrats two hundred eighty-seven.

Under this proposal, voters would know that they are electing a government and an opposition. Let me admit at once that the election would be rigged to produce a majority government even though some voters seem to prefer, or at least to be indifferent to, divided government. But let me also insist that elections are now rigged to produce divided governments. It is true that ticket-splitting voters, measured by the number of congressional seats with split electoral results, has doubled since the 1930s.[11] But it is also true that the overwhelming majority of the electorate still vote for candidates for the presidency and for Congress who bear the same party label. In 1956, an exceptionally high year for ticket splitting, 79 percent of the voters preferred presidential and congressional candidates of the same party.[12] The facts are that divided governments are foisted on the public by a minority of not more than 20 to 25 percent of the voters.

More controversial will be the proposal to reduce the power of the Senate that has many admirers among scholars and perhaps has increased its public support by the Watergate investigation of 1973. The chief reason for the change is, once more, to create conditions favorable to party government. In this way there will be one prime forum for debating public policy, for seating the opposition, and for registering the confidence reposed in government by the national legislature (and, through the legislature, by the public). It is extremely difficult to have two theaters for testing the viability of government as the moves of both Britain and France to reduce the power of their second chambers show. It compounds confusion if the government has to fight for its program in two chambers with entirely different power bases. More important, it disturbs and perhaps destroys that perception of government that the voter must have in order to develop a sense that he is sharing, through his party, in running the country. It might also be pointed out in an age that places great emphasis on the principle of one person, one vote, that the Senate becomes increasingly anomalous. In 1790 half the states with the smallest populations (dividing South Carolina, the middle state) had 22 percent of the total population of the United States; in 1970, the smallest half of the states had only 15 percent of the total.[13]

What would happen to the many able senators? They would move into the reconstituted House. Political talent gravitates toward power. In the House, under the new rules, they could aspire to be members of the cabinet or of the shadow cabinet; their honorable ambitions to be president would find a natural outlet in the House. There, too, they would gain not only the legislative experience but also the administrative experience demanded by modern government.[14]

Election of the president—and of congressmen-at-large—in a national constituency would end the special leverage now enjoyed by more populous states by virtue of the unit rule that gives the entire electoral vote of each state to the party with a plurality of the presidential vote. The past justification of this leverage as needed to countervail the rural–small town advantage vested in Congress is losing credibility because of changes in the economy and would be demolished by the new government with its congressmen-at-large and its emphasis on disciplined parties. The extraordinary influence now vested in racial, ethnic, economic, or regional blocs by their strength in critical states would disappear or be transferred in a diminished form to the national arena. In view of the vast electoral turnout that the new scheme would ensure, such leverage would be much more difficult to organize into plausible threats. Moreover, efforts to identify a national voting bloc and to use its powers to pressure candidates or parties would have to be heavily advertised. Inevitably, this would court counterattacks. At the same time, the new scheme would give every voter everywhere a sense of equal significance in the vital act of creating a government.[15]

What chance would third parties have under the proposed Constitution? Not much. But then they have had little chance under the present Constitution as is indicated by the fact that the average total vote for all minority candidates from 1828 through 1964 was only 5.2 percent of the total popular vote.[16] The present electoral college invites a minority candidate with sectional strength but a small fraction of the total vote to try to throw the election of the president into the House of Representatives where he can blackmail the winner. This situation, which is widely considered to be a flaw in the present Constitution, would not occur under the proposed document. If a third party candidate should poll a significant number of votes, only the runner-up for the presidency would have the congressional seat, the title of leader of the opposition, and the accouterments of office. History has raised the question only once since the Civil War—in 1912 Theodore Roosevelt would have been declared the leader of the opposition rather than William Howard Taft.

A Theory of Representation and the Division of Political Labor

The proposals for reform arise from the seriousness of the great political issues raised in earlier chapters. Their adoption should strengthen the president's hand in important respects while significantly controlling his initiative, the autonomy of the bureaucracy, the forces inimical to coherent policy, and the thrust of private group pressures. Moreover, the reforms should make for better theory and practice respecting public opinion, representation, and the division of political labor. The travail of public opinion would be reduced by relieving the public of the impossible demands now placed upon it, by providing an essential and practicable political role for the public, and by greatly diminishing the frustration of the public produced by the studied confusion of the present governmental system. The pressures to eliminate corruption stemming from party government should reassure the public. At the same time, a theory of representation should emerge that should provide a satisfactory answer to the question, How is the community as a whole to be represented?[17] Rather than fixing responsibility on the president alone and then flagrantly fragmentizing it among the public at large, the new Constitution will charge governing parties with finding conditional and contingent solutions to the pressing social and economic problems of the modern polity.

Underlying the discussion of the role of public opinion and of the theory of representation to which it leads is the question of the division of political labor. Generalizing from English experience, Ernest Barker wrote that "government by discussion proceeds through four main stages—first of party, next of the electorate, then of parliament, and finally of cabinet." On the relationship between electorate and party, he noted the difficulties of reconciling the electorate's freedom of choice of individuals with its selection of a governing party as well as the inherent ambivalence in the exercise of free discretion by the same act that also delegates discretion. But he was clear that delegation was necessary.

Just as, in the act of selection, or, as it may also be termed, the moment of "taking over" from the party, the electorate has at once to follow the guidance of the party and to exercise its own judgment, so in the act of instruction, or the moment of "handing over" to the parliament, the electorate has both to guide parliament and to vest it with its own deliberative discretion. . . . But, in a more particular sense, the electorate does not give detailed instructions or specific mandates. It creates a legislature; but it does not dictate legislation or participate in legislation. It elects a body for the purpose of doing something beyond what it does itself, and something different from what it can do itself.[18]

Discussion of radical political reforms seems to be dictated by the awesome shortcomings of present institutions. By the same token efforts to find correctives force the argument into fundamental questions of political theory concerning the nature of man, of society, and of government. Much debate should center on these questions—and it should do so with considerable urgency not only for reasons already delineated but for others as well, especially the growing vulnerability of present institutions to crises.

Crises

Until very recently much optimism was voiced about the ability of the American system to cope with crises. Herbert Agar wrote that in a country so large and heterogeneous as the United States, "most politics will be parochial, most politicians will have small horizons. . . . For the most part the members of the Senate and House must represent their own states and districts." But when "good times" fail and "the bombs fall or the banks close or the breadlines grow by the millions," the country "must recapture the distributed sovereignty and act like a strong and centralized nation."[19]

The government can meet crises, Agar insisted, because the president, the one man elected at large by voters, becomes "the voice of the people." And he quoted Pendleton Herring: "Our system can respond quickly to emergency conditions once the public is convinced of the need. Presidential leadership sustained by a united people has power for any crisis."

As long as crises were occasional and episodic, the formula seemed to work, although even then it was subject to the charge that it rested on a reification of public opinion and a continuation of good luck on which the country cannot safely rely.[20]

More recently, Richard E. Neustadt has given a contrary appraisal of the ability of the system to cope with crises. In the great Depression of the 1930s and World War II, crises united the country. But the Korean war failed to bring consensus and in the late 1950s the cold war became a way of life. However dangerous the events, the people no longer felt them as crises. Indeed, our politics had fundamentally changed.

The weakening of party ties, the emphasis on personality, the close approach of world events, the changeability of public moods, and above all the ticket-splitting, none of this was "usual" before the Second World War.

In consequence, Neustadt thought that "crisis consensus" would probably be unattainable by future presidents.

We may have priced ourselves out of the market for [productive] crises on the pattern Roosevelt knew—productive in the sense of strengthening his chances for sustained support *within* the system.

Judging from the fifties, neither limited war nor limited depression is productive in these terms. Anything unlimited will probably break the system.[21]

If crises threaten to break the system, all the more reason to consider fundamental reform. In certain specific ways party government will help the country cope with crises. For one thing it will organize and orient public opinion so that a degree of unity can be obtained. The same ability that enables the opposition to mount a concerted criticism of government also empowers it to collect the political forces of the country behind a unified leadership, if this is necessary. Moreover, party government will help the country to cope with crises by permitting the replacement of a leader who has become politically disabled and also by providing a means of escaping from the tyranny of fixed calendar elections. Both points need some elaboration.

Presidential Disability and Presidential Removal

Concern about presidential disability flagged between Woodrow Wilson's collapse in 1919 and Dwight D. Eisenhower's heart attack of 1955 followed by an operation for ileitis in 1956 and a stroke in 1957. Ensued the Twenty-fifth Amendment (1967) that attempts to provide for the removal of presidents unable to discharge their duties.[22] Untested, the amendment might work if the president is physically disabled. But what if a president becomes *politically* disabled? When the nation is in great peril a healthy president might lose his will to act, his grasp of events, or his nerve. He might panic in times of grave civil disorders or external threats. Or he might become obsessed with the use of force as an answer to problems or simply too reckless in the use of force—or he might be too permissive, letting events ride until they are beyond whatever control was initially possible.

The proposal that the president's congressional party should be able to replace him would take care of this difficulty. Its wisdom is justified by recent British history. In 1940 Winston Churchill replaced Neville Chamberlain as prime minister and then summoned the British to an effort of incalculable benefit to the western world. Similarly, Lloyd George replaced Herbert Asquith as prime minister during World War I. Admiration for Lloyd George was less unanimous than for Churchill, yet British historians generally agree that the substitution was needed in 1917. In 1956 when the British-French-Israeli attack on Egypt failed, Prime Minister Anthony Eden, who was somewhat discredited politically by the event (and whose health also suffered), could give way to Harold Macmillan.

Much flexibility exists in a government by political parties that, in addition to their mass bases and their national organizations, have corps of leaders so trained and tempered in the art of government that they come to accept not only the duty to choose and follow a leader but also the obligation to replace him if he fails. The risk that ambitious men will readily conspire to replace their chief is nullified by the rarity of the examples. A prime minister in Great Britain or a president in America is the most valuable political property of his party. To remove him his associates have to risk their own careers. No one has expressed the proposition more succinctly than Winston Churchill:

The loyalties which center on number one are enormous. If he trips he must be sustained. If he makes mistakes they must be covered. If he sleeps he must not be wantonly disturbed. If he is no good he must be pole-axed.[23]

Calendar Elections

Party government would help the country cope with crises by enabling not only the removal of politically inadequate leaders but also the substitution of flexible election dates for those fixed by the calendar. When the country is fighting for its life the extra danger of a quadrennial election may be extreme. Since 1812 we have held only two presidential elections during major wars. Clearly, we can no longer count on such good fortune. The new danger inherent in calendar elections is compounded also by "the close approach of world events." The great powers will henceforth be mutually capable of mounting devastating strikes on a moment's notice. The same is true of smaller harassments. The present determination of electoral dates by the inevitable wheel of alternate Octobers, with months given over to campaigns and interregnums, contains a threat to national survival. The risk is compounded by the Twenty-second Amendment.

Party government permits an alternative. Elections within reasonable intervals can be required by the Constitution with their timing left to statute law that means, subject to certain safeguards, to the discretion of the governing party. Potential enemies would then be deprived of much of their advantage, first, because they would no longer be able to plan harassments according to the calendar and, second, because the periods of vulnerability in campaigns would be telescoped from interminable months to a few weeks.[24]

Conclusion

On behalf of what universal idea are the Italians in Rome? asked Theodor Mommsen.[25] If a similarly malicious question were applied to the United States, every American could answer that he inherits the universal idea of constitutional democracy. As noted earlier, the words are inseparable. Limited government came to us largely from England, although we have shaped its content. According to C. H. McIlwain, England became national while it was still feudal so that the limits of the feudal contract were wrought into the frame of government.[26] We escaped the feudal heritage, but happily we persisted in maintaining the constitutional ideal. Democracy or rule by numbers is likewise ancient, but America has given it a peculiar stamp with the emphasis on equality. If some of the sources are also English—"the poorest he that is in England hath a life to live as the richest he"[27]—the equalizing spirit took charge in America as it never has in England. Constitutionalism remains the most valuable secular development of mankind. Egalitarianism is the most explosive idea in the world today.[28]

How Americans will bear their precious burden of ideas will depend on how well they learn to live with the tensions between the limits imposed especially in the Bill of Rights and the drives implicit in popular government. Only part of the answer is provided by majority rule.

The justification of majority rule in politics is not to be found in its ethical superiority. It is to be found in the sheer necessity of finding a place in civilized society for the force which resides in the weight of numbers.[29]

With us, the force of numbers is not ultimate. Our nation cannot wipe out the absolute proscription against using torture to extract confessions and still remain a constitutional democracy. If torture is used in our democratic constitutional government (as it has been and may be again), it is illegitimate, an aberration; whereas in practice under authoritarian regimes of either wing—and in theory under democracy defined as simply a means of making decisions of whatever scope—torture is a perfectly proper way of obtaining information or enforcing commands.

The force of numbers is also limited by recognizing that most questions decided by majorities are settled only conditionally. That thought may be small comfort to the losers; but it is vital to the health of the polity because it recognizes the contingent and tentative character of policies that must, nevertheless, be formulated and applied to pressing social and economic problems. This is part of the rationale underlying the case for party government with its emphasis as much on the opposition as on the administration.

These points answer the argument that there is no alternative between absolute majority rule and minority rights,[30] an example of the fallacy of either/or. Our constitutional democracy requires both. The marriage between popular government and the Bill of Rights recognizes that the only way to prevent the human condition from degenerating into bestiality is to force men to live with many of their natural divergencies and contradictions. Nevertheless, Austin Ranney has written that

responsible and disciplined parties will appeal only to a people committed to the desirability of unlimited majority-rule, and . . . the American people, far from believing in majority-rule, are devoted to the preservation of minority *rights* against majority rule.[31]

The first clause can be dismissed as an effort to stack the deck. But what of the second, namely, that Americans have rejected majority rule (which is equated with party government) in favor of minority rights? This is a curious statement. Millions of Americans have lived with equanimity in situations where local majorities oppressed local racial or ethnic minorities. We accept without qualms the majority principle in deciding state, national, and local elections as well as in voting in our legislative bodies, in judicial panels, and in referenda. But we have also preserved minority rights, even though they have not always been equally accessible to all minorities; and we have done so with institutions that make "due process of law" a meaningful phase. It cannot be asserted too dogmatically that the union of the majority principle and minority rights is the essence of our civil experience. A tango without both partners would, indeed, be the last.

What kind of government will Americans want a generation from now? In 1969 nearly 71 million Americans were less than eighteen years old. By 1987—the two hundredth anniversary of the Constitution—those who survive will all have reached voting age, swelling the potential electorate by perhaps 67 million or some 40 percent of the total. Let us assume that Thoughtful Americans point now toward a fundamental decision about the framework of their government fifteen or twenty years hence. If so, the decision should then be founded on reasoned analyses of the polity—not only as it is now but as it might be. The most obvious place to make the analyses is in the colleges and universities. In 1930 out of 22.5 million Americans between the ages of fifteen and twenty-four only 1.1 million were enrolled in colleges and universities. Of 24.5 million in the same age bracket in 1966, those enrolled had risen to 5.5 million. By 1987 a sizable fraction of the eighteen to thirty-six cohort will have had university experience. It is from sources such as these that great amounts of new blood should be pumped into the constituent group.

But what will Americans have learned a generation from now about their political system? Americans are said to have fully considered and rejected the case for party government, for example, because Woodrow Wilson's *Congressional Government* had gone through twenty-five printings by 1925.[32] On the contrary. Precious few have heard or read Wilson's arguments. If they study political science beyond the level of civics courses, they learn from "teaching books."

In 1964 the teaching books in American government fail in at least three of the same ways the teaching books of thirty and more years ago failed. They continue to fail as efforts to "make good citizens," because handbooks are not guides and guides are not inspiration. They continue to fail as books of ideology or indoctrination or pure and simple debate, because they go to such lengths to avoid a point of view. . . . But most important, there is no trend away from the failure to encourage political inquiry and understanding.[33]

This book does not pretend to be a text, but it has a point of view and does aim to encourage political inquiry and understanding. Let the debate proceed!

"Gentlemen," said the aging Edmund Burke, "what shadows we are, what shadows we pursue." One remembers Tolstoy's characterization of Czar Alexander's adviser, Speransky, who never considered that all he thought and all he believed might be meaningless nonsense. The enormousness, perhaps the enormity, of this undertaking has never been far from my mind. And yet there is a compelling need for architectonic analysis. All of us feel the thrust of powerful drives of individualism, of group or tribal interest, of egalitarianism, of collectivism, and even of racism. Excepting racism, each has its virtues; but, following Aristotle, each has its perversions. Individualism can become solipsistic and verge into anarchy and violence; "that timid, staring creature, man" may have a bomb in either hand. Group appetite can become "an universal wolf." Equality can breed a deadening uniformity. Collectivism can degenerate into a totalitarian state. The task of politics and government is to contain, moderate, and sublimate these drives. Political theory must illuminate the art of government, and political science must guide its application to particular polities, each largely *sui generis*. Perhaps above all the need is for a revision of ancient political myths to inspire the belief that a new world is possible and that it will come—something that goes beyond *vox populi, vox dei* to express and ennoble the dilemmas of the human condition and yet to reconcile them with a call to action. If a poet exists who is not up to his eyeballs in self-pity, this may be his hour.

Notes

Introduction

1. V. O. Key, Jr., *The Responsible Electorate* (Cambridge, Mass.: Harvard University Press, 1966).

2. Ibid., p. 30.

1. The Constitutional Potential of Party Government

1. "The National Commitments Resolution," 91st Cong., 1st sess., Calendar No. 118, report No. 91–129 (to accompany S. Res. 85) 16 April 1969. Text of Secretary of State William P. Rogers on "Authority for Bombing in Cambodia," *New York Times,* 1 May 1973. (Qualified somewhat by the War Powers Act of 1973.)

2. See the exchange between Senator Sam Ervin, Jr., and John J. Wilson in the Watergate *Hearings,* 25 July 1973.

3. Richard E. Neustadt, *Presidential Power* (New York: Wiley, 1960), especially chap. 3.

4. Alexander Hamilton, *Federalist Papers No. 70.*

5. Quoted in Neustadt, *Presidential Power,* p. 106.

6. These include *Federalist Papers No. 67 to No. 77;* Henry Jones Ford, *The Rise and Growth of American Politics* (New York: Macmillan, 1898); Woodrow Wilson, *Constitutional Government in the United States* (New York: Columbia Univ. Press, 1908); Wilfred E. Binkley, *The President and Congress* (New York: Vintage Books, 1962), first published as *The Powers of the President* (New York: Doubleday, 1937); E. P. Herring, *Presidential Leadership* (New York: Farrar and Rinehart, 1940); Edwin S. Corwin, *The President: Office and Powers* (New York: New York Univ. Press, 1940, 1957); Harold J. Laski, *The American Presidency* (New York: Harpers, 1940); Louis Brownlow, *The President and the Presidency* (Chicago: Public Administration Service, 1949); A. N. Holcombe, *Our More Perfect Union* (Cambridge,

Mass.: Harvard Univ. Press, 1950); James M. Burns, *Presidential Government* (Boston: Houghton Mifflin, 1965); Rexford G. Tugwell, *The Enlargement of the Presidency* (Garden City, N.Y.: Doubleday, 1960); and Louis W. Koenig, *The Chief Executive* (New York: Harcourt, Brace, 1964).

7. Early recognition of the problem appeared in Holcombe, *Our More Perfect Union,* p. 424; *Toward a More Responsible Two-Party System,* Report of the Committee on Political Parties of the Amer. Pol. Sci. Asso. (*APSR,* September 1950, supplement), pp. 14, 93; E. S. Corwin, *The President: Office and Powers,* chap. 7; and Robert Dahl, *Congress and Foreign Policy* (New York: Harcourt, Brace, 1950), chaps. 7 and 8.

8. Warren Miller, University of Michigan's Institute for Social Research, a study reported in Boyce Rensberger, "Study Finds Most Lack Trust in the U. S.," *New York Times,* 5 Nov. 1971.

9. Justice Oliver Wendell Holmes, Jr., quoted in Robert A. Horn, *Groups and the Constitution* (Stanford: Stanford Univ. Press, 1956), pp. 2–3.

10. Gaddis Smith, review of *The Pentagon Papers,* edited by the *New York Times,* by the Beacon Press (Boston); and by the Department of Defense (Washington, D.C.). *New York Times Book Review,* 28 Nov. 1971, p. 30.

11. George E. Reedy, *The Twilight of the Presidency* (New York: New American Library, 1970).

12. W. Ivor Jennings, *The British Constitution* (Cambridge: University Press, 1942), p. 77.

13. Eric Sevareid, "The Final Troubled Hours of Adlai Stevenson," *Look,* 30 Nov. 1965. Compare Richard Walton, "The Last One Hundred Seventy Days of Adlai Stevenson," *Esquire,* Sept. 1968, p. 133.

14. General David M. Shoup, with Colonel James A. Donovan, "The New American Militarism," *Atlantic,* April 1969.

15. Richard E. Neustadt, "Politicians and Bureaucrats," in David B. Truman, ed., *The Congress and America's Future* (Englewood Cliffs, N. J.: Prentice-Hall, for the American Assembly, 1965).

16. "A leading Republican on Foreign Affairs remarked . . . 'There's a Chinese Wall between the two houses. There is more bipartisanship in Congress than there is bicameralism.' " H. Bradford Westerfield, *Foreign Policy and Party Politics* (New Haven: Yale Univ. Press, 1955), p. 123.

17. An early exposition of the inability of public opinion to decide such issues was provided by A. Lawrence Lowell. See Austin Ranney,

The Doctrine of Responsible Party Government (Urbana: Univ. of Ill. Press, 1954), pp. 51–52.

18. Roland Young, *This is Congress* (New York: Knopf, 1943), p. x.

19. Herbert Agar, *The Price of Union* (Boston: Houghton Mifflin, 1950), p. xiv.

20. This analysis draws on Neustadt, *Presidential Power,* chap. 5.

21. *McCulloch* v. *Maryland,* 4 Wheat. 316 (1819).

22. Of the laws of the commonwealth the most important, wrote Rousseau, "was not graven on the tablets of marble or brass, but on the hearts of the citizens. This forms the real Constitution of the State . . ." *The Social Contract,* book II, chap. 12.

23. W. Ivor Jennings, *The British Constitution,* p. 78.

2. On the Difficulty of Arguing with Presidents

1. John P. Roche, special consultant to President Lyndon B. Johnson, ridicules the view of Johnson's "isolation" and his protection by "courtiers" from reality. "The Jigsaw Puzzle of History," *New York Times Magazine,* 24 Jan. 1971.

2. Richard E. Neustadt, *Presidential Power* (New York: Wiley, 1960).

3. James David Barber, *Presidential Character* (Englewood Cliffs, N. J.: Prentice-Hall, 1972).

4. George E. Reedy, *The Twilight of the Presidency* (New York: World, 1970).

5. Neustadt, *Presidential Power* (New York: Wiley, 1960, 1964; Signet ed.), p. 43; E. S. Corwin, *The President: Office and Powers* (New York: New York Univ. Press, 1957), pp. 297–98; Rexford Guy Tugwell, *The Enlargement of the Presidency* (Garden City, N. Y.: Doubleday, 1960), p. 488. Cf. Charles M. Hardin, "Presidential Confrontation," *The Center Diary,* Center for the Study of Democratic Institutions, Santa Barbara, May-June 1966, p. vii.

6. *New York Times,* 8 June 1973.

7. Rexford Guy Tugwell, *The Democratic Roosevelt* (New York: Doubleday, 1957), pp. 97, 192, 308–33.

8. Ibid., pp. 90–91.

9. Raymond Moley, *After Seven Years* (New York: Harper, 1939), p. 55.

10. Ibid., pp. 343, 396–97. Henry Morgenthau interpreted his own relationships with Roosevelt almost identically as Tugwell and Moley did. John Morton Blum, *Roosevelt and Morgenthau* (Boston: Houghton Mifflin, 1970), pp. 200–201.

11.   Samuel I. Rosenman, *Working with Roosevelt* (New York: Harper, 1951), pp. 8–10.

12.   Robert E. Sherwood, *Roosevelt and Hopkins,* (2 vols.; New York: Harper, 1948, 1950; Bantam ed., 1950), 1: 3, 4, 260–61.

13.   Ibid., pp. 361–63.

14.   Frances Perkins, *The Roosevelt I Knew* (New York: Viking, 1946), p. 256.

15.   Harold L. Ickes, *The Secret Diary of Harold L. Ickes* (2 vols.; New York: Simon and Schuster, 1954), 2: 308–9.

16.   Blum, *Roosevelt and Morgenthau,* pp. 199–200.

17.   Richard F. Fenno, Jr., *The President's Cabinet* (Cambridge, Mass.: Harvard Univ. Press, 1959; Random House, Vintage ed.), pp. 238–46.

18.   Henry L. Stimson and McGeorge Bundy, *On Active Service in Peace and War* (New York: Harper, 1947), p. 199.

19.   Ibid., pp. 346, 357, 364–74, 414.

20.   Ibid., pp. 419–32.

21.   Ibid., p. 526.

22.   Harry S. Truman, *Memoirs,* vol. 1, *Year of Decisions* (New York: Doubleday, 1955), pp. 328–330.

23.   Eisenhower, *The White House Years: Mandate for Change* (Garden City, N. Y.: Doubleday, 1963), p. 134.

24.   Rowland Evans, Jr., and Robert D. Novak, *Nixon in the White House* (New York: Random House, 1971; Vintage ed., 1972) p. 11.

25.   After Jefferson until Jackson presidents continued a considerable part of their predecessors' cabinets and counted the votes of heads of departments equally with their own. "In short, the *presidency was in commission.*" Corwin, *The President: Office and Powers,* p. 19.

26.   Theodore C. Sorensen, *Kennedy* (New York: Harper and Row, 1965), pp. 281–84.

27.   Fenno, *The President's Cabinet,* p. 247. Fenno reports only two occasions when policies were seriously discussed in the cabinet with Roosevelt present: November 1937, with the second deep depression of the decade developing, and November 1941, when the break with Japan appeared imminent. Pp. 126–27. Cf. Ickes, *The Secret Diary of Harold L. Ickes,* 2: 278–79 and Blum, *Roosevelt and Morgenthau,* p. 179. See also Tugwell, *The Democratic Roosevelt,* p. 14.

28.   "Organizing for National Security, Inquiry of the Subcommittee on

National Policy Machinery, Committee on Government Operations, U. S. Senate, *Hearings* (1961), 1: 569.

29. John Hersey, "Profiles: Mr. President—II—Ten O'clock Meeting," *New Yorker,* 14 April 1951, p. 40.

30. Patrick Anderson, *The President's Men* (Garden City, N. Y.: Doubleday, Anchor ed., 1969), pp. 136–37. What follows on Clifford is also drawn from Anderson, pp. 134–57, including quotations from Lilienthal and Keyserling.

31. Fenno, *The President's Cabinet,* pp. 111–12, 130, 144–45, 148. See also John Hersey, "Profiles: Mr. President: III—Forty-eight Hours," *New Yorker,* 21 April 1951, pp. 52–53.

32. Harry S. Truman, *Memoirs, Year of Decisions,* 1: 327, 554, 560.

33. Ibid., p. 552. James F. Byrnes, *Speaking Frankly* (New York: Harper, 1947), p. 238, and Byrnes, *All in One Lifetime* (New York: Harper, 1958), pp. 342–45.

34. David E. Lilienthal, *The Journals of David E. Lilienthal,* vol. 2, *The Atomic Energy Years* (New York: Harper and Row, 1964), p. 2; Louis W. Koenig, *The Truman Administration: Its Principles and Practices* (New York: N. Y. Univ. Press, 1956), pp. 21–22.

35. Walter Millis, with the collaboration of E. S. Duffield, ed., *The Forrestal Diaries* (New York: Macmillan, 1951) pp. 280–81, 415–38, 502–40. Further corroboration would be provided by an analysis of the controversies over the military budget of 1949 and 1950. See, for example, p. 430.

36. "The President and the Secretary of State," in Don K. Price, ed., *The Secretary of State* (American Assembly, Columbia University, 1960), pp. 33–37 and passim. See also Dean Acheson, *Present at the Creation* (New York: Norton, 1969), pp. 88, 111, 137.

37. Acheson, *Present at the Creation,* p. 344.

38. Ibid., p. 406.

39. Ibid., p. 437.

40. Ibid., pp. 169–70. From Truman's succession in April 1945 until the State of Israel emerged at midnight, 14 May 1948, the Palestinian question was repeatedly on Truman's mind. Truman, *Memoirs,* vol. 2, *Year of Trial and Hope,* pp. 133–64. Robert Silverberg, *If I Forget Thee, O Jerusalem* (New York: Morrow, 1970) pp. 266–408. Truman was "well aware" that not everyone in the White House agreed with him on the subject on which he also recorded unparalleled outside pressure. Pressure aside, the question is, How many persons faced Harry Truman on the issue and argued with him? Silverberg (pp. 386–88) and Truman (pp. 160–61) record only one, the visit of Eddie Jacobson, Truman's old friend and former partner, who prevailed on him to see Dr. Chaim

Weizmann. Officials might circumvent Truman (Silverberg, pp. 388–91); but no one, including Forrestal, who "almost obsessively discussed Palestine with anyone who would listen . . ." (Silverberg, pp. 345–69), confronted Truman on the issue. Walter Millis, *The Forrestal Diaries,* index under Palestine; note esp. p. 364.

41. "Organizing for National Security," Inquiry of the Subcommittee on National Policy Machinery, Committee on Government Operations, U. S. Senate, *Hearings* (1961), 1: 582.

42. Adolph A. Berle and Malcolm Moos, "The Need to Know and The Right to Tell," *Political Science Quarterly,* June 1964.

43. Krock, *Memoirs,* p. 306.

44. Quoted in Anderson, *The President's Man,* p. 189, and see Anderson, pp. 187–89, for next paragraph.

45. Eisenhower, *The White House Years: Waging Peace* (Garden City, N. Y.: Doubleday, 1963), p. 311.

46. Felix Belair, Jr., "Eisenhower Rebuts 'Nonsense' that He Left Too Much to Staff," *New York Times,* 23 Oct. 1968.

47. *Waging Peace,* p. 246.

48. Fenno, *The President's Cabinet,* Vintage ed.; see pp. 96–97, 103–13, 137–41, 148, for Eisenhower's cabinet.

49. John Emmet Hughes, *The Ordeal of Power* (New York: Dell, 1962), pp. 59, 122.

50. Quoted by Fenno, *The President's Cabinet,* p. 118. Fenno commented that Eisenhower's remark confirmed "the absurdity of taking a vote in . . . Cabinet . . . with each vote counting as one, when the President obviously doesn't look at it that way."

51. Arthur Larson, *Eisenhower: The President Nobody Knew* (New York: Popular Library, 1968), pp. 26–27, 128–32. Neustadt, *Presidential Power,* chap. 7.

52. Felix Belair, Jr., "Eisenhower Rebuts 'Nonsense' . . ." *New York Times,* 23 Oct. 1968.

53. Eisenhower, *Waging Peace,* pp. 362–66. Compare Eleanor Lansing Dulles on the extreme closeness of the two men who complemented each other, despite differences of temperament. *John Foster Dulles: The Last Year* (New York: Harcourt, Brace & World, 1963), p. 29. Andrew H. Berding, *Dulles on Diplomacy* (Princeton, N. J.: Van Nostrand, 1965), chap. 2, "Eisenhower and Dulles—Two of One Mind."

54. Eisenhower, *Waging Peace,* pp. 405–7. Eisenhower did get somewhat exasperated over Dulles's handling of the Suez matter in 1956; but he was critical of Dulles's lack of adroitness rather than his intentions. *Waging Peace,* pp. 33–34.

55. Sherman Adams, *Firsthand Report* (New York: Harper, 1961; Popular Library, 1962), pp. 92–95, and chap. 6.

56. Larson, *Eisenhower: The President Nobody Knew,* p. 72.

57. Hughes, *Ordeal of Power,* p. 91.

58. Eisenhower, *Crusade in Europe,* pp. 475–77.

59. Eisenhower, *Waging Peace.* See, for example, pp. 64–65, 293, 330, 397, 468, 547.

60. Theodore Sorensen, *Decision-Making in the White House* (New York: Columbia Univ. Press, 1963), pp. 55–67.

61. Robert F. Kennedy, "Thirteen Days: The Story About How the World Almost Ended," *McCall's,* Nov. 1968, pp. 170–71.

62. Schlesinger, *A Thousand Days* (Boston: Houghton Mifflin, 1965), pp. 255–56, 258–59.

63. Anderson, *The President's Men,* p. 234.

64. Ibid., p. 320.

65. Ibid., p. 394.

66. Thus the consummately experienced Adolph A. Berle wrote that "a President can get the best from [his staff]—and they can best function—only when the exchange is wholly candid." In Berle's experience, "great decision making usually boils down to a tired Chief of State on one side of the desk and a trusted aide or friend on the other." Adolph A. Berle and Malcolm Moos, "The Need to Know and the Right to Tell," *Political Science Quarterly,* June 1964.

67. For the Taft confrontation, Sherman Adams, *Firsthand Report,* pp. 29–31; Robert J. Donovan, *Eisenhower: The Inside Story,* pp. 112 ff. For the Knowland confrontation, Adams, *Firsthand Report,* pp. 402–3.

68. Ickes, *The Secret Diary of Harold L. Ickes,* 2: 278–79.

69. MacArthur, *Reminiscences* (New York: McGraw-Hill, 1964) pp. 100–101. "Neither the President nor I ever spoke of the meeting," MacArthur continued, "but from that time on he was on our side."

70. *Capitalism, Socialism and Democracy* (New York: Harper, 1942), p. 257.

71. Carl Sandburg, *Abraham Lincoln, The War Years* (4 vols.; New York: Harcourt, Brace, 1939), 1: 365. Mason and Slidell, Confederate emissaries, were en route to England on the British steamship *Trent* when they were seized by the U.S.S. *San Jacinto,* 25 November 1861. The seizure provoked talk of war in England that abated when Seward ordered the men released on a technicality.

3.   Government by Presidential Instinct

1. William P. Gerberding, "Franklin D. Roosevelt's Conception of the Soviet Union in World Politics" (Ph. D. thesis, Department of Political Science, University of Chicago, 1959). References are to pp. 18, 62, 126–30, 152, 170, 210, and 249.

2. Raymond Moley, *After Seven Years* (New York: Harper, 1939), p. 95.

3. Tang Tsou, *America's Failure in China, 1941–1950* (Chicago: Univ. of Chicago Press, 1963). See pp. 38–39, 58–59, 71, 94–95, 123–24.

4. Fox Butterfield, chapter 1, "The Truman and Eisenhower Years," in *The Pentagon Papers* (New York: *New York Times,* 1971), pp. 7–10.

5. Gar Alperovitz, *Atomic Diplomacy: Hiroshima and Potsdam* (New York: Simon and Schuster, 1965), p. 230.

6. Harry S. Truman *Memoirs,* vol. 1, *Year of Decisions* (Garden City, N. Y.: Doubleday, 1955) pp. 14–17, 84–85. Walter Millis, ed., *The Forrestal Diaries* (New York: Macmillan, 1951), pp. 48–51, and Barton W. Bernstein and Allan J. Matusow, *The Truman Administration, A Documentary History* (New York: Harper and Row, 1966), p. 159.

7. Truman, *Memoirs,* vol. 1, *Year of Decisions,* p. 419, and Alperovitz, *Atomic Diplomacy,* pp. 14, 56, 113, 179, 236–37.

8. Bernstein and Matusow, *The Truman Administration,* p. 222; Alperovitz, *Atomic Diplom*acy, pp. 14, 237.

9. Bernstein and Matusow, *The Truman Administration,* pp. 222–32. For partial corroboration of the correctness of Stimson's views in the light of hindsight see Dean Acheson, *Present at the Creation* (New York: Norton, 1969), pp. 123–25, 132.

10. Louis J. Koenig, *The Chief Executive* (New York: Harcourt, Brace, 1964), pp. 350–51.

11. Robert Alan Arthur, "The Wit and Sass of Harry S. Truman," *Esquire,* Aug. 1971.

12. Quoted in William P. Gerberding, "Viet Nam and the Future of United States Foreign Policy," *Virginia Quarterly Review,* Winter 1968, pp. 19–42.

13. George E. Reedy, *The Twilight of the Presidency* (New York: New American Library, 1971), p. 27. Compare Richard Barnet, "The Game of Nations," *Harper's,* Nov. 1971, and his reference to James C. Thomson, Jr., at p. 56.

14. Richard E. Neustadt, *Presidential Power* (New York: Wiley,

1960), pp. 126–27. Much of what follows on Korea is drawn from this source, chap. 6, sect. 3–4.

15. Ibid., p. 145.

16. Acheson, *Present at the Creation,* pp. 466–68. Acheson attacked criticisms by politicians and academicians that the State Department had tried to dominate the military conduct of the war and, on the other hand, that the Chiefs of Staff had tried to dominate its diplomatic course. On the contrary, he wrote, "So insistent was each upon having guidance from the other that it gave rise to some . . . avoidance of responsibilities. . . . Conflict was not unknown, as these pages amply show; but when the going was tough each showed great deference to the other in the assumption of responsibility" (p. 517).

17. Patrick Anderson, *The President's Men* (Garden City, N. Y.: Doubleday, 1969; Anchor ed.) p. 215.

18. Chalmers Roberts, "The Day We Did Not Go to War," *Reporter,* 14 Sept. 1954, pp. 31–35.

19. D. D. Eisenhower, *The White House Years: Waging Peace* (Garden City, N. Y.: Doubleday, 1963) pp. 346–47.

20. D. D. Eisenhower, *The White House Years: Mandate for Change* (Garden City, N. Y.: Doubleday, 1963). See chap. 14. At first, Eisenhower conditioned American action on British support, p. 347; later, it was enough that the British should acquiesce, p. 359, n. 8; and still later—even though Eisenhower declared that "unilateral intervention would have been sheer folly"—he would have gone in if China had given regular air support to the Vietminh, p. 373.

21. Ibid., chap. 19, esp. pp. 464, 476–77.

22. Eisenhower, *Waging Peace,* p. 610.

23. Eisenhower, *Crusade in Europe* (Garden City, N. Y.: Doubleday, 1948), p. 443; cf. *Mandate for Change,* pp. 312–13.

24. Eisenhower, *Waging Peace,* p. 369.

25. Arthur Larson, *Eisenhower: The President Nobody Knew* (New York: Popular Library, 1968), p. 83.

26. Eisenhower, *Mandate for Change,* p. 248.

27. Ibid., chap. 28, "A New Look at America's Defenses," esp. pp. 446, 451, 454.

28. Eisenhower, *Waging Peace,* p. 286.

29. Ibid., p. 278 (Eisenhower's italics).

30. Larson, *Eisenhower: The President Nobody Knew,* pp. 82–83.

31. Eisenhower, *Crusade in Europe,* pp. 475, 477.

32. See, for example, Eisenhower, *Waging Peace,* pp. 64–65, 293, 330, 397, 468, 547.

33. Emmet John Hughes, *The Ordeal of Power* (New York: Dell, 1962), pp. 88 ff., 102–3.

34. Eisenhower, *Waging Peace,* p. 107.

35. Roscoe Drummond and Gaston Coblentz, *Duel at the Brink* (Garden City, N. Y.: Doubleday, 1960), p. 29.

36. Allen S. Whiting, "Time for a Change in Our China Policy," *New York Times Magazine,* 15 Dec. 1968, p. 28.

37. See *The Pentagon Papers,* pp. xix, 6, 27, 254.

38. Roger Hilsman, *To Move a Nation* (Garden City, N. Y.: Doubleday, 1967), pp. 482, 489.

39. Kenneth O'Donnell, "LBJ and the Kennedys," *Life,* 7 Aug. 1970. Senator Mansfield confirmed the story, including the president's anger at his criticism. John H. Averill in the *Los Angeles Times,* 3 August 1970.

40. See references in previous note.

41. Kennedy was deeply concerned about public opinion at the time; his "main worries, as in August [1963], were failure and the appearance of complicity" in the plot to remove Diem. *The Pentagon Papers,* p. 182, and Ralph L. Stavins, "Kennedy's Private War," *New York Review of Books,* 22 July 1971.

42. Sander Vanocur, "Kennedy's Voyage of Discovery," *Harper's,* April 1964.

43. Neustadt, *Presidential Power,* chap. 3.

44. Major differing interpretations are in Marguerite Higgins, *Our Vietnam Nightmare* (New York: Harper and Row, 1965), pp. 189–97, and Hilsman, *To Move a Nation,* pp. 99, 484 ff., on which *The Pentagon Papers* relies heavily.

45. On 31 August 1963, Paul M. Kattenburg, a diplomat who headed the Vietnam Interdepartmental Working Group, proposed American disengagement in a National Security Council meeting, thus becoming the first official "on record in a high level Vietnam policy meeting to pursue to its logical conclusion the analysis that the war effort was irretrievable . . . with or without President Diem." President Kennedy was not present, and one wonders if Kattenburg would have spoken up before him. As it was, he was squelched by Vice President Johnson and by Secretaries Rusk and McNamara. *The Pentagon Papers,* p. 174.

46. Graham T. Allison, "Conceptual Models and the Cuban Missile Crisis," *APSR* (Sept. 1969), p. 689.

47. The analysis draws upon Sorensen, *Kennedy,* chap. 24, "The Confrontation in Cuba." Other sources are Allison, "Conceptual Models . . . ," Hilsman, *To Move a Nation,* Arthur Schlesinger, Jr., *A Thousand Days* (Boston: Houghton Mifflin, 1965), Robert F. Kennedy, "Thirteen Days," *McCall's,* Nov. 1968, and Dean Acheson, "Dean Acheson's Version of Robert Kennedy's Version of the Cuban Missile Affair," *Esquire,* Feb. 1969.

48. Dean Acheson warmly disagreed on the quality both of the debate and of the debaters. Discussion "within the 'Ex-Com' after a couple of sessions seemed to me repetitive, leaderless, and a waste of time." He was happy when he had a chance to see the president alone. He agreed that Ex-Com members were all "equals" and were uninhibited. But "in any sense of constitutional and legal responsibility they were not equal and should have been under the direction of the Head of Government or his . . . Secretary of State and his military advisers."

49. See, for example, reviews of *The Pentagon Papers* by Eugene G. Windchy in *New Republic* for 7 and 14 Aug. 1971, Gaddis Smith, in *New York Times Book Review,* for 28 Nov. 1971, Arthur Schlesinger, Jr. in *New York Review of Books,* 21 Oct. 1971, as well as the comments by Daniel Ellsberg, "Ellsberg Talks," in *Look,* 5 Oct. 1971.

50. See chaps. 4–6.

51. "Analyzing Presidents: From Passive-Positive Taft to Active-Negative Nixon," *Washington Monthly* (Nov. 1969), adapted from a paper read at the American Political Science Association convention, Washington, 1969. A leading authority on the presidency, Richard E. Neustadt, made a similar analysis of Mr. Nixon's character in 1970. Israel Shenker, "Harvard Expert on the Presidency Views Nixon Policy with Fear," *New York Times,* 17 May 1970.

52. Reedy, *The Twilight of the Presidency;* quotations are from the first two chapters.

53. Alexander J. Groth, "Britain and America: Some Requisites of Executive Leadership Compared," in *Political Science Quarterly* (June 1970).

54. The experience of the Rockefeller Foundation, I believe, is also in point. The proposed programs are gathered in a docket for presentation to the trustees. The docket is first discussed by the principal officers who are obligated, after examination, to approve and support it collegially. Their debate is much more searching than it would otherwise be because they anticipate thorough questioning by the trustees.

4. The Problem of Bureaucracy

1. "Politicians and Bureaucrats," in David B. Truman, ed., *The Congress and America's Future* (Englewood Cliffs, N. J.: American Assembly, Columbia University, and Prentice-Hall, 1965). I rejected the term "feudalism" because that has a ring of the past and a connotation of contractual relationships, limitation, and rigidity whereas the thing under discussion is protean, explosive, current, and dynamic. Other terms to describe essentially the same phenomenon are "whirlpools of policy," E. S. Griffith, *Congress: Its Contemporary Role* (3d ed.; New York: New York Univ. Press, 1961), pp. 50–51, 158; "creeping pluralism," J. Leiper Freeman, *The Political Process: Executive Bureau-Legislative Committee Relations* (New York: Doubleday, 1955); "interest group liberalism," Theodore J. Lowi, *The End of Liberalism* (New York: Norton, 1969), chap. 3; and "private power," Grant McConnell, *Private Power and American Democracy* (New York: Knopf, 1966).

2. This was the spirit that informed Max Weber's classic analysis. See Weber, "The Essentials of Bureaucratic Organization: An Ideal-type Construction," reprinted from *The Theory of Social and Economic Organization* (trans. by A. M. Henderson and Talcot Parsons) in Robert K. Merton et al., *Reader in Bureaucracy* (Glencoe, Ill.: Free Press, 1952). Weber is a common point of departure. See the critiques of his theory by Friedrich and others in Merton et al.; by Charles Jacob in *Policy and Bureaucracy* (New York: Van Nostrand, 1966), chap. 1; by Francis E. Rourke, Introduction to *Bureaucratic Power in National Politics* (Boston: Little, Brown, 1965); and in Dwight Waldo, *Ideas and Interests in Public Administration* (New York: McGraw-Hill, 1953), chap. 2. The same ideas guided C. J. Friedrich's discussion of bureaucracy as the "core of modern government" in *Constitutional Government and Democracy* (Boston: Ginn, 1950) as well as Dwight Waldo's philosophical inquiry in *The Administrative State* (New York: Ronald Press, 1948).

3. *Capitalism, Socialism and Democracy* (3d ed.; New York: Harper and Row, 1950), pp. 205–7.

4. Neustadt does not stress the latter function much, although he emphasizes the career identification of bureaucrats with their agencies and the consequent inward focusing of loyalties. Freeman mentions the ideological aspects of bureaucracy, p. 2. Compare W. Y. Elliott on the coorganic theory of politics in *The Pragmatic Revolt in Politics* (1928). Drawing on Chester I. Barnard, Edward C. Banfield employs "ideal benefactions," *Political Influence* (New York: Free Press, 1961), p. 264. I was first struck by the phenomenon in studying agricultural agencies ("Reflections on Agricultural

Policy," *APSR* [Aug. 1948]) and later saw the relevance in other agencies.

5. R. E. Neustadt, "The Presidency and Legislation—the Growth of Central Clearance," *APSR* (Sept. 1954).

6. A. M. Schlesinger, Jr., *The Age of Roosevelt,* vol. 2, *The Coming of the New Deal* (Boston: Houghton Mifflin, 1959), p. 528.

7. R. E. Neustadt, "Approaches to Staffing the Presidency," *APSR* (Dec. 1963).

8. Clem Miller, *A Member of This House,* quoted in Neustadt, "Politicians and Bureaucrats," p. 103.

9. The Interstate Commerce Commission was nearly powerless from its inception in 1887 until the Hepburn Act of 1906, partly because of congressional limitations on its original grant of powers, and even more because the courts construed what powers it had virtually out of existence. Merle Fainsod, Lincoln Gordon, and Joseph C. Palamountain, Jr., *Government and the American Economy* (New York: Norton, 1959), pp. 258 ff. The Antitrust Division of the Justice Department was long starved for funds. "Not until its fiftieth year was as much as $1,000,000 appropriated to the purposes of the Sherman Act." Walton Hamilton and Irene Till, *Antitrust in Action,* TNEC monograph no. 16, 71st Cong., 3d sess. (1941), p. 23.

10. Charles M. Hardin, *Food and Fiber in the Nation's Politics,* vol. 2, Technical Papers, Nat'l. Advis. Comm. on Food and Fiber (Washington, D.C.: GPO, 1967), pp. 55–56.

11. Irving K. Fox and Orris C. Herfindahl, "Attainment of Efficiency in Satisfying Demands for Water Resources," *Amer. Econ. Rev., Proceedings,* Vol. 54 (May 1964), pp. 198 ff.

12. W. L. Cary, *Politics and the Regulatory Agencies* (New York: McGraw-Hill, 1967), p. 3.

13. Marion Clawson, *Uncle Sam's Acres* (New York: Dodd Mead, 1951), pp. 302 ff. Clawson and Burnell Held, *The Federal Lands* (Baltimore: Johns Hopkins Press, 1957), pp. 96 passim.

14. For example, recognition of the bargaining agent in labor disputes by the National Labor Relations Board. Fainsod, Gordon, and Palamountain, *Government and the American Economy,* pp. 191 passim.

15. Max Lowenthal, *The Federal Bureau of Investigation* (New York: Sloane, 1950), chap. 26.

16. Far from being "independent" agencies, regulatory commissions "are stepchildren whose custody is contested by both Congress and the Executive, but without very much affection from either. . . . Furthermore, they are often starvelings. . . . Even in 1965, the

budget of the six totaled only 96 million dollars in a national budget of 96 billion. . . ." Cary, *Politics and the Regulatory Agencies,* pp. 4, 61.

17. Griffith, *Congress: Its Contemporary Role,* pp. 50–51, 158. Griffith first developed the idea of whirlpools in *The Impasse of Democracy* (1939).

18. A. F. Bentley, *The Process of Government* (Chicago: Univ. of Chicago Press, 1908), p. 359.

19. *Public Administration and the Public Interest* (New York: McGraw-Hill, 1936), chap. 23, pp. 379–84.

20. *Bureaucracy in a Democracy* (New York: Harper, 1950), pp. 24, 560, 567, 571–72. When Hyneman wrote, the problem of divided government had not reemerged. See chap. 9, below.

21. *APSR* (Dec. 1950), pp. 990–1004.

22. The dangers of government by clique were delineated by Alexander Hamilton in *Federalist Papers* No. 70. Political scientists whose interpretations in varying degrees support the analysis in the text include J. Leiper Freeman, *The Political Process: Executive Bureau-Legislative Committee Relations,* pp. 14–15. Avery Leiserson, "Political Limitations on Executive Reorganization," *APSR* (Feb. 1947); Louis G. Gawthorp, *Bureaucratic Behavior in the Executive Branch* (New York: Free Press, 1969), p. 264; V. O. Key, Jr., "Legislative Control," in Fritz Morstein-Marx, ed., *Elements of Public Administration* (Englewood Cliffs, N. J.: Prentice-Hall, 1946, 1959); Paul Appleby, *Policy and Administration* (University, Ala.: Univ. of Ala. Press, 1949), pp. 29–30, 144–45; Theodore J. Lowi, *The End of Liberalism,* pp. 88–89, 222; Grant McConnell, *Private Power and American Democracy,* chap. 7 and p. 338; Herbert Kaufman, "The Growth of the Personnel System," in Wallace Sayre, ed., *The Federal Government Service: Its Character, Prestige, and Problems* (Englewood Cliffs, N. J.: Prentice-Hall, 1965); Daniel P. Moynihan, *Maximum Feasible Misunderstanding* (New York: Free Press, 1970), pp. xviii, xxii–iii; and Elliott A. Krause, "Functions of a Bureaucratic Ideology: 'Citizen Participation,' " *Social Problems* (Fall, 1968). Those viewing the phenomenon with equanimity include Ernest F. Griffith, *Congress: Its Contemporary Role,* William L. Cary, *Politics and the Regulatory Agencies,* pp. 22–23; Marver Bernstein, *Regulating Business by Independent Commissions* (Princeton: Princeton Univ. Press, 1955), p. 163; Charles E. Jacob, *Policy and Bureaucracy,* pp. 104–5, 172; Francis E. Rourke, *Bureaucratic Power in National Politics* (Boston: Little, Brown, 1965), pp. xiii and passim; and Samuel Huntington, "The Marasmus of the ICC: The Commission, the Railroads, and the Public Interest," *Yale Law Journal* (April

1952), as well as his "Interservice Competition and the Political Role of the Armed Services," *APSR* (March 1961).

23. Charles M. Hardin, *Food and Fiber in the Nation's Politics.*

24. Arthur Maass, *Muddy Waters* (Cambridge, Mass.: Harvard Univ. Press, 1951).

25. Grant McConnell, *Private Power and American Democracy;* see index under Forest Service.

26. Ibid., chap. 7.

27. Helen Leavitt, *Superhighway—Superhoax* (New York: Doubleday, 1970), and William V. Shannon, "The Untrustworthy Highway Fund," *New York Times Magazine,* 15 Oct. 1972.

28. Examples include federal communications policy, the Atomic Energy Commission, federal housing policy, and the Federal Bureau of Investigation.

5. The Military Bureaucracy

1. *Economy in the National Government* (Chicago: Univ. of Chicago Press, 1952), p. 139. Also Seymour Melman, *Pentagon Capitalism* (New York: McGraw-Hill, 1970); Bruce M. Russett, *What Price Vigilance? The Burdens of National Defense* (New Haven: Yale Univ. Press, 1970). William Proxmire, *Report from Wastelands: America's Military-Industrial Complex* (New York: Praeger, 1970). William McGaffin and Erwin Knoll, *Scandal in the Pentagon* (New York: Fawcett, 1970). Sidney Lens, *The Military-Industrial Complex* (Philadelphia and Kansas City: Pilgrim Press and the National Catholic Reporter, 1970). Richard A. Kaufman, "We Must Guard Against Unwarranted Influence by the Military-Industrial Complex," *New York Times Magazine,* 22 June 1969. Donald McDonald, "Militarism in America," *Center Magazine,* Jan. 1970. Edward A. Kolodziej, *The Uncommon Defense and Congress: 1945–1963* (Columbus: Ohio State Univ. Press, 1966). Warner R. Schilling, Paul Y. Hammond, and Glenn Snyder, *Strategy, Politics, and Defense Budgets* (New York: Columbia Univ. Press, 1962), and Elias Huzar, *The Purse and the Sword* (Ithaca: Cornell Univ. Press, 1950).

2. Despite large percentage reductions, American military personnel and budgets typically remained considerably higher after wars than they had been before the hostilities, the "ratchet effect." Russett, *What Price Vigilance,* pp. 2–4.

3. Seymour Melman, "Pax Americana," *New York Times,* 3 Nov. 1970.

4. The Federal Reserve Bank of Saint Louis, "Federal Budget Trends,"

4 Nov. 1970, and Committee on Economic Development, *The National Economy and the Vietnam War* (1967).

5. James A. Donovan, *Militarism: U.S.A.* (New York: Scribners, 1970), p. 124.

6. Interview in Davis, California, 28 March 1966. Later he changed his mind. See, for example, his *The Limits of Power* (New York: Holt, Rinehart & Winston, 1967), chaps. 3 and 9.

7. David M. Shoup, with James A. Donovan, "The New American Militarism," *Atlantic Monthly,* April 1969, and Donovan, *Militarism, U.S.A.,* chap. 7, "Military Gamesmanship," chap. 9, "A War for Everybody," and chap. 10, "The Great Bombing Hoax."

8. *The Report to President and the Secretary of Defense on the Department of Defense by the Blue Ribbon Defense Panel* (Washington, D.C.: G.P.O., 1970), p. 33 (henceforth the Fitzhugh Report).

9. Donovan, p. 151.

10. William R. Emerson, "F.D.R." in Ernest R. May, ed., *The Ultimate Decision: The President as Commander-in-Chief* (New York: Braziller, 1960), pp. 148 ff. Emerson qualifies the statements somewhat more than I have indicated. His quotation is from Mark S. Watson, *The War Department: Chief of Staff: Pre-war Plans and Organization in World War II* (Washington: Historical Division, Dept. of the Army, 1950).

11. This paragraph is drawn from Donovan, chaps. 6 and 7; the quotation from Leahy is from p. 115. See also William Beecher, "Laird Said to Tighten Rein on the Joint Chiefs of Staff," *New York Times,* 14 June 1970. According to the Fitzhugh Report (pp. 15–16), it was the Secretary of Defense rather than Congress who put the military service chiefs back into operations after the 1958 reorganization.

12. Donovan, p. 127.

13. This analysis draws heavily on Donovan, chaps. 4 and 5, especially pp. 75–76, 133–34.

14. See the experience of Rear Admiral Arnold E. True (ret.). Eugene E. Windchy, *A Documentary on the Incidents in the Tonkin Gulf* (Garden City: N. Y.: Doubleday, 1971), pp. 44–45, 47–48, and of Lieutenant-Colonel Anthony B. Herbert in James T. Wooten, "How a Supersoldier was Fired from His Command," *New York Times Magazine,* 5 Sept. 1971, as well as a *Playboy* interview, 11 July 1972. A. Ernest Fitzgerald, a civilian engineer in the Department of Defense, was punished for revealing cost overruns on the C–5A cargo plane (*New York Times,* 11 Nov. 1969).

15. "The Ordeal of the Army," *New York Times,* 2 April 1971.

16. Alfred Vagts, *A History of Militarism* (New York: Norton, 1937).

Samuel J. Huntington, *The Soldier and the State* (Cambridge, Mass.: Harvard U. Press, 1957). Morris Janowitz, *The Professional Soldier* (N. Y.: Free Press, 1960, 1964).

17. "The New American Militarism," *Atlantic Monthly,* April 1969.

18. "The Programming of Robert McNamara," *Harper's,* Feb. 1971; cf. Ralph E. Lapp. "The Vicious Acronyms," *New Republic,* 21 June 1969; John Kenneth Galbraith, "How to Control the Military," *Harper's,* June 1969.

19. *House Hearings,* Agric. Approp., Fiscal 1965, Part 1, p. 2300. In December 1971 it transpired that Congressman William H. Natcher (D., Kentucky) had used his strategic position on the appropriations committee to hold up the Washington, D. C., subway for two years.

20. *House Hearings,* Agric. Approp., Fiscal, 1965, Part 5, p. 15.

21. *Congressional Quarterly, Legislators and the Lobbyists* (2d ed., 1968), "The Military-Industrial Lobby," pp. 68–69.

22. *Congressional Quarterly, Legislators and the Lobbyists* (1st ed., Sept. 1965), "The Military Lobby," pp. 28–29.

23. John W. Finney, "Pentagon Bares Cost of Germ War Study," *New York Times,* 5 March 1969. Harry Howe Ransom, *Can American Democracy Survive The Cold War?* (Garden City, N.Y.: Doubleday, Anchor ed., 1964), pp. 180–82.

24. Lewis A. Froman, Jr., and Randall B. Ripley, "Conditions for Party Leadership: The House Democrats," *APSR* (March 1965). Edward J. Kolodziej, *The Uncommon Defense in Congress,* chap. 8. Proxmire, *Report from Wastelands,* chap. 5.

25. *Congressional Quarterly, Legislators and the Lobbyists* (1968), p. 55. On crucial issues, generals and admirals are called in. C.Q.'s informant, then employed as an industrial lobbyist, said that as a Pentagon lobbyist he had had "50 times the influence . . . I have now."

26. Elias Huzar, *The Purse and the Sword* (Ithaca: Cornell Univ. Press, 1950), p. 171. Walter Millis, *Arms and Men: A Study in Military History* (New York: Putnam, 1956), p. 199. Arthur Smithies, *The Budgetary Process in the United States* (New York: McGraw-Hill, 1955), p. 236. A strong defense of congressional oversight of the military was made by Samuel P. Huntington, *The Soldier and the State* (Cambridge, Mass.: Harvard Univ. Press, 1957), pp. 402, 409–12, 418–21; but in his article, "Strategic Planning and the Political Process," *Foreign Affairs,* Jan. 1960, he reversed himself. See chap. 6 below, n. 62.

27. *The Uncommon Defense and Congress* (Columbus: Ohio Univ. Press, 1960), pp. 76, 97, 99, 470–73, 495, 504–5, and passim.

28. Kaufman, "We Must Guard Against Unwarranted Influence by the Military-Industrial Complex."

29. Joseph Kraft, "The Nixon Supremacy," *Harper's*, March 1970, p. 49.

30. Joseph Kraft, "Laird Serves up a Turkey," *Sacramento Bee*, 20 Jan. 1971.

31. J. K. Galbraith, "How to Control the Military," *Harper's*, June 1969, p. 35. Galbraith quoted Ralph Dungan, formerly U. S. ambassador to Chile.

32. Lens, pp. 65–66.

33. "Thirteen Days," *McCall's*, Nov. 1968.

34. Letter to the editor, *New York Times*, 22 July 1969.

35. Donovan, chap. 3. See also the Fitzhugh Report, chap. 6 and pp. 234 ff.; the Hébert probe, reported in *C.Q., Legislators and the Lobbyists* (1960), p. 25, and Proxmire, *Report from Wastelands*, chaps. 6 and 7.

36. Donovan, p. 55, and chap. 3 generally, also *Congressional Quarterly, Legislators and the Lobbyists* (1960), p. 27, and (1968), pp. 55, 57.

37. Lens, chap. 5; Proxmire, p. 9.

38. Robin Clarke, *The Silent Weapons* (New York: McKay, 1968), pp. 9, 219–20, and Seymour M. Hersh, *Chemical and Biological Warfare* (New York: Bobbs-Merrill, 1968), chap. 8.

39. Irving Louis Horowitz, "The Life and Death of the Project Camelot," *International Education: Past, Present, Problems and Prospects*, House Doc., No. 527, 89th Cong., 2d Sess. (Prepared by the Committee on Education's Task Force on International Education, Congressman John Brademas, chairman.) Also James Ridgway, *The Closed Corporation, America's Universities in Crisis* (New York: Ballantine Books, 1969), pp. 63 ff., 133–35, 216 ff.

40. Lens, p. 120, see especially chap. 6, "The Labor Lieutenants." The chief exception has been the United Auto Workers Union under the late Walter P. Reuther and his successor, Leonard Woodcock.

41. See, e.g., David B. Truman, *The Governmental Process* (New York: Knopf, 1951), pp. 139–55.

42. V. O. Key, Jr., *Politics, Parties, and Pressure Groups* (N. Y.: Crowell, 1964), pp. 108–9.

43. Justin Gray, *The Inside Story of the Legion* (N. Y.: Boni and Gaer, 1948), chap. 8.

44. "The Selling of the Pentagon" was attacked at once and was shown a second time, with criticisms included, on 27 February 1971. Con-

gressman F. Edward Hébert, chairman of the House Armed Services Committee, called it a "vicious piece of propaganda," and said that all he wanted "was accuracy." Replied the president of CBS News, Richard S. Salant, "He got it." Hébert also called the film "the most un-American thing I have ever seen on the tube." Secretary of Defense Melvin Laird said that it was not un-American but that more professionalism could have been shown. Agnew called the film a "subtle but vicious broadside against the nation's defense establishment," said that it was distorted, and proclaimed that he wanted to "tell the American people that they cannot rely on CBS for facts. . . ." After the appended criticisms, Salant of CBS declared that no one had shown that any of the things the film recorded did not happen.

In March the Committee on Interstate and Foreign Commerce, House of Representatives, Congressman Harley O. Staggers (D., West Virginia) chairman, subpoenaed CBS to supply all material used in preparing the film. Frank Stanton refused to supply materials other than those actually used. The committee subpoenaed again in June; Stanton remained obdurate: "compliance would have a chilling effect" on CBS's efforts to get and report the news. President Nixon was reported opposed to the Staggers's probe. In July the Interstate and Foreign Commerce Committee proposed to cite Stanton and CBS for contempt for refusing the subpoena; but the House voted to recommit, 226–181, thus killing the bill. Sources: the film, "The Selling of the Pentagon," with appended criticisms and a rejoinder; *Facts on File* (1971), pp. 169, 273, 407, 531. Robert Sherrill, "The Happy Ending (Maybe) of 'The Selling of the Pentagon,' " *New York Times Magazine,* 16 May 1971.

45.   "The New American Militarism."

46.   John Kenneth Galbraith, "How to Control the Military," *Harper's,* June 1969. On the simplistic distortion provided by the Navy's official anticommunism see excerpts from the *Blue Jackets' Manual* and the *Naval Officers' Guide* supplied by Donovan, pp. 218–19. On military ideology generally see Janowitz, *The Professional Soldier,* chap. 5.

47.   Donovan, p. 217.

48.   Donovan, pp. 4–5. Once begun, a military ideology can clearly draw on all the glorious military traditions back to Thermopylae and the siege of Troy.

49.   Ibid., p. 37.

50.   Ibid., p. 69.

51.   Ibid., p. 34.

52.   "The New American Militarism."

53.   Ibid.

54. Proxmire, *Report from Wastelands,* p. 221, italics in original.

55. Ibid., italics supplied.

56. Ransom, *Can American Democracy Survive the Cold War?,* pp. 180–82.

57. In 1964, the total national contributions to congressional electoral campaigns (exclusive of primaries) averaged about $4,000 per candidate. Estimated from Kevin L. McKeough, *Financing Campaigns for Congress: Contribution Patterns of National Level Party and Non-Party Committees, 1964* (Citizens' Research Foundation, 245 Nassau St., Princeton, N. J., 1970).

6. The Influence of the Military Bureaucracy— and a Corrective

1. David M. Shoup, "The New American Militarism" (written with James A. Donovan), *Atlantic Monthly,* April 1969.

2. Sidney Lens, *The Military-Industrial Complex* (Philadelphia: Pilgrim, 1970), pp. 17–18, 35–38.

3. Richard E. Neustadt, *Presidential Power* (New York: Wiley, 1960), p. 176 and passim.

4. *Militarism, U.S.A.* (New York: Scribner's, 1970), p. 152.

5. "The Road from War," review of *Vietnam, 1965–1970,* by Robert Shaplen, *New York Times Book Review,* 4 Oct. 1970.

6. Donovan, *Militarism: USA,* p. 157.

7. Shoup, "The New American Militarism."

8. Donovan, *Militarism: USA,* pp. 152–55.

9. "American Militarism: What Is It Doing To Us?", *Look,* 12 Aug. 1969, p. 16.

10. Joseph Kraft, "Washington Insight: Negotiating Out of Vietnam," *Harper's,* Sept. 1965, p. 42. Italics added. Some indication of Kraft's sources may be inferred from his informed and extremely laudatory account of McGeorge Bundy in *Harper's,* November 1965.

11. "Tonkin Bay: The Mystery Grows," *New York Review of Books,* 28 March 1968; "The Supine Senate," *New York Review of Books,* 13 Feb. 1969. Anthony Austin, *The President's War* (A New York Times Book, 1971). For a showing of the great permissiveness of the Tonkin Gulf Resolution compared to the Formosa Resolution of 1955, the Middle East (Eisenhower) Resolution of 1957, and the Cuban Resolution of 1962, see pp. 10–11, 85. Eugene G. Windchy, *A Documentary of the Incidents in the Tonkin Gulf* (Garden City, N. Y.: Doubleday, 1971). *New York Times, The Pentagon Papers* (1971), chap. 5.

12. *New York Times, The Pentagon Papers,* pp. 244, 285.

13. Austin, *The President's War,* pp. 87–88.

14. Windchy, *A Documentary of the Incidents in the Tonkin Gulf,* p. 219.

15. Austin, *The President's War,* pp. 331–32.

16. *New York Times, The Pentagon Papers,* pp. 240–41.

17. The attacks promise to continue. See U. S. Grant Sharp, "The Story Behind the Bombing," *New York Times,* 6 Aug. 1971.

18. Austin, *The President's War,* pp. 145–46.

19. Ibid., pp. 254-57.

20. Ibid., p. 268.

21. Ibid., pp. 179, 186, 206–7, 217 and passim.

22. Townsend Hoopes, *The Limits of Intervention* (New York: McKay, 1969), pp. 27–28. Hoopes calls the incident a "consequential inadvertency" seemingly "unavoidable" because the men involved were "overworked."

23. Norman Cousins, "How the U. S. Spurned Three Chances for Peace in Vietnam," *Look,* 29 July 1969. Compare David Kraslow and Stuart H. Loory, *The Secret Search for Peace in Vietnam* (New York: Random House, Vintage ed., 1968).

24. Townsend Hoopes, *The Limits of Intervention,* p. 62.

25. Austin, *The President's War,* p. 194.

26. See the review of Hedrick Smith and William Beecher, incorporating reports of seven *New York Times* reporters, "The Vietnam Reversal of 1968," *New York Times,* 6 and 7 March 1969. Townsend Hoopes, *The Limits of Intervention,* and Don Oberdorfer, *Tet!* (Garden City, N. Y.: Doubleday, 1971), esp. pp. 249–50, 257, 266.

27. Terence Smith, "New U. S. Tactics Intensified Fighting," *New York Times,* 23 March 1969. On 7 March 1969, the CBS news reported, in effect, that General Abrams had seized the opportunity of the interregnum between the election and the Nixon inaugural so to escalate the fighting that the incoming administration would have no alternative but to fight on to a military victory.

28. "Lavelle: A Stock Character," in *Sacramento Bee,* 22 June 1972; see also articles by Seymour M. Hersh, 10, 12, 13, and 15 June 1972, and by James Reston, 14 June 1972, all in *New York Times.*

29. Secret American bombing beginning in 1969 in Cambodia was disclosed by the Senate armed services committee in 1973; some considered the scandal greater than Watergate.

30. Other areas and countries could be included in these illustrations. For examples from Latin America, see chap. 5.

31. *New York Times*, 29 June.

32. Donald McDonald, "Militarism in America," *Center Magazine,* Jan. 1970, p. 16.

33. John W. Finney, "U.S. to Sign Pact with Spain Today," and "U.S. and Spain Sign Accord on Bases," *New York Times,* 6 and 7 Aug. 1970. Compare the description by Rowland Evans and Robert Novak of the concerted administration efforts at "Undermining Fulbright," *Davis Enterprise,* Davis, California, 19 Jan. 1971.

34. *The Ultimate Folly* (New York: Knopf 1969), p. vii. See also Frederic J. Brown, *Chemical Warfare: A Study in Restraints* (Princeton: Princeton Univ. Press., 1968); Seymour M. Hersh, *Chemical and Biological Warfare, America's Hidden Arsenal* (New York: Bobbs-Merrill, 1968); Robin Clarke, *The Silent Weapons* (New York: McKay, 1968).

35. Seymour M. Hersh provides much further documentation of the military bureaucracy, including the influence of the Chemical Corps, the links to industry (often blandly denied), the use of propaganda including parades of the horribles, and the ties to the little group of congressional insiders. Chairman Sikes was avid for funds for CBW but was monumentally indifferent to the defense of civilians from CBW (*Chemical and Biological Warfare,* pp. 188, 189, 190, 191–92, 194 ff., 197, 205).

36. McCarthy, *The Ultimate Folly,* p. 141.

37. Seymour M. Hersh, *Chemical and Biological Warfare,* p. 38.

38. *The Ultimate Folly,* pp. 126–32. This is indirectly borne out by J. H. Rothschild, *Tomorrow's Weapons* (New York: McGraw-Hill, 1964). Chap. 7, "What The Russians Are Doing," devotes three pages to prospective offensive use of CBW (mainly statements of Russian officials that CBW would be used in any future war) and nearly six pages to civilian defense. General Rothschild was formerly head of the Army Chemical Corps research and development command.

39. "The Atomic Arms Race: A 'Mad Momentum' May Be under Way," *New York Times Magazine,* 6 Dec. 1967.

40. Andrew Hamilton, "The Arms Race: Too Much of a Bad Thing," *New York Times Magazine,* 6 Oct. 1968, p. 35.

41. Sidney Lens, *The Military-Industrial Complex,* pp. 53–54.

42. "Strategic Weapons: Prospects for Arms Control," *Foreign Affairs,* April 1969, p. 414. Italics added.

43. David Halberstam, "The Programming of Robert McNamara," *Harper's,* Feb. 1971, pp. 53–54. Compare Richard E. Neustadt's testimony, Hearings, subcommittee on national security and international operations, Committee on Governmental Operations, Senate, 89th Cong. 1st Sess., Part 3 (1965), pp. 135–36.

44. Halberstam; italics supplied.

45. Andrew Hamilton, "The Arms Race: Too Much of a Bad Thing," *New York Times Magazine,* 6 October 1968.

46. Richard M. Nixon, "United States Foreign Policy for the 1970's: the Emerging Structure of Peace," The White House, Feb. 1972 (mimeo), pp. 174–82.

47. "Statement of Secretary of Defense Melvin R. Laird before the House Armed Services Committee," 17 Feb. 1972 (mimeo), p. 40.

48. Ralph E. Lapp, "Can SALT Stop MIRV?" *New York Times Magazine,* 1 Feb. 1970.

49. Dr. Jerome B. Wiesner, science adviser to President Kennedy, and Dr. George Rathjens, formerly chief scientist for the Defense Department, in a paper prepared for the American Association for the Advancement of Science, 1969.

50. Joseph Kraft, "Laird Prepares for New 'War,'" *Sacramento Bee,* 13 June 1972. In 1973 came more of the same. See Richard J. Levine "The Price of Peace," *Wall Street Journal,* 17 July 1973. Levine quoted Chairman George Mahan of the House Appropriations Committee: "You just can't break through the military bureaucracy very well."

51. I. F. Stone, "McNamara and Tonkin Bay: The Unanswered Questions," *New York Review of Books,* 29 March 1968, pp. 5–6.

52. See, however, the review article, based on Mark Sacharoff's bibliography on alleged war crimes in Vietnam, Neil Sheehan, "Should We Have War Crime Trials?," *New York Times Book Review,* 28 March 1971.

53. Quoted by Donald McDonald, "Militarism in America," *Center Magazine,* Jan. 1970, p. 31. Fulbright's speech, on the floor of the Senate, was given 13 Dec. 1967.

54. *American Economic Review,* May 1968, quoted in Donald McDonald, "Militarism in America," p. 25.

55. "Politicians and Bureaucrats," in David B. Truman, ed., *Congress and America's Future* (1965), p. 120.

56. Janowitz, *The Professional Soldier* (New York: Free Press, 1960).

57. See his review of books by Proxmire, Seymour Melman, Sidney Lens, and J. S. Baumgartner, *New York Times Book Review,* 24 May 1970.

58. "How to Control the Military," *Harper's,* June 1969.

59. The single-purpose organizations in congressional districts aimed at control of the military are somewhat reminiscent of Moisei Ostrogorski's "temporary parties for single issues," advanced as a cure of democracy's problems (*Democracy and the Organization of*

Political Parties: Vol. 2, *The United States,* "Conclusion", Part 12)
and are subject to the same criticisms. See, e.g., S. M. Lipset's introduction to his edition of Ostrogorski (N. Y.: Doubleday, Anchor
ed., 1964), 1:lix ff. A similar criticism is implicit in E. M. Sait's
prescient discussion of efforts to crush political machines. Even if
temporarily successful, such efforts either leave the machine intact,
or if they kill it off, they destroy party spirit with the same blow.
And this may wreck democratic government; "for individual responsibility without party responsibility means chaos" (*American
Parties and Elections* [New York: Appleton-Century, 1942], p.
470). It has not meant chaos, however; bureaucracy has emerged to
fill the vacuum, and the only way to control it is by the superior
organization of revitalized and centralized political parties.

60. *What Price Vigilance: The Burdens of National Defense* (New
     Haven: Yale Univ. Press, 1970), pp. 178, 186ff.

61. Charles E. Jacob found the traditional confidence in civilian control
     of the military somewhat compromised by the cold war, the grow-
     ing congressional and public acceptance of the peacetime draft and
     high military budgets, and the military industrial complex. The
     pluralistic politics of defense he found "natural enough"; but a
     "genuine cause for concern" lay in "the *concentration* of political
     power capable of being wielded by the military in association with
     big industry" (*Policy and Bureaucracy* [chap. 7 esp. p. 179; his
     italics]). While the inference favoring party government is not so
     obvious as with Russett, it clearly runs in that direction.

62. Samuel J. Huntington, "Strategic Planning and the Political
     Process," *Foreign Affairs,* January 1960. This article marked a sharp
     departure from Huntington's defense of the separation of powers in
     The Soldier and the State (Cambridge, Mass.: Harvard Univ. Press,
     1957), pp. 402, 409–12, and 418–21.

7. "Greater Resistance to Pressure"

1. "Toward a More Responsible Two Party System," *APSR,* Supple-
    ment, September 1950. A "phenomenal growth of interest organiza-
    tions in recent decades" required a "reinforced party system" to
    "cope with multiple organized pressures" (see pp. 2, 13, 34, 86).

2. William Yandell Elliott, ed., *United States Foreign Policy, Its
    Organization and Control* (New York: Columbia Univ. Press,
    1952), p. 299.

3. Theodore J. Lowi, *The End of Liberalism* (New York: Norton,
    1969), p. 54.

4. James Q. Wilson, "Corruption is not Always Scandalous," *New
    York Times Magazine,* 28 April 1968.

5. W. Ivor Jennings, *Party Politics,* Vol. 1, *Appeal to the People*

(Cambridge: University Press, 1960), p. 111. Compare John W. Gardner, "You Are Being Had," *New York Times,* 4 July 1971.

6. Arthur F. Bentley, *The Process of Government* (Chicago: Univ. of Chicago Press, 1908; Bloomington, Ind.: Principia Press, 1949) pp. 370–71; cf. pp. 226–27, 279, 422, 477.

7. David B. Truman, *The Governmental Process* (New York: Knopf, 1951), pp. 50–51. In his foreword to the 2d edition (1971) Truman substantially modified this position (pp. xlv–xlvi).

8. E. C. Banfield, "In Defense of the American Party System," in Robert Goldwin, ed., *Political Parties, U.S.A.* (Chicago: Rand-McNally, 1964), p. 35.

9. Leo Weinstein in "The Group Approach, Arthur F. Bentley," and Leo Strauss, "An Epilogue," in Herbert J. Storing, ed., *Essays on the Scientific Study of Politics* (New York: Holt, Rinehart & Winston, 1962). See also Lowi, *The End of Liberalism.*

10. Sidney Baldwin, *Poverty and Politics* (Raleigh: Univ. of North Carolina Press, 1968). AFBF attacks on FSA are related on pp. 341–56, passim. Baldwin carefully qualified the role of the AFBF in the outcome, p. 411. Grant McConnell was much more generous in allocating credit to the AFBF. *The Decline of Agrarian Democracy* (Berkeley: Univ. of Calif. Press, 1953), p. 177. For AFBF's own claims, see Orville M. Kile, *The Farm Bureau Through Three Decades* (Baltimore: Waverly Press, 1948), p. 264.

11. See Baldwin, *Poverty and Politics*; Charles M. Hardin, "American Agriculture," in Stephen D. Kertesz and M. A. Fitzsimons, eds., *What America Stands For* (South Bend: Univ. of Notre Dame Press, 1959); and Don F. Hadwiger, "The Freeman Administration and the Poor," *Agricultural History,* Jan. 1971.

12. Compare Theodore J. Lowi's remark that "all established interests are conservative" (*The End of Liberalism,* p. 66). Cf. Grant McConnell, *Private Power and American Democracy* (New York: Knopf, 1966), pp. 339, 341; and E. E. Schattschneider, *The Semi-Sovereign People* (New York: Holt, Rinehart & Winston, 1960, 1964), p. 35.

13. *The People Left Behind* (Washington, D. C.: GPO, 1967), p. ix.

14. Erwin Knoll, "The Oil Lobby Is Not Depleted," *New York Times Magazine,* 8 March 1970. Morton Mintz and Jerry S. Cohen, *America, Inc.* (New York: Dial, 1971). Robert Engel, *The Politics of Oil.* Daniel Jack Chasan, *The Alaskan Oil Boom* (New York: Praeger, 1971).

15. Herbert E. Alexander, *Financing the 1964 Election* (Princeton: Citizen's Research Foundation, 1965), pp. 91–92.

16. "Houston's Superpatriots," *Harper's,* Oct. 1961, reprinted in Robert

A. Rosenstone, ed., *Protests from the Right* (Beverly Hills: Glencoe Press, 1968), p. 55.

17. Benjamin R. Epstein and Arnold Foster, *The Radical Right* (New York: Random House, Vintage ed., 1967), p. 7. See also Harry and Bonaro Overstreet, *The Strange Tactics of Extremism* (New York: Norton, 1964), p. 128. George Thayer, *The Farther Shores of Politics* (New York: Simon and Schuster, 1967), pp. 149–52.

18. Erwin Knoll, "The Oil Lobby Is Not Depleted," and Daniel Bell, "The Dispossessed" (1962), in Daniel Bell, ed., *The Radical Right* (New York: Doubleday, 1963: Anchor ed., 1964), p. 31, n. 16.

19. Robert Sherrill, "A Lobby on Target," and "High Noon on Capitol Hill," *New York Times Magazine,* 15 Oct. 1967, and 23 June 1968. Unless otherwise noted, reference is to these articles.

20. Louis Harris reported that the public favored "strict control and regulation of hand guns" by 66 to 33 percent but also agreed, 49 to 43 percent, with the statement, "The way things are today, people should own guns for their own protection." Nevertheless, nearly two-thirds of the population in cities and suburbs do not own guns (*Sacramento Bee,* 3 June 1971).

21. Ben A. Franklin, "Tydings Seeks to Counter Gun Lobby," and "Gun Lobby Hails Tydings Defeat," *New York Times,* 6 Sept. and 8 Nov. 1970. Arlen J. Large, "The Gun Lobby Works to Defeat Lawmakers who Support Controls," *Wall Street Journal,* 11 Sept. 1970.

22. *To Establish Justice, To Insure Domestic Tranquility* (Washington, D. C.: GPO, 1968), pp. xviii, xxvi, 169–86.

23. Presidential Commissions, *Hearings,* Subcommittee, Admin. Practices and Procedures, Senate Judiciary Committee, 92d Cong., 1st Sess., 1971, at p. 161. On the development of armed groups with revolutionary potential see George Thayer, *The Farther Shores of Politics,* chap. 6, and Martin Waldron, "Militants Stockpile Illegal Guns Across the United States," *New York Times,* 28 Dec. 1969. For some connection between such groups as the Minutemen and the NRA see Sherrill's articles.

24. William Yandell Elliott, *The Pragmatic Revolt in Politics* (New York: Macmillan, 1928) and *The Need for Constitutional Reform* (New York: McGraw-Hill, 1935); E. E. Schattschneider, *Party Government* (New York: Rinehart, 1942) and *The Semi-Sovereign People* (1960); Hanry S. Kariel, *The Decline of American Pluralism* (Stanford: Stanford Univ. Press, 1961), pp. 288–89.

25. Grant McConnell, *Private Power and American Democracy,* provides a recent analysis much in point. Criticizing the confusion of public and private in American political thought, the unusual weight our system affords to minority interests and especially to their

controlling elites, and the inflated value placed on small constituencies, McConnell recommends enlarging the effective political
constituency and strengthening both the presidency and the national
parties (see, for example, pp. 339–42, 347–49, 351–52, 355–56).

26.   *The End of Liberalism.* References will be to this volume unless
otherwise noted. On p. 73 Lowi briefly considers and rejects majoritarian government as an alternative to interest group liberalism.
A more elaborate rejection, which I shall answer in chap. 9, is contained in "Party, Policy, and Constitution in America," in William
N. Chambers and Walter D. Burnham, eds., *The American Party
Systems* (New York: Oxford Univ. Press, 1967).

27.   *The End of Liberalism,* pp. ix–x and chaps. 3 and 10.

28.   If space permitted, I could make similar arguments asserting the
primacy of reform in the party system to cope with the rise of the
regulatory state that, Lowi says, required that the "hallowed role of
the legislature" be reduced and the "even more hallowed separation
of powers" revised (p. 129); with the need for metropolitan government founded on a "unitary principle—where all autonomy
within the region is eliminated" (p. 267); with the need to move
away from a plebiscitary presidency (p. 85); with the need for a
new organization of social classes to support Lowi's revolution of
juridical democracy (p. 270); and with the problems of the "lack
of will" (i.e., of political will, I take it) as well as the lack of a
sense of legitimacy needed by political leaders if they are resolutely
to "wield the authority of democratic government . . ." (pp. 270–
75).

29.   "In Defense of the American Party System," in Goldwin, ed.,
Political Parties, U.S.A., pp. 35–36.

30.   "The active participation of private parties in the conduct of public
business, whether as interest group representatives or as civic
leaders, is a peculiarly American phenomenon. In many other
countries it is taken for granted that public affairs are to be managed
solely by . . . elected or appointed [officials]. . . . In London, for
example, there is not even a chamber of commerce or a taxpayers'
association, and no businessman would dream of 'giving leadership'
to a local council behind the scenes." Edward C. Banfield and
James Q. Wilson, *City Politics* (Cambridge, Mass.: Harvard Univ.
Press, 1963), pp. 245–46.

31.   "Pressure Groups and Parties in Britain," *APSR,* March 1956, pp.
1–23, at p. 3. For the history see Beer, "The Representation of Interests in British Government—Historical Background," *APSR,*
Sept. 1957.

32.   Samuel H. Beer, *British Politics in the Collectivist Age* (New
York: Knopf, 1965; Random House, 1969), p. 78.

33. "Parties, Pressure Groups and the British Political Process," *Political Quarterly,* Jan.–March 1958, pp. 5–16, at pp. 5, 9.

34. "Pressure Groups and Parties in Britain," *APSR,* March 1956, p. 9. The classic interpretation has been vigorously challenged by Michael R. Gordon, "Civil Servants, Politicians, and Parties," *Comparative Politics,* Oct. 1971, commenting on the "pluralistic stagnation of the new group politics"—but he notes that these are not matters "on which Americans can feel superior" (p. 58).

35. *APSR,* Sept. 1962, pp. 621–33, at pp. 630–31.

36. If Pennock had divided the British total by 350,000 farms rather than 290,000, a figure more comparable to the 5,900,000 he used for the United States, he would have got $2,045 per British farm rather than $2,469. He did not count American subventions of farm exports, which sharply enlarge our outlays per farm. He did not take sufficient account of the difference between Great Britain's use of production payments, letting farm prices fall by permitting imports, with American price support policies that meant that the subsidy was paid twice, once by the government and once by the consumer. See Charles M. Hardin, "Present and Prospective Policy Problems of U.S. Agriculture," *Jour. of Farm Econ., Proceedings Number,* 1965, at p. 1,103; cf. Donald R. Kaldor, "The Free Market as a Farm Policy Alternative," National Agric. Advisory Commission, U.S.D.A., *Farm Policy in the Years Ahead* (1964), p. 8, and Marion Clawson, *Policy Directions for U.S. Agriculture* (Baltimore: Johns Hopkins Press, 1968), p. 211. Between 1958–61 and 1964–67, I calculate that British subsidies increased 12 percent per farm; in the U. S. from 1956–63 to 1964–67 the increase was 54 percent. Sources: *Agric. Statistics for England and Wales,* 1967–68, HMSO, 1969, Table 63 A, and Central Statistical Office, *Annual Abstract of Statistics,* No. 106, 1969, HMSO, 1970, p. 289. For the U. S., farm numbers are from *Statistical Abstract,* 1970, p. 589; for budget outlays *U.S. Budget in Brief,* Fiscal Year 1972, p. 62.

37. *The State and the Farmer* (London: Allen and Unwin, 1962), p. 208.

38. Allen Potter, *Organized Groups in British National Politics* (London: Faber and Faber, 1961), pp. 212–13.

39. On the veterans see Graham Wooton, "Ex-Service Men in Politics," *Political Quarterly,* Jan.–March 1958, and John H. Millett, "British Interest Groups: A Case Study," *Political Science Quarterly,* March 1957. On the public roads lobby see Samuel E. Finer, *Political Quarterly,* Jan.–March 1958. On the medical profession, Harry Eckstein, *Pressure Group Politics: The Case of the British Medical Association* (Stanford: Stanford Univ. Press, 1960). See also Potter, *Organized Groups in British National Politics,* and J. D. Stewart, *British Pressure Groups* (Oxford: Oxford Univ. Press, 1957).

40. "Parties, Pressure Groups, and the British Political Process," *Political Quarterly,* Jan.–March 1958, esp. pp. 14–15. McKenzie referred especially to Samuel J. Eldersveld's concern that American pressure groups tend to splinter and to complicate policy-making and to hide it from public scrutiny, in Henry Ehrmann, ed., *Interest Groups on Four Continents* (Pittsburgh: Univ. of Pittsburgh Press, 1958). See also McKenzie, *British Political Parties* (New York: St. Martin's Press, 1955), chap. 10. Compare J. D. Stewart, *British Pressure Groups,* chap. 10, and Finer in Ehrmann, ed., *Interest Groups on Four Continents.*

41. *Anonymous Empire* (London: Pall Mall, 1958), pp. 92–106, 126–27.

42. Gabriel A. Almond summarized the conclusions in "A Comparative Study of Interest Groups and the Political Process," *APSR,* March 1958, pp. 270–82. Quotations from p. 278, italics added.

43. Mancur Olson, Jr., *The Logic of Collective Action* (Cambridge, Mass.: Harvard Univ. Press, 1965). See "The 'Special Interest' Theory and Business Lobbies," pp. 141–48, and literature there cited. Numerous disclosures in recent years show the prevalence of the business "fix" in American politics.

44. *Anonymous Empire,* pp. 126–27. Calhoun recognized the problem of anarchy and sought to avoid it. Ralph Lerner, "Calhoun's New Science of Politics," *APSR* (Dec. 1963).

45. Edward C. Banfield, *The Unheavenly City* (Boston: Little, Brown, 1968), chap. 11.

46. Representative of the evolution are "Congress and the Budget—a Planner's Criticism," *APSR* (Dec. 1949); Banfield, *Political Influence* (New York: Free Press, 1961), and *The Unheavenly City* (1968).

47. Samuel H. Beer, *British Politics in the Collectivist Age* (New York: Random House, 1965; Vintage ed., 1969); Malcolm Maclennan, Murray Forsyth, and Geoffrey Denton, *Economic Planning and Policies in Britain, France, and Germany* (New York: Praeger, 1968), quoted in Suzanne Berger, "The French Political System," in Samuel H. Beer et al., *Patterns of Government* (3d ed.; New York: Random House, 1972), p. 418.

48. Herbert Stein, *The Fiscal Revolution in America* (Chicago: Univ. of Chicago Press, 1969).

49. Don K. Price, *The Scientific Estate* (Cambridge, Mass.: Harvard Univ. Press, 1965).

50. Walter W. Heller, *New Dimensions of Political Economy* (New York: Norton, 1966), pp. 42–47.

51. See *British Politics in the Collectivist Age,* pp. 352–70.

52. Ibid., p. 347. For examples of reciprocal political education between parties and groups (Labour and trade unions) see pp. 169, 200, 209, 211, and 241.

53. Ibid., p. 370 and chap. 13 generally.

54. Ibid., p. 350.

55. Ibid. (1969 edition, epilogue), pp. 391 ff.; he returned to a glimmer of optimism only in his closing sentence (p. 434).

56. Samuel H. Beer, "The British Political System," chap. 11, "The Challenge to Collectivist Politics," in Beer et al., *Patterns of Government* (3d ed.; quotations are from p. 322).

57. Calculated from Table 373, p. 234, and Table 369, p. 232, *Statistical Abstract of the United States, 1972.*

58. Finer, "The Political Process in Great Britain," in Ehrmann, ed., *Interest Groups on Four Continents,* p. 120. *Statistical Abstract of the United States,* 1972, Table 340, p. 216, Table 387, p. 241, and Table 389, p. 242.

59. Jack Rosenthal in *New York Times,* 6 Nov. 1972. A report of the Center for Policy Studies at the University of Michigan attributed only 1 percent of the "explained variance" in the presidential vote of 1972 to busing (pp. 28–29). The argument is involved and, I think, obscure. It is suggested that race was declining in salience as an issue in 1972 (pp. 21–22). But it was also said that "McGovern . . . was exceptionally unpopular among Wallace supporters. . . ." He got an "amazing 65 percent less of the two-party vote than he could normally have expected from this group" (p. 64); Arthur H. Miller, Warren E. Miller, Alden S. Raine, and Thad A. Brown, "A Majority Party in Disarray: Policy Polarization in the 1972 Election." Among numerous newspaper accounts that support the position in the text are John Herbers, "School Busing Becomes a National Issue that May Affect the '72 Presidential Race," Jerry M. Flint, "School Busing Divides Michigan Democrats. . . ," and Paul Delaney, "Nixon Renews Bus Issue: Stand Called Diversionary," in the *New York Times* for 3 Oct. 1971, 2 Nov. 1972, and 11 Sept. 1973, respectively. For the salience of the busing issue in Massachusetts, the one state McGovern won, but where the state's racial imbalance law rather than a federal court order was the object of discontent, see Robert Rheinhold, "More Segregated than Ever," in *New York Times Magazine,* 30 Sept. 1973.

60. Steven V. Roberts in the *New York Times,* 15 Aug. 1973, p. 19. See also on the same page a report of an Oliver Quayle poll taken for NBC that found voter-preference, if the presidential race were then rerun, to be 51 percent for McGovern against 49 percent for Nixon.

8. The Travail of Public Opinion

1. James Bryce, *The American Commonwealth* (2 vols.; New York: Macmillan, 1893, 1910), 2:267.

2. Don K. Price, "Irresponsibility as an Article of Faith," in Harlan Cleveland and Harold D. Lasswell, eds., *Ethics and Bigness* (New York: Harper, 1962).

3. Herbert Agar, *The People's Choice* (Boston: Houghton Mifflin, 1933); Clinton Rossiter, *The American Presidency* (New York: Harcourt, Brace, 1956); E. S. Corwin, *The President: Office and Powers* (New York: New York Univ. Press, 1957); Henry Jones Ford, *The Rise and Growth of American Politics* (New York: Macmillan, 1914). For the interplay between presidents and public opinion see especially Richard E. Neustadt, *Presidential Power* (New York: Wiley, 1960, 1964) chap. 5; and Elmer E. Cornwell, Jr., *Presidential Leadership of Public Opinion* (Bloomington: Indiana Univ. Press, 1965), e.g., pp. 4, 61, 73, 86, 98, 111.

4. Quoted in Grant McConnell, *Private Power and American Democracy* (New York: Knopf, 1966), pp. 12–13. Italics supplied. Cf. Ernest R. May, "Cleveland and McKinley executed the will of the people as reflected by resolutions passed by Congress. On the Hawaiian issue of 1893 and the Philippine issue of 1898 each initially took a position that he should postpone decision until the public will became plain, and neither met much criticism for doing so" (*American Imperialism* [New York: Atheneum, 1968], p. 26).

5. Quoted in Louis W. Koenig, *The Chief Executive* (New York: Harcourt, Brace & World, 1968), p. 190; cf. Cornwell, *Presidential Leadership of Public Opinion,* pp. 58–59; James McGregor Burns, *Presidential Government* (Boston: Houghton Mifflin, 1965), p. 266.

6. Jackson subcommittee on national policy machinery, Senate Committee on Government Operations, "Organizing for National Security," vol. 1, *Hearings* (1961), p. 111.

7. Walter Millis, et al., *Arms and the State* (New York: 20th Century Fund, 1958), p. 308.

8. Richard R. Rovere and Arthur M. Schlesinger, Jr., *The General and the President* (New York: Farrar, Straus & Young, 1951), pp. 6–10.

9. William S. White, *The Citadel* (New York: Harper, 1955), p. 244.

10. Rovere and Schlesinger, *The General and the President,* pp. 172–82. Italics supplied.

11. Walter Millis et al., *Arms and the State,* p. 325. John E. Mueller reports that the polls in April 1951 suggested public support for MacArthur was twice as great as for Truman. MacArthur's support fell off with the Senate hearings but rose again when peace talks proved unproductive. By early 1952, "when the polling agencies grew bored with the issue," polls showed overwhelming public support for MacArthur and rejection of Truman. "Presidential Popularity from Truman to Johnson," *APSR* (March 1970), pp. 18–34, at p. 29, n. 39. However, MacArthur, who had won the Wisconsin Republican presidential primary in 1944 (dashing Wendell Willkie's hopes) and the Illinois primary in 1948, was crushed in the Wisconsin primary of 1952 and made virtually no showing elsewhere. James W. Davis, *Presidential Primaries: The Road to the White House* (New York: Crowell, 1967), pp. 294–98; see also Index under MacArthur. This is an excellent example of the frequent conflict between what the polls report the public thinks and how the public is willing to act.

12. John Dewey, *The Public and Its Problems* (Chicago: Holt, 1927; Gateway ed., 1946), p. 124. Compare Walter Lippmann, *The Phantom Public* (New York: Harcourt, Brace, 1925), and Lindsay Rogers, *The Pollsters* (New York: Knopf, 1949).

13. Dewey, *The Public and Its Problems,* esp. pp. 12–13, 121.

14. David B. Truman, *The Governmental Process* (New York: Knopf, 1951), p. 220. Cf. Arthur F. Bentley, *The Process of Government* (Chicago: Univ. of Chicago Press, 1908), chap. 8 and esp. pp. 243–44. Ernest R. May relies on the concept, *American Imperialism,* chap. 2.

15. Bentley, *The Process of Government,* p. 243.

16. See, for example, Walter DeVries and V. Lance Tarrance, *The Ticket Splitter: A New Force in American Politics* (Grand Rapids, Mich.: Eerdmans, 1972), esp. chap. 5; Dan Nimmo, *The Political Persuaders* (Englewood Cliffs, N. J.: Prentice-Hall, 1970), chaps. 3–5; and Mark R. Levy and Michael S. Kramer, *The Ethnic Factor: How America's Minorities Decide Elections* (New York: Simon and Schuster, 1972, 1973), chap. 8 and the epilogue on the 1972 election.

17. Nimmo, *The Political Persuaders,* pp. 118, 144.

18. Lloyd A. Free and Hadley Cantril, *The Political Beliefs of Americans* (New Brunswick: Rutgers Univ. Press, 1967), pp. 44–45.

19. Corwin, *The President: Office and Powers,* p. 421. See also C. Herman Pritchett, *The American Constitution* (New York: McGraw-Hill, 1959), pp. 40, 336–39. In 1955 the Bricker Amendment came within one vote of achieving the two-thirds necessary to pass the Senate.

20. V. O. Key, Jr., *Public Opinion and American Democracy* (New York: Knopf, 1961), pp. 82–84.

21. Ibid., chap. 4.

22. Dale E. Hathaway, E. E. Peterson, and Lawrence Witt, "Michigan Farmers and the Price Support Program. II, Farmers' Attitudes" (Agric. Exper. Sta. Tech. Bull. no. 235, East Lansing, Dec. 1952).

23. Free and Cantril, *Political Beliefs of Americans,* pp. 122, 196.

24. Alan F. Westin, "The John Birch Society: 'Radical Right' and 'Extreme Left' in the Political Context of Post World War II," in Daniel Bell, ed., *The Radical Right* (New York: Doubleday, 1963; Anchor ed., 1964), pp. 239–40. See in the same volume, Seymour Martin Lipset, "Three Decades of the Radical Right. . . ," at pp. 421–39.

25. *New York Times,* 31 July 1964.

26. For the difficulty of sorting out how people really feel about communism see, e.g., Free and Cantril, *The Political Beliefs of Americans,* pp. 25, 79, 97, 105, 106, 119, 120.

27. Earl Latham, *The Communist Controversy in Washington* (Cambridge, Mass.: Harvard Univ. Press, 1966), pp. 1–2, 357.

28. Angus Campbell et al., *The Voter Decides* (Evanston: Row, Peterson, 1954), p. 52. Free and Cantril found only 8 percent mentioning communism as a personal fear, but 22 percent as a fear for the nation (war scored 50 percent and "lack of law and order" only 5 percent—this was 1964). But when the sample was asked how much danger they thought Communists were "right here in America to this country at the present time," they cranked up the proper responses: 28 percent thought "a very great deal" and 34 percent "a good deal." Free and Cantril, *The Political Beliefs of Americans,* pp. 105, 106, 119–20.

29. Kurt Riezler, "Decisionmaking in Modern Society," *Ethics* (Jan. 1954), part 2 (one of the most illuminating discussions of public opinion).

30. Tom Harrison, quoted in F. G. Wilson, "Public Opinion and the Intellectuals," *APSR* (June 1954), pp. 321–39, at p. 324.

31. Homer, quoted by James Bryce, *The American Commonwealth* (1910 edition), 2:251.

32. "The Historical Background of Modern Social Psychology," in Gardner Lindzey, ed., *Handbook of Social Psychology* (Reading: Addison-Wesley, 1954), 1:45.

33. David E. RePass says that the "agree" or "disagree" questions typically posed to the public to elicit its ideas on issues often fail to measure any real attitudes. "Issue Salience and Party Choice," *APSR* (June 1971), pp. 389–400, at p. 391.

34.   Theodore H. White, *The Making of the President* (New York: Atheneum, 1965; Signet ed., 1966), pp. 81–82.

35.   V. O. Key, Jr. (with the assistance of Milton C. Cummings, Jr.), *The Responsible Electorate* (Cambridge, Mass.: Harvard Univ. Press, 1966), chaps. 3 and 4. David E. RePass concluded that the "voting public has at least a few issues in mind at the time of an election. . . ." Thus 23 percent of the public were "aware of four or more issues." But these were issue areas (war and peace, race relations, schools, social security, and the like) rather than specific issues; moreover, of twenty-five such areas, the average number even perceived by individuals was only 2.5. "Issue Salience and Party Choice," pp. 398, 400.

36.   Key, *Public Opinion and American Democracy* (New York: Knopf, 1961), pp. 14, 536. If space permitted, further documentation of Key's conclusion that a piece of the puzzle is missing could be supplied by analyzing research findings. Thus the Michigan Survey Research Center developed an elaborate scheme for explaining the "electoral decision" and concluded that the Republican's charge of corruption in government had a strong influence in deciding the 1952 election (Angus Campbell et al., *The American Voter* [New York: Wiley, 1960], pp. 524–25). But in 1954 the Survey Research Center made a contrasting—and, I think, a sounder—evaluation of the 1952 election, namely, that the fact that many Republican voters mentioned "corruption" does not mean that the issue was determinative of their vote. Indeed, an analysis will show that at best the corruption issue might have significantly influenced only about 90 of the 692 of the SRC sample who claimed that they had voted for Eisenhower (Campbell et al., *The Voter Decides* [Evanston: Row, Peterson, 1954], p. 52). In the same way, Ernest R. May's finding that shifts in public opinion accounted for the swing toward, and then away from, imperialism (in the sense of acquiring American colonies) in the late 1890s and the early 1900s is doubtful precisely because of Key's missing piece of the puzzle. May was able to adduce almost no evidence of a link between the foreign policy elites and the larger public that he thought had been activated at the time (*American Imperialism: A Speculative Essay* [New York: Atheneum, 1968]). See especially chap. 1 for the problem, chap. 2 for the theory of public opinion employed, and chaps. 3–9 for an examination of influential opinion. See, for my conclusions, esp. pp. 190, 210–11.

37.   Aaron Wildavsky, "The Two Presidencies," *Trans-Action* (Dec. 1966).

38.   Neustadt, *Presidential Power*, p. 58 and index.

39.   Neustadt's pedagogy is outlined in *Presidential Power*, chap. 5, esp. pp. 100–105, and used to analyze presidential actions in much

of the rest of the book with many examples of failures as well as some successes. See also Cornwell, *Presidential Leadership of Public Opinion,* pp. 54, 71, 96, 112, 116, 141, 147–49, 167–68, 179, 183, 196, 246, 263–64.

40.   John E. Mueller, "Presidential Popularity from Truman to Johnson," *APSR* (March 1970), pp. 18–34, at p. 19.

41.   John E. Mueller, "Popular Support for Wars in North Korea and Vietnam, *APSR* (June 1971), pp. 358–75, at p. 365.

42.   Mueller, "Presidential Popularity from Truman to Johnson."

43.   Richard M. Nixon's high point was 68 in November 1969. By early 1971 his average was hovering around 50 and in late June it fell to 48 percent approval, which was lower than any of his four predecessors had fallen at the end of the first twenty-nine months in office. By mid-1972, however, Nixon had sharply recouped, and in January 1973 he scored 68. Then came the plunge to 40 in July.

44.   "Public Opinion and the War in Vietnam" (*APSR,* June 1967), pp. 317–33, at p. 333.

45.   Verba et al., "Public Opinion and the War in Vietnam," p. 333. Heinrich Bruening, former chancellor of the Weimar Republic, described a similar phenomenon to me. When he was forced, as he believed, to issue deflationary decrees in 1930, the immediate reaction would be favorable because the government had acted; in a very few days it would turn unfavorable as wage cuts were felt; as unemployment dropped and the economy improved, opinion would turn favorable again (three weeks or so later); in the longer run adverse tendencies would set in once more, restricting economic activity; and opinion would again turn adverse. Then it was time for a new decree.

46.   Walter Lippman, *The Public Philosophy* (Boston: Little, Brown, 1955), chap. 2 and Lindsay Rogers, *The Pollsters,* chap. 18.

47.   "Gallup Calls Public Disillusioned and Cynical," *New York Times,* 10 Feb. 1968.

48.   Peter Kihss, "Louis Harris Tells Publishers of New Coalition for Change," *New York Times,* 22 April 1971. See also Louis Harris, "Regard for Leadership in Institutions Falls," *Sacramento Bee,* 25 Oct. 1971.

49.   Samuel Lubell, *The Hidden Crisis in American Politics* (New York: Norton, 1970), p. 12.

50.   "64% of Poll Say U.S. Is on Wrong Track," *New York Times,* 9 July 1971. Cf. a study by the Michigan Institute for Social Research (Warren Miller reporting) discussed in Boyce Rensberger, "Study Finds Most Lack Trust in U.S.," *New York Times,* 15 Nov.

1971. See also two papers prepared by Arthur H. Miller et al. of the Center for Policy Studies at the University of Michigan, "Social Conflict and Political Estrangement, 1958–1972" and "A Majority Party in Disarray: Policy Polarization in the 1972 Election," both published in 1973.

51.   Albert H. Cantril and Charles W. Roll, Jr., *Hopes and Fears of the American People* (New York: Universe Books, 1971). Cf. John Herbers, "Survey Finds Fear of U.S. Breakdown," *New York Times,* 26 June 1971, and David C. Anderson, "Scrutinizing the 'Crisis of Confidence,'" *Wall Street Journal,* 2 Aug. 1971. Questions were asked permitting a comparison with the 1964 poll that attempted to tap the aspirations and fears of Americans both personally and for the nation. Interestingly, both the 1964 and the 1971 polls found Americans optimistic about their personal situation; but the outlook for the nation had worsened. Free and Cantril, *The Political Beliefs of Americans,* chap. 7.

52.   "The Textbook Presidency and Political Science," Amer. Pol. Sci. Assoc., 1970 (mimeo.), pp. 29–30.

53.   Free and Cantril, *The Political Beliefs of Americans,* p. 187.

54.   *Sacramento Bee,* 22 Jan. 1968. "The drop in esteem for Congress since the flood of Great Society Legislation . . . has been precipitous. Since the high-water mark in 1965, a decline of thirty percentage points has taken place." And in 1970 congressional mail showed a rise in anguish. "Congressional aides, whose job it is to read and answer the mail, said they cannot remember a time when such a general feeling of unrest existed among constituents." David E. Rosenbaum, "Mail to Congressmen Registers Anguish," *New York Times,* 28 May 1970.

55.   *Leviathan,* part I, chap. 13, Everyman's ed., p. 64.

56.   Boyce Resberger, "1 of 5 Men Said to Favor Violence to Effect Change" in *New York Times,* 26 May 1971, reporting on Monica D. Blumenthal's paper, part of a study conducted by the University of Michigan's Institute for Social Research.

57.   Free and Cantril, *The Political Beliefs of Americans,* pp. 193–94. Probably the strongest aspiration of most Americans who are employed and healthy is to advance the education of their children. Asked to choose among reasons explaining success, 71 percent named education (even ahead of the 66 percent for "initiative, effort, hard work" and the 59 percent for "character, will power"); and 76 percent selected lack of education as the prime cause of human failure.

58.   Peter Schrag, "The Forgotten Americans," *Harper's,* August 1969.

59.   Andrew N. Greeley, program director, NORC, the University of Chicago, "Turning Off 'The People,'" *New Republic,* 27 June

1970. Compare Michael Novak, "White Ethnic," *Harper's,* Sept. 1971.

60. (Boston: Atlantic-Little, Brown, 1971). I am indebted to the review by David C. Anderson, " 'Middle America': A Closer Look," *Wall Street Journal,* 18 July 1971.

61. In 1970 CBS news queried a national sample and found that over half would deny the right of individuals to criticize government if the criticism were thought (by whom?) to be against the national interest. Fifty-five percent would prevent newspapers from printing stories against the national interest. About 75 percent thought that "extremist groups" (how and by whom defined?) should not be permitted to conduct nonviolent demonstrations against the government. James Reston, "Washington: Repeal the Bill of Rights?" *New York Times,* 19 April 1970.

62. Walter Dean Burnham, *Critical Elections and the Mainsprings of American Politics* (New York: Norton, 1970), pp. 192–93.

63. Walter Lippmann, *The Phantom Public,* p. 57. Lindsay Rogers, *The Pollsters,* p. 89. Willmoore Kendall, "On the Preservation of Democracy for America," *Southern Review,* June 1939. Rogers quotes Puffendorf who justifies majority rule because hardly any other way of settling issues exists.

64. Dewey, *The Public and Its Problems,* pp. 177–78.

65. See John C. Ranney's argument that democracy was not simply the registration of the popular will but the entire process by which a people and their agents inform themselves, make compromises, and finally decide issues. "Do the Polls Serve Democracy?" *P.O.Q.* (1946) 10: 249–60.

66. Sidney Verba et al., "Public Opinion and the War in Vietnam," at p. 331. Italics added.

67. Mueller, "Popular Support for the Wars in Korea and Vietnam," p. 370.

68. Walter Dean Burnham, *Critical Elections and the Mainsprings of American Politics,* pp. 188–89.

69. Marvin Zetterbaum, *Tocqueville and the Problem of Democracy* (Stanford: Stanford Univ. Press, 1967), pp. 142–43.

70. C. H. McIlwain, "Medieval Estates," chap. 23 in vol. 7, *Cambridge Medieval History.*

71. *Ancient Law* (Everyman's ed.), pp. 15–16, 18, 77, 82, 90, 96.

72. "Great Britain . . ." in S. Neumann, *Democratic Party Systems* (Chicago: Univ. of Chicago Press, 1955), p. 56.

73. Louis Hartz, *The Liberal Tradition in America* (New York: Harcourt, Brace, 1955).

74. New York Times, *The Pentagon Papers* (1971), pp. xi–xvi and, for example, pp. 242, 246–47, 249, 251–53, 257. Ralph L. Stavins, "Kennedy's Private War," *New York Review of Books,* 22 July 1971, pp. 24–25. Suzannah Lessard, "A New Look at John Kennedy," *Washington Monthly,* Oct. 1971. Anthony Austin, *The President's War* (New York Times Book, 1971), p. 297.

9. The Feasibility of Party Government

1. Donald E. Stokes, "Party Loyalty and the Likelihood of Deviating Elections" in Angus Campbell et al., *Elections and the Political Order* (New York: Wiley, 1966), p. 126. Donald E. Stokes and Warren E. Miller, "Party Government and the Saliency of Congress," first appeared in *Public Opinion Quarterly* (Winter 1962) and "Constituency Influence in Congress," *APSR* (March 1963); chaps. 11 and 16, respectively, in Augus Campbell et al., *Elections and the Political Order.* Milton E. Cummings, Jr., *Congressmen and the Electorate* (New York: Free Press, 1966), p. 198. William Nisbet Chambers, "Party Development and the American Mainstream," Chambers and Burnham, eds., *The American Party System,* (New York: Oxford Univ. Press, 1967), pp. 3, 31–32.

   Walter Dean Burnham stresses the decline of party loyalties but exaggerates the "independents" by omitting those who classify themselves as "weak" Democrats or Republicans. Compare *Critical Elections and the Mainspring of American Politics* (New York: Norton, 1970), p. 121, with Angus Campbell et al., *The American Voter* (New York: Wiley, 1960), p. 124. (My colleague John R. Owens called this point to my attention). Burnham notes that 52 percent of the independents oppose the development of new parties (p. 131, n. 36).

2. A. N. Holcombe, *Our More Perfect Union* (Cambridge, Mass.: Harvard Univ. Press, 1950), pp. 239–51. Chambers, *The American Party System,* p. 10.

3. Compare the stress on "the habit of party loyalty" that shaped the mutual loyalty of English governmental ministers and made "party the real secret of the step upwards from Cabal to Cabinet," G. M. Trevelyan, "The Two-Party System in English Political History," quoted in Leslie Lipson, "The Two-Party System in British Politics," *APSR* (June 1953), p. 343.

4. Aristotle, *The Politics* (Everymans ed.), book 3, chap. 4.

5. C. O. Jones, "Inter-party Competition for Congressional Seats," *Western Political Quarterly* (Sept. 1964), pp. 461–76, at p. 474.

6. Louis M. Seagull, "The Emergence and Persistence of Republicanism in the Deep and Rim South," a paper presented at the APSA meeting, Los Angeles, Sept. 1970, based on a Ph.D. thesis, "Southern

Republicanism: Party Competition in the American South, 1940–1968," Univ. of Chicago, 1970.

7.   Ibid.

8.   Edwin Carl Ladd, Jr., and associates, "The American Party Coalitions: Social Change and Partisan Alignments, 1935–1970," paper, APSA meeting, 1970, p. 36.

9.   Alexander Heard, *Toward a Two-Party South?* (Chapel Hill: Univ. of N. Carolina Press, 1952), pp. 246–47. There is some argument over whether class voting declined in the United States between the 1930s and the 1960s. Angus Campbell et al. say it has (*The American Voter,* p. 347; but they find it rising somewhat in the south, perhaps reflecting "growing industrialization and urbanization...," p. 368.) Robert R. Alvord finds that it has not declined (*Party and Society* [Chicago: Rand McNally, 1963], chap. 8). Alvord thought class voting might rise in the South as the middle class identify more with the Republicans (pp. 238–39). See also V. O. Key on rising class politics in Louisiana and Texas (*Southern Politics* [New York: Knopf, 1949]); cf. on Tennessee Norman L. Parks, "Tennessee Politics since Kefauver and Reece, a Generalist's View," in *Jour. of Politics* (Feb. 1966). George Gallup advised the Republicans that southern white-collar workers are "their natural hunting ground, where they can hope to expand into a majority party" (Christopher Lydon, "Polls on Election Found Accurate," *New York Times,* 8 Nov. 1970).

10.   *American Political Science Review* (1950, vol. 44, no. 3, part 2). In 1970 the twentieth anniversary of the report was observed by a panel of the APSA. Evron M. Kirkpatrick criticized it in " 'Toward a More Responsible Two-Party System': Political Science, Policy Science, or Pseudo-Science?" (see *APSR,* Dec. 1971); Gerald M. Pomper, with some reservations, praised its prescience and its intention, "After TwentyYears: The Report of the APSA Committee on Political Parties," *Jour. of Politics* (Nov. 1971). Both papers contain ample citations of literature on the report.

11.   Ibid., pp. 15, 30. Italics in original. Comments include Austin Ranney, "Toward a More Responsible Two-Party System: A Commentary," *American Political Science Review* (June 1951, vol. 45, no. 2), pp. 488–99; Edward C. Banfield, "In Defense of the American Party System," in Robert A. Goldwin, ed., *Political Parties USA* (Chicago: Rand McNally, 1961, 1964); Nelson W. Polsby and Aaron B. Wildavsky, *Presidential Elections* (New York: Scribner's, 1964, 1968); and James Q. Wilson, *The Amateur Democrat* (Chicago: Univ. of Chicago Press, 1962; Phoenix ed., 1966).

12.   *The Amateur Democrat,* p. 340, and see generally chap. 12, "The New Party Politics: An Appraisal."

13. "In Defense of Party Government," p. 21.

14. Their quotation is from the CPP report already cited. Numerous other examples include Austin Ranney, *The Doctrine of Responsible Party Government* (Urbana: Univ. of Ill. Press, 1954), p. 68. Leon Epstein, *Political Parties in Western Democracies* (New York: Praeger, 1967), pp. 270–71 and passim. See also the discussions of Professors Miller and Stokes in n. 36 and of Professor Lowi in n. 38, below. For Don K. Price, see *The Scientific Estate* (Cambridge, Mass.: Harvard Univ. Press, 1965), p. 189.

15. Herbert Agar, *The Price of Union* (Boston: Houghton Mifflin, 1950), p. xiv.

16. Richard E. Neustadt, *Presidential Power* (New York: Wiley, 1960), pp. 187–89. Compare Robert A. Dahl in Robert A. Dahl, ed., *Political Oppositions in Western Democracies* (New Haven: Yale University Press, 1966), p. 54.

17. Ranney and Kendall, *Democracy and the American Party System,* pp. 522–23.

18. In addition to examples of the influence of political institutions on attitudes provided at the end of chap. 8 see the French experience as observed by Philip Williams, *Politics in Postwar France* (London: Longmans, Green, 1954), pp. 328–29, and by Suzanne Berger in Samuel H. Beer et al., *Patterns of Government* (New York: Random House, 1973), p. 414.

19. Joseph A. Schumpeter, *Capitalism, Socialism, and Democracy* (New York: Harper, 1942), pp. 269, 294, and, generally, chaps. 20–23. For the British application see Allen Potter, "Great Britain: Opposition with a Capital 'O'," in Robert A. Dahl, ed., *Political Oppositions in Western Democracies,* pp. 8, 22, 31–33, and David Butler and Donald Stokes, *Political Change in Britain* (London: Macmillan, 1969), pp. 23, 29, 32, 38, 40, 43.

20. Samuel Lubell, *The Hidden Crisis in American Politics* (New York: Norton, 1970), p. 279. Among the voluminous literature on the subject see W. J. Cash, *The Mind of the South* (New York: Knopf, 1941), and V. O. Key, *Southern Politics in State and Nation* (New York: Knopf, 1949).

21. Gunnar Myrdal, *An American Dilemma* (New York: Harper, 1944), chap. 1.

22. David B. Truman, *The Congressional Party* (New York: Wiley, 1959), pp. 280, 285, 306. Duncan MacRae, Jr. (with Fred H. Gouldner), *Dimensions of Congressional Voting* (Berkeley: Univ. of Calif. Press, 1958), p. 232. Julius Turner, *Party and Constituency: Pressures on Congress* (Baltimore: Johns Hopkins Press,

1951), p. 34. David R. Mayhew, *Party Loyalty Among Congressmen* (Cambridge, Mass.: Harvard Univ. Press, 1966), chap. 6.

23.   Lewis A. Froman, Jr., *Congressmen and Their Constituencies* (Chicago: Rand McNally, 1963), pp. 88–89.

24.   The National Rifle Association may be an exception under present arrangements with off-year elections. In presidential years the vote for congressmen is one-third to one-half again as large as the midterm turnout (Cummings, *Congressmen and the Electorate*, p. 199).

25.   Neustadt cited a long list of issues but did not spell out how the crosscurrent among their supporters would prevent stable majorities. On many of the issues that he cites I think a consolidation of differences along party lines is progressing, as I shall argue later (see *Presidential Power*, chap. 8).

26.   A. N. Holcombe, *Political Parties of Today* (New York: Harper, 1924), pp. 355–56.

27.   V. O. Key, Jr., *Politics, Parties, and Pressure Groups* (New York: Crowell, 1942, 1947), pp. 131–32. Also Key's *Public Opinion and American Democracy* (New York: Knopf, 1961), pp. 496–99.

28.   Raymond A. Bauer, Ithiel de Sola Pool, and Lewis Anthony Dexter, *American Business and Public Policy* (New York: Atherton Press, 1964), chap. 20, "Lessons of the Community Studies," pp. 315, 316, and 319. Horizontal: from firm to firm, Chamber of Commerce to Trade association, etc., rather than vertical: organizational spokesmen direct to Washington.

29.   Lewis Anthony Dexter, who made the major contribution to *American Business and Public Policy* on congressional-constituent relationships, noted elsewhere some "important instances when congressmen were changed by their districts." In 1955 some farm belt congressmen switched to support reciprocal trade, perhaps prodded by the Farm Bureau (which, incidentally, had supported reciprocal trade since the late 1930s), and certain southern congressmen, moved by complaints of textile mills, voted for the first time against reciprocal trade. Nevertheless, Dexter suggests that one of the shifters, Congressman Henderson Lanham of Georgia, did so largely as a result of a superficial inquiry about effects on the textile industry without inquiring what the effects would be on his farmer constituents who would normally expect to profit from expanded foreign trade. So the implication is somewhat ambivalent. "Congressmen and Their Constituencies" in Robert L. Peabody and Nelson R. Polsby, eds., *New Perspectives on the House of Representatives* (Chicago: Rand McNally, 1962, 1969), pp. 21–23.

30.   The late Senator McKellar had a rule that no letter from his district was to go unanswered longer than forty-eight hours.

The late Clem Miller noted that while in his district he was engaged "continuously in the job of being a representative of individuals. I collected a list of problems on which individuals asked valid intercession with their impersonal, bureaucratic government—pensions, social security, civil service, and so on. Personal problems large and small, they are all important to the possessor" (*Member of the House: Letters of a Congressman,* p. 135).

Professors Miller and Stokes concur. Many congressmen are able to nurse their districts effectively by doing things unrelated to policy issues. Ethnic identification "may cement a legislator in the affections of his district, whatever (within limits) his stand on issues. And many congressmen keep their tenure of office secure by skillful provision of district benefits ranging from free literature to major federal projects. In the full study of which this analysis is part, we have explored several bases of constituency support that have little to do with policy issues" ("Constituency Influence in Congress," *APSR,* [March 1963]).

31.   Thomas B. Gilpatrick, "Price Support Policy and the Mid-West Farm Vote," first published in the *Mid-West Journal of Political Science* (November 1959) and reprinted in Charles G. Mayo and Beryl Crowe, *American Political Parties: A Systematic Perspective* (New York: Harper & Row, 1967), p. 418.

32.   Ibid., p. 478. The "countervailing forces" Gilpatrick mentioned were, in this example, the American Farm Bureau Federation and the state farm bureaus. But it is doubtful that the Farm Bureau swung many votes. In a study of the 1963 wheat referendum, Don F. Hadwiger and Ross B. Talbot concluded that neither the Farm Bureau nor the Agricultural Stabilization and Conservation Service of the USDA was successful in persuading the farmers to vote their way; indeed, "in Kansas counties where local ASCS groups campaigned hardest [for favorable votes], the percentage of 'no' votes increased most; and where the Farm Bureaus worked hardest [for negative votes], the percentage of 'no' votes increased least" (*Pressures and Protests: The Kennedy Farm Program and the Wheat Referendum of 1963* [San Francisco: Chandler, 1965], p. 311).

33.   This section draws on Donald F. Stokes and Warren E. Miller, "Party Government and the Saliency of Congress" and "Constituency Influence in Congress"; see above, n. 1.

34.   Lewis Anthony Dexter worked twenty man-days for a congressional primary candidate in 1956. During the period "only four people raised any national or international issues whatsoever with him or with me (others who worked for him . . . had similar reports to make)." ("Congressmen and Their Constituents" in Robert L.

Peabody and Nelson R. Polsby, eds., *New Perspectives on the House of Representatives* [Chicago: Rand McNally, 1962, 1969], p. 20).

35. Sixty-seven percent of the voters were aware of the incumbent candidates who lived in the same community; only 45 percent, of incumbents living in other communities. Forty-seven percent of the voters were aware of nonincumbent candidates living in the same community; only 22 percent, of nonincumbent candidates living outside ("Party Government and the Saliency of Congress," in Angus Campbell, *Elections and the Political Order,* p. 208).

36. Stokes and Miller make exactly the opposite interpretation of their findings. They argue that the relationship in America between voter and congressmen works against the development of responsible party government. They postulate that party government depends on an alert and rational electorate that selects among parties according to its preference for program and then scrutinizes congressmen to see to it that they adhere to the program. If we consider the prime function of elections to be to make governments, thus qualifying the mandate theory that has put so much of the debate about party government beside the mark, then the relationships between voters and congressmen that Miller and Stokes describe far from working against party government would actually strengthen it. The strength comes from the fact that most voters are loyal partisans and also from the inference that since they do not know specifically how congressmen behave or vote anyway, congressmen may as well vote the party line.

37. "After 20 Years: The Report of the APSA Committee on Political Parties," a paper prepared for the APSA meeting, Los Angeles, 1970, pp. 14 ff. Published in *The Journal of Politics* (Nov. 1971).

38. "Party, Policy, and Constitution in America" in William Nisbet Chambers and Walter Dean Burnham, eds., *The American Party Systems: Stages of Political Development* (New York: Oxford University Press, 1967), pp. 238 and following, especially pp. 259–74. Lowi says that American parties perform a single function that he calls constituent or constitutional (institutionalizing, channeling, and "socializing" conflict over control of the regime). In Europe parties perform this function but also assume responsibility for making policies. In America, "Parties present few issues to electorates as referenda or quasireferenda and therefore represent few real majorities before, during, or after elections. In mixing up the deviants among a congeries of issues, the party represents 'artificial majorities'; and those, of course, are not majorities in any sense but a numerical one. . . . This means that, electorally, American parties represent outcomes *in general;* parties seldom shape or represent outcomes *in particular.* Representing *in general* is not the same as responsible policy making by party or even the shaping of policy

along lines of electoral influence or electoral choice." Lowi's argument, like many others, hinges on a strict construction of the mandate theory and hence is vulnerable to criticisms of that theory
already noted.

39. Ibid., figs. 5 and 6, pp. 261–62.

40. *The Real Majority* (New York: Coward-McCann, 1970). For
what follows see pp. 40, 174–75, 207–8, 282–83, and 292.

41. Ibid., pp. 174–75.

42. In 1970 the much-advertised Social Issue proved less compelling at
the polls than the Economic Issue. Lydon, "Polls on Election Day
Found Accurate," *New York Times,* 8 Nov. 1970; Roy Reed,
"Democrats Void Nixon Administration's 'Southern Strategy' in
All but One State"; and Max Frankel, "Aftermath of a Bitter Cam-
paign," *New York Times,* 5 Nov. 1970.

43. Scammon and Wattenberg, *The Real Majority,* pp. 40, 282–83.

44. *Party Loyalty Among Congressmen* (Cambridge, Mass.: Harvard
Univ. Press, 1946), p. 150; see especially chap. 6.

45. As Mayhew shows, the mutual tenderness among Democrats was
profound for farmers and westerners, less so for labor and for city
interests, whereas southern Democrats, especially those from the
more rural districts with the heaviest concentrations of non-voting
Negroes, often voted with Republicans to kill proposals. The
Democrats needed only some 230 congressmen to take care of the
farmers and westerners; they had to have 260 to move on public
housing and well over 300 to pass the National Labor Relations
Act (1935) and the Fair Labor Standards Act (1938) (ibid.,
pp. 165–67).

46. Ibid., p. 160.

47. Telling criticisms of the priorities in recent federal budgets may be
found in the Committee on Economic Development, *The National
Economy and the Vietnam War* (1968), in the annual volumes
of the Brookings Institute, e.g., Charles L. Schultze et al., *Setting
National Priorities, the 1972 Budget* (Washington, D. C.: Brookings, 1971), Robert S. Benson and Harold Wolman, eds., *Counter-
budget* (New York: Praeger, 1971), and Leonard Ross, "Old Priorities Never Die," *New York Times Book Review,* 31 Oct. 1971.

48. If space permitted, an elaborate criticism could be made of mistakes in our economic policy that have apparently been aggravated
by our political system.

10. Reform

1. C. J. Friedrich, *Constitutional Government and Democracy* (Boston: Ginn, 1950). See index under "Constituent group."

2. I anticipate criticisms such as David B. Truman's that advocates of sweeping constitutional reform "do not indicate how we can get from here to there" (*The Governmental Process* [New York, Knopf, 1951], p. 530). With respect, I propose to get from here to there by educating the "potential group" described by Truman in 1951 and, more sharply and succinctly, in 1971 (ibid., index under "Interest Groups: potential," and, in the 1971 edition, "Introduction to the Second Edition," pp. xxxviii, xlii, and xlv). And to those who, with Henry Steele Commager, consider it "wildly improbable" that Americans would embrace sweeping constitutional reform, let me say, again with respect, that on Saturday, 20 October 1973, there was little that any longer seemed "wildly improbable" (Commager, "The Presidency After Watergate," *New York Review of Books,* 18 Oct. 1973, p. 51). In the light of events, prudence surely enjoins us to make an analysis *much more thorough than we have ever made before* of the *constitutional* alternatives that may exist. There may be harsher alternatives. At the risk of incurring the charge, which I do not think will properly lie against this book, of advocating a "devil" theory, I must say that circumstances may arise in which we ought to consider a military coup something less than "wildly improbable."

3. Allen Potter, "Great Britain: Opposition with a Capital 'O'," in Robert A. Dahl, ed., *Political Oppositions in Western Democracies* (New Haven: Yale Univ. Press, 1966), esp. p. 13. K. B. Smellie, *A Hundred Years of English Government* (London: Duckworth, 1950), chap. 5. W. Ivor Jennings, "On the House of Lords," *Parliament* (Cambridge: University Press, 1957), chap. 12.

4. David Butler and Donald Stokes, *Political Change in Britain* (London: Macmillan, 1969), chap. 1.

5. British experience suggests that constituency parties come to insist as strongly as national parties that their candidate accept and support the program of the national party. Leon D. Epstein, *Political Parties in Western Democracies* (New York: Praeger, 1967), p. 219.

6. V. O. Key, Jr., *Politics, Parties, and Pressure Groups* (New York: Crowell, 1964), p. 568.

7. John Gardner, "You Are Being Had," *New York Times,* 4 July 1971.

8. W. Ivor Jennings, *Party Politics,* vol. I, *Appeal to the People* (Cambridge: University Press, 1960), p. 111.

9. Rexford G. Tugwell, "The Model Constitution," *Center Magazine,* Sept. 1970, p. 28. Chester I. Barnard, "Bureaucracy in a Democracy: Book Review Article," *APSR* (Dec. 1950), pp. 990–1004.

10. Compare Richard E. Neustadt's proposal in "The Presidency at Mid-

Century," *Law and Contemporary Problems* (Autumn 1956), pp. 610–45, at p. 641.

11.   Walter DeVries and V. Lance Tarrance, *The Ticket Splitter: A New Force in American Politics* (Grand Rapids, Mich.: Eerdmans, 1972), p. 30.

12.   Milton C. Cummings, Jr., *Congressmen and the Electorate* (New York: Free Press, 1966), p. 13.

13.   Respecting nominations to the U.S. Supreme Court, when presidents and Senate majorities belong to the same party, the Senate has nearly always approved appointments (98 of 108 approved between 1790 and 1970). Between 1894 and 1968 the Senate rejected only one Supreme Court nominee. If presidential nominations to the federal courts were published ninety days before appointments were made, the opposition, the bar, and the press would have time to bring forth the kind of information that eliminated certain nominees in 1968 and 1970. See, generally, Robert Scigliano, *The Supreme Court and the Presidency* (New York: Free Press, 1971), pp. 96–105.

14.   Richard E. Neustadt, *Presidential Power* (New York: Wiley, 1960), chap. 7. Michael R. Gordon, "Civil Servants, Politicians, and Parties," *Comparative Politics* (Oct. 1971).

15.   Thoughtful analyses of proposals to change present methods of presidential election are provided by Neal R. Peirce, *The People's President* (New York: Simon and Schuster, Clarion ed., 1968), and Alexander M. Bickel, *The New Age of Political Reform* (New York: Harper & Row, 1968). Both, however, deal with the problem on the assumptions of maintaining general constitutional arrangements and not as part of a proposal for comprehensive constitutional change.

16.   William Nisbet Chambers and Walter Dean Burnham, eds., *The American Party Systems* (London: Oxford Univ. Press, 1967), p. 31.

17.   Samuel H. Beer, "The Representation of Interests in British Government: Historical Background," *APSR* (Sept. 1957), p. 614. See also Alfred de Grazia, *Public and Republic* (New York: Knopf, 1951), p. 251. The other question, how are particular interests to be represented, has been vigorously answered by the formation of pressure groups.

18.   *Reflections on Government* (New York: Oxford Univ. Press, 1942; Galaxy ed., 1958), pp. 37, 43–44. See also Alfred de Grazia, *Public and Republic,* p. 251 and especially chap. 9. John C. Ranney used the division of labor to illuminate the role of public opinion in

democracies ("Do the Polls Serve Democracy?," *Public Opinion Quarterly* [1946], pp. 249–60).

19. Herbert Agar, *The Price of Union* (Boston: Houghton Mifflin, 1950), pp. xiv, xvi.

20. In a remarkable concession, appearing in a footnote on pp. 279–80, Agar acknowledged that the American system has worked so far by virtue of a "remarkable series of accidents. . . . It is a question whether the United States should continue to stake the future on such haphazard strokes of good fortune."

21. Neustadt, *Presidential Power,* p. 186.

22. "On several occasions in our history when the President was disabled, the Ship of State simply drifted" (John D. Feerick, *From Failing Hands* [New York: Fordham Univ. Press, 1965], p. 20).

23. Churchill, *The Second World War,* vol. 2, *Their Finest Hour* (Boston: Houghton Mifflin, 1949), p. 15.

24. The risk of foreign harassment is not the only disadvantage borne of calendar elections that induce protracted campaigns that subject candidates to unnecessary physical strain, greatly increase electoral costs, and distort the essential process of political debate. The last point needs amplification. The important and valuable emotional commitments in campaigns do not provide the best conditions for the rational discussions that constitutional democracies, above all other types of government, must stress.

25. G. A. Borgese, *Goliath: The March of Fascism* (New York: Viking, 1937), p. 78.

26. "Medieval Estates," chap. 23 of *Cambridge Medieval History,* vol. 7.

27. A. D. Lindsay, *The Modern Democratic State* (New York: Oxford Univ. Press, 1947), p. 118.

28. See the comments on the disruptive projection of the western way of life into China in Tang Tsou and Morton H. Halperin, "Mao Tse-Tung's Revolutionary Strategy and Peking's International Behavior," *APSR* (March 1965), pp. 80–99, at p. 99.

29. Walter Lippmann, *The Phantom Public,* p. 57, quoted by Lindsay Rogers, *The Pollsters* (New York: Knopf, 1949), p. 89.

30. Austin Ranney and Willmoore Kendall, *Democracy and the American Party System,* chap. 2, esp. p. 37.

31. Austin Ranney, *The Doctrine of Responsible Party Government* (Urbana: Univ. of Ill. Press, 1954), p. 160. Compare his remark

that "Lowell's denial of their major premise—that Americans want effective majority-rule democracy—is one of the most devastating and fundamental criticisms ever made of the party government school . . ." (p. 67).

32. Ibid., p. 160, footnote.

33. Theodore J. Lowi, "American Government, 1933–1963: Fission and Confusion in Theory and Research," *APSR* (Sept. 1964), pp. 589–99, at p. 597.

Index of Names

Subject Index